AN ISLAND CABIN

ARTHUR HENRY

Introduction by MAGGIE WALKER
Afterword by STEPHEN JONES

THREE SHORT STORIES BY

THEODORE DREISER

A DOER OF THE WORD
THE VILLAGE FEUDISTS
A CRIPPLE WHOSE ENERGY GIVES INSPIRATION
(THE NOANK BOY)

FLAT
HAMMOCK
PRESS

Flat Hammock Press
5 Church Street
Mystic, CT 06355
(860) 572-2722
www.flathammockpress.com

Printed in the United States of America

10 9 8 7 6 5 4 3 2 1

ISBN-13: 978-0-9818960-1-4

INTRODUCTION

BY MAGGIE WALKER

On that sparkling blue and gold day in 1994, the rocky islet emerging from Fishers Island Sound, a mile from the little fishing village of Noank, appeared as an uninhabited quarter acre covered with scrub. But when my husband, Mark, and I set foot on the little beach of the 'Isle of Quirk,' I knew I was walking in the footsteps of my beloved grandfather. Stephen Jones who had brought us here in his boat, *Lawrence*, was custodian of this important part of my family's and literary history's heritage.

Arthur Henry's book, *An Island Cabin*, first published in 1902, was and still is famous in these parts for being a delightful yarn full of good salt air, sun—and wind-burnished characters, and nature's whimsical storms and calms. It has a suspenseful plot in which five disparate friends from the Big City occupy a simple summer cabin—but they do not all revel in nature's embrace.

For most readers of more than one hundred years ago, the identity of four of these characters was unknown. Arthur Henry is clearly the author, the 'I' and the 'me', but he gives his friends pseudonyms. Even though the book was serialized in the *New York Post* prior to publication, only the *cognoscenti* could have identified them. But this was of no significance since one of these friends had not yet achieved recognition as the seminal American naturalist who decisively broke with Victorian literary tradition. He was none other than Theodore Dreiser (named 'Tom' in this book) who for ten years prior had been

Henry's closest friend and literary collaborator. *An Island Cabin* tells the momentous story of the end of their collaboration.

Other pseudonymous characters include: Anna Mallon (called 'Nancy'), Henry's future wife who provided the small cash needed to build the cabin; Beezie ('Elizabeth'), Anna's best friend, helpmate, and chaperone; and Jug, Dreiser's wife ('Ruth').

The drama of the Dreiser-Henry friendship is described in the first full-length biography of Henry's life, *Dreiser's 'Other Self': The Life of Arthur Henry*, published in 2005 by Fithian Press, co-written by Mark and me. Over a number of our retirement years, writing this book was an exciting adventure, like fitting together many pieces of a very difficult jigsaw puzzle. Some core pieces were in my library, most importantly Henry's unpublished autobiographical novel written in his old age. However, these were meaningless until we had gathered up the scattered bits and pieces from numerous other sources and the picture became whole.

Mark died in 2007, but I know he would have been as proud and excited as I am that this third edition of my grandfather's delightful and insightful book is now available to a new generation.

PUBLISHER'S PREFACE

By Stephen Jones

> Noank... now inspired me to go on and explore other fishing communities. I'd see if there, too, in those towns where men fished on their own hook... liberty still endured. Or had these communities been done in by exaggerated land values and a complexity of other modern forces? Of course, I had to recognize that Noank was a funny kind of anti-success story in terms of its unpretentious leaders and small-scaled institutions.
>
> —Russell Bourne
> "Noank: Each Man on His Own Hook"
> *The View from Front Street*

For a century, various people including artists, visual, verbal, and musical—and recently the zoning board—have been trying to "capture" the charm that Arthur Henry (1867-1934) and Theodore Dreiser (1871-1945) found in 1900 Noank. To preserve this charming maritime atmosphere, nowadays it seems that some sort of rear guard action is an almost weekly occurrence. The rise in waterfront real estate with its attendant invasion by "people from away," has threatened to do what the "playing out" of the fishing fleet in Dreiser's day could not accomplish and change what the regulations call "the character of the neighborhood."

It may come as a surprise to those unfamiliar with the Noank work of these two Midwestern newspapermen that any such self-confessed landlubbers "from away" could have anything to contribute to an appreciation of this tiny, insular Yankee port as it was a hundred years ago.

When they "discover" Noank, the two newspaper men are in their early thirties, and were but recently arrived on the Atlantic coast. They are attempting to parley a modest success in the flatlands into greater fame as book writers in Manhattan. Arthur Henry, then the better known of the two, wrangles a book deal based on a proposal that he live on an island. This island turns out to be "a barren hummock" of some ¼ acre of scrub, rock and sand ¾ of a mile off the little maritime village of Noank, an obscure hamlet at the southeastern corner of Connecticut found for him by his girlfriend's mother.

In Noank, Henry manages to persuade a local artisan, for a few hundred dollars, to build him a cabin, complete with attic sleeping loft, veranda and fireplace and chimney. As almost an afterthought, he commissions an ancient rigger to knock out a small, flat-bottomed rowboat capable of sailing from the Town Landing Place out to the island. He brings with him two women, neither of whom is married to him, his writing pad, a small amount of cash and to bundle it all together, a kind of half-baked ideology which he has been working out for the past few years which he insipidly calls "the doctrine of happiness,"

Despite various complications, only some of which he shares in his memoir *An Island Cabin*, Henry manages to remain on the island he calls "Quirk" from May until the second week of October. Those are the days when Henry finds Noank serving "a long line of schooners and smacks... bearing steadily up and down the Sound and all kinds of smaller craft criss-crossing over it." Ashore, the village reflects this maritime focus in large and small ways, from the great Palmer Shipyard at the lower end of the peninsula to the jumble of portable lobster gear stored in the tiny back garden sheds all along "the grassy lanes." He never knows just what to expect, but when he stumbles across something, everything seems more in harmony with the neighborhood:

During most of the month of June, in passing Mr. Potter's

house, going to and from a nearby dock, I had seen a good-sized sailboat, bereft of canvass and rigging, reposing in his dooryard, its mast and rigging rising to a level with the eves.

There were boats that, in such a place, would look like pigs in a parlor, but this one seemed as much at home as did the old yellow cat asleep by the door...

The people who live in such a place are, of course, as much a part of it as the furniture and it is their pace of living that to Henry is the key. It is not merely a matter of the arbitrary eccentricity of what Dreiser here calls "the rural soul." In addition to the artisans there are the old salts such as the laconic squarerigger Captain Louie and his scoundrel parrot; a nearby island philosopher-caretaker Sam; and, John MacDonald the busy supervisor of the great Palmer Shipbuilding Yard, who takes the time out one day on the steps of the barbershop to ask the writer a favor:

I want to ask something of you. I want you to get the sentiment in... Life is just full of it, but it is hard for a man to always see it. Now, take the shipyard for instance. I know there is sentiment there enough around me every day. And I wish I could feel it more and not do anything to the contrary. But I've over three hundred men at work... I have to keep things going, and I am just forced contrary to sentiment. Now, you come down there some day, and get it all out of me, and write it down where I can have it to read when things don't go right, will you?

There are assorted passing sloop sailors and voices in the harbor night. Here is our hero rowing ashore one evening and pontificating to one of his women about how organic their wisdom has been growing by the minute. He has yet to assimilate the fact of lobster cars floating at sea level:

"Look out!" cried Nancy.

The boat stopped short with a bump, and I was thrown upon my back in the bottom of it, my feet in the air.

"You'll find it handier to go around those things," said a gruff voice close to me.

The pitch here is perfect and if you commit a similar kinesthetic screw-up today and are fortunate enough to be witnessed by one of the old Noankers, this is pretty much the cadence in which you will be apprised of the situation.

Along the way, Henry augments his entourage with his old writing pal Theodore Dreiser and his wife and their maid and three cats and two dogs. In *An Island Cabin* this invitation to the man Henry calls "Ted" seems like the most maddening of blunders, but the depth of the two men's previous relationship must be understood. So close was this connection that Dreiser characterized Henry as his "other self." Henry had been his editor on *The Toledo Blade* and they had spent long hours together socializing and dreaming up big time careers for themselves as book writers. The year before they came to Noank, Dreiser, on a bet with Henry, has just written and managed to force Doubleday & Doran to publish his first book, the novel *Sister Carrie*, now a staple in the canon of American realism, but then an embarrassment to the publishing industry. While on the island Dreiser attempts to recoup his literary losses by going ashore and interviewing the local color. Three pieces "The Village Feudists," "A Doer of the World," and "A Cripple Whose Energy Gives Inspiration" (also titled "The Noank Boy") result and eventually have found their way into the Dreiser canon. They are here republished in one volume along with Henry's memoir for the reciprocal light they cast. Also included is a review of some local adventures in scholarship on these four works

Nothing is as perplexing these days in the world of literature than the division between fiction and non-fiction. It is a distinction that has suffered what mariner's call a bearing drift. In a way Theodore Dreiser was responsible in 1925 for beginning some of this with a long prose narrative based on newspaper and court accounts of a murder trial in upstate New York that he fleshed out with remembrances of meals, streets, fire hydrants etc. that he himself had witnessed. But the "novel" *An American Tragedy* was not Dreiser's first venture into the realm we seem compelled to call since Capote's *In Cold Blood*, "non-fiction." (John Hersey was probably correct in claiming his *Hiroshima* as the first modern non-fiction novel. If Daniel Defoe were around, he'd probably have his hand up for his working up of Alexander Selkirk's shipwreck.)

The naive notion that Henry's book is "true" whereas Dreiser's sketches are not "true" has proved useless. Arthur Henry changes the names of his principle characters, fudges the finances, omits a visit from his wife while his mistress is present, but keeps the names of the locales and the place. Essentially Dreiser changes no names and seems to use no composite characters.

The dozen sketches Dreiser published together as *Twelve Men* in 1919 and from which two pieces on Noank are reissued here, was originally given a fiction number under the Dewey decimal system by the Library of Congress, and so it is still classified by the Noank Historical Society. However, of recent years, rare book dealers have taken to listing it as non-fiction. The University of Pennsylvania which houses the major Dreiser collection, has somewhat dodged the issue by listing it as a category that almost seems invented for especially for Dreiser, "American Realism." Arthur Henry's *An Island Cabin*, on the other hand, has always been classified as non-fiction.

Except in a rhetorical spat, a work does not become fiction by nature of factual mistakes or debatable opinions. Conversely, the employment of real names for people, gadgets and places does not make for non-fiction. The *it* in "it really happened" is often a matter of focus as much as fact. (Who is looking where and when with what preconceptions or later persuasions?) There is Hemingway's *obiter dicta* about "true" books which are true emotionally if not so factually. There is Frank Mankiewicz's comment that Hunter Thompson's *Rolling Stone* reporting on George McGovern's run for president was the factually less true but the most accurate. As for the "real" in *really*, semanticists have long recognized four meanings of the word *true*: empirical, logical, subjective and directive. The Latin root of *fact* and *fiction* is the same, *to make*. The Latin root of *real* is *res* which gives the nod to *thing* as the privileged truth. And none of this semantic housekeeping addresses the bottomless metaphysical pit of *what is true?* In an age where we classify Sebastian Junger's *The Perfect Storm* as non-fiction and Joseph Conrad's "Youth" as fiction, the old membrane between the genres seems unmanageably porous. But what is perhaps the most interesting aspect of *An Island Cabin* is not the ephemeral idyll on the Isle o' Quirk with its ambiguous *fin de siécle* hanky-panky, as the book's refracted view of the hard working village on the far shore.

In the Afterword we attempt, among other matters, to distinguish on a case by case basis some of the quarrels over the empirical truth of these four pieces. The effort is by no means exhaustive and scholars are invited to tramp the paths. (Watch out for ticks and the poison ivy.)

—*Schooner Wharf*
Mystic, Connecticut

AN
ISLAND CABIN

ARTHUR HENRY

From Ram Island at low, low tide. As now, one hardly need wet a foot to skip over to the big island. This is the "narrow run" which at high tide was the watery passageway of the jaunty old gent in the sailboat which so impressed Arthur Henry.

CHAPTER I

WHILE the world on shore is gasping in the heat I am sitting on the porch of my island cabin, the sound of the incoming tide in my ears, the cool salt air sweeping about me.

There are those so poor that they must walk through the blazing streets to their work in stores and factories. There are those rich enough to idle the summer in mountain and water-side resorts. I belong to neither of these classes, nor to any of the grades between. I am so poor in pocket that, were I in the city, I should often walk to save my nickel, and yet my days are filled with such comfort and delight as only the possessor of millions is supposed to enjoy.

I am lord of an Isle. The nearest mainland is a mile away. I have not seen a policeman nor disagreed with my neighbor for a month. There are days together when the wide stretch of water between me and all laws and customs is rough enough to swamp a boat. Every stone and inch of earth, the great rocks and smooth white beach of my little kingdom are mine to do with as I will. The wind and water bring food and fuel to my borders, requiring of me only the effort of taking it.

For years I had heard of little islands along the coast from Connecticut to Maine that were owned by no one and could be had for the claiming. I had heard of them vaguely. They took form in my fancy, dotting a fanciful sea, green-hooded isles with a wall of rocks and a sandy beach. They were my possessions in Spain. Some time, when I became rich, I would select my own and settle there, with my income and my books, in peace. It is a question if one's dreams can be bought with a surplus. I got mine for three hundred dollars, and I believe that I enjoy their possession because I had no more.

For years I had heard of them and longed for one of my own and done nothing, held, like most of those I know, grinding at the mill, by a fancied necessity. And so it might have been forever had not a vagrant impulse intervened.

It was a raw Sunday in December. I had spent the day with my friends, Nancy and Elizabeth. A friend of Nancy's had told her of a number of unclaimed islands off the Connecticut coast. "He says if you want an island, go up to Noank and see Captain Green, an old sailor, who knows those waters."

We got time-tables and maps and found Noank to lie half-way between New London and Stonington, just where Fishers Island Sound joins the sea.

"Some day," I said, "we'll get us an island, you, Elizabeth and I, or, if Mother Grundy objects, we'll get two of them close together."

"Some day is a long time off," said Nancy. "I wish we had one now."

On my way home in the afternoon, I found myself near the slip of the Stonington boat. I had seven dollars in my pocket. The fare to Noank and return would be six dollars. I had passed this way often in the heat of the summer, looked at the boat, dreamed my dream and turned away. Now, when the icy wind stung my face, I went aboard and bought my ticket. To be sure, I had never known before just where to go, but I have often wondered at my proceeding.

At sunrise, I left the train at Noank and walked along a winding, narrow street, over a hill, through the town. Lights were still shining in kitchen windows, for the day had not yet penetrated the houses, and the village, accustomed to rising at four o'clock during the fishing season, was astir early even on this winter morning when it might have slept. Snow lay upon trees and bushes, covered the stone walls and picket fences that bordered the streets, and hid the fields, rising over the hills to the west. The east half of the town is a sharp slope to the water-side, and I could look down every side street across Fishers Island Sound and out to sea. Descending a hill at the southeastern end, I passed through the shipyard, and came out upon a point of land where stands the Noank lighthouse, and, just this side of it, the home of Captain Green. On one side of the road was his house; on the other, his workshop, resting partly on land and partly on piles over the water. He was once a Norse sailor—a captain in the merchant marine. He is now a rigger of boats. I found him at this early hour opening a coil of rope in his shop. He had just extinguished his lamp, for the light of sunrise, glancing across the sea and Sound, fell upon his work through the eastern windows. A fire was roaring in the stove. The wind and water were noisy at the door.

"Good morning, Captain," said I.

He lifted his grizzled head into the red light falling through the window back of him, and peered at me for a moment, silent.

"Come closer," he said, "so's I can see who ye be."

"You never saw me before," said I, "but I have come up from New York to see you."

I was close to him now, and saw that his eyes were of a clear blue, keen, shrewd and questioning. His face was red and rugged, a strong, well-preserved Norse face, seasoned by a life of sunlight, rain and salt air.

I told him my errand and asked him if he could help me.

"There's islands off here, true enough—little hummocks and reefs—but I don't know as there's any fit to live on."

"Where are they, Captain? Can you see them from here?"

He threw the door open and a strong, cold wind swept in. A handful of spray came over the door-sill. Far to our right lay the long, low ridge of Fishers Island, its eastern point reaching into the ocean. To the left of us ran the Connecticut coast, coming to a point about seven miles away at Watch Hill. Looking straight before us, between the nose of Fishers Island and Watch Hill, we could see the ocean. In this direction, a mile away, were four islands, one of about five acres, the others just rocky hummocks, rising from the water and capped with soil.

"The large one is Mystic Island," said the Captain. "It belongs to a Norwich man. The three dumplings are no one's, so far as I know."

I looked at the distant islands in the tossing water with a growing wonder and excitement. Could it be that I was soon to possess one?

"If I build a house on one of those," I asked, "will it be mine?"

"You can rig her up and claim her and she's yours."

"I wish I could get out there now and select one. Can you take me?"

He looked at me quizzically.

"If the *Eric Lief* was afloat we could we could sail out easy."

He glanced at his sloop hauled high on shore for the winter and I followed his glance wistfully.

"It's a trim boat," I said.

"Aye, it is. I made her myself—every bit of her."

"I could tell that by her staunch look. She favors you. I wish she were afloat."

"You want to get out there bad, don't you?"

"Yes, I do."

"Well, I'll row you. We can make it, I guess."

He took a pair of oars from their pegs, gave me a rubber coat and hat, clothed himself in a suit of tarpaulin, and climbed down the wet steps outside to a slippery landing, where a small boat was lying. He pushed it off into the water and held it away from the boards.

"Get in there quick," he commanded.

I jumped into the tossing boat, and he followed, pushing vigorously with an oar. A moment's wrestle with the waves, and we were safely off, wet from head to foot, and with a good cargo of water.

"Bail her out," he said, kicking a pail toward me. He was pulling steadily. The boat was tossing and lunging and the spray was falling over us. I did not know then the task he had undertaken. I have since tried this voyage against wind and tide, and failed. The Captain was steadily gaining way, and he was seventy years old.

"They are strong enemies," I said, "the wind and the tide."

Fully five minutes later he murmured, as if to himself:

"Not enemies, no, they are old friends of mine."

An hour's pull brought us to the nearest of the islands. We landed on a sandy beach in the lee. The wind did not reach us here. It was calm and warm in the sunshine. Clambering up the rocks, we found a quarter of an acre of smooth, rich earth, covered with a thick brush. The windward shore was solid rock, with wide, smooth ledges, precipitous walls, and huge boulders. Here the wind blew a gale, and the surf beat furiously. It was bitter cold, and the scene across the white-caps to the ocean was wild and desolate. But the sounds around me, the cold, the endless stretch of water, filled me with delight, and I fixed upon this island as my abode. I christened it "The Isle o' Quirk."

Back in the Captain's shop, I drew a plan for a cabin, and that afternoon secured a carpenter to build it before spring for two hundred and seventy-five dollars.

The last week in May the cabin was completed. Early Saturday morning we were in Noank—Elizabeth, Nancy and I. The day before we had spent two hours shopping. It cost us thirty dollars to buy what we needed—a kitchen-table, a hammock, water pails, two rustic settees, two camp chairs, agate-ware plates, coffee cups, kettles, and frying pans, steel knives, aluminum spoons and forks, a hatchet, a coil of rope, the ticking for four narrow beds, and the bedding. The department store in New York shipped these goods without charge, and we found them waiting for us at the depot. We opened our trunk on the platform, and got out the ticks.

"Where can I get these filled?" I asked of the station master, who stood watching us with a friendly interest."

You're the Isle o' Quirk people, ain't you?" he asked.

"Yes. Where can I get some straw?"

"There's a farmer just down the road there, second house from the corner—he fills ticks."

We found him at his breakfast and called him to the kitchen door.

"Can I get these ticks filled?"

He looked at us in silence until I repeated my question. Then he said slowly, as if there was some almost insurmountable obstacle in the way:

"Yes, I guess you can."

"How much?"

He thought a long time over this, looked at his wife, at the ticks, at the barn, and then at us.

"Well, I guess about a dollar and a quarter for the four of them."

"When can I get them? I want them delivered to Ashbey's dock. He will take us to the island."

"I kinder thought you was the Quirk Island folks," he said, with an expression of relieved curiosity.

"How soon can you have them there?"

"Well, some time to-day or to-morrow, if it don't rain."

"Oh, come. We must have them over this morning. Come out to the barn and fill them now. We'll help you."

"Well, mebbe I can," he said, slowly.

We got him to the barn, threw down the straw, and saw the ticks filled and put on his wagon and his ox team yoked.

At the station, we found our boxes loaded on a one-horse wagon. Perched on the seat was a sturdy, bustling little Irishman, with a broad, contorted mouth and a shrewd eye.

"Where to?" he asked, picking up the reins. He scarcely waited for me to say Ashbey's dock before he was off.

"That's Bill," said the station master.

"He seems a brisk fellow."

"Yes, Bill's wide-awake. There's another fellow gone to expressing here now—got a new wagon and a faster horse. Bill was afraid you'd hire him, so he loaded up and was ready."

We followed our things along the winding street, through the town. It was a gray, windy day, but never have I met a finer welcome from the spring. Noank is a bower of trees and vines and bushes. Every house in it has been hauled from the sea in fish nets, and set here with all the sailor's love of his haven. They are clean, snug and well-preserved with white paint. The yards are carefully tended; the stone walls and white picket fences straight and whole.

The apple trees were in full bloom. Hundreds of bushes, burdened with purple, pink, salmon and white blossoms crowded the yards. Nearly every house was half hidden by wistaria vines. The air was heavy with perfumes. I have never heard so many song-birds. Except for these and the sound of the northwest wind among the trees, and the water under the hill the little town was very quiet. We saw no one as we wound through it. We found Bill at the dock and sent him for Mr. Ashbey.

"Is that it?" asked Nancy in a whisper of excitement, holding her hat from the snatches of strong wind and pointing across the water.

"It is," I replied.

We stood in silence, our eyes fixed upon the little island, a mile away. We could see the house plainly. Its wide porches gave it the appearance of a bird with spreading wings.

When Ashbey came, he looked at the flying clouds and the choppy sea, and shook his head.

It's pretty rough. I don't know as we can make it with this load."

"Let's try it," I urged.

"Are the women afraid?"

"No, indeed," said Nancy eagerly.

"All right, we can do it safely if you're not afraid."

We piled the boxes and trunk in his catboat, and put the bed ticks across a sharpie, fastened to our stern by a tow line. Twenty minutes later we stood on the beach of the island. Crossing the sand, we clambered up a path through the bushes, over the rocks and reached the porch of the cabin. Down on the beach, in the lee, it was warm and still. Here on the porch we felt the sweep of a strong, cold wind, and thirty feet away, where the rocky north shore rose boldly from the sea, the waves were pounding tumultuously. As far as the eye could see in this direction stretched the water, rolling in great, white-capped billows from the ocean. Dark clouds were moving swiftly over us. The Connecticut coast, to the left, and Fishers Island, to the south, were almost lost in the gray mist.

"I wish we could have a heavy storm," I said.

"Well, I guess you will," said Ashbey. "You'd better get some wood in the first thing you do. I'll get back home, if you don't mind."

He hurried down to the boat, threw the boxes and trunk on the beach, left me the sharpie with its load, and put back to Noank.

Nancy and Elizabeth were in the cabin, and I heard the sounds of clearing and cleaning. I knocked the boxes open with a stone, and carried in the things. Before this was done the rain had begun. I gathered a great pile of drift wood and stored it on the porch. Suddenly the storm broke. The rain fell in torrents and the wind rose to a tempest. As we closed the doors and windows of the cabin, and stood looking at each other and listening to the tumult of sounds outside, our eyes lit with delight. This was a grand welcome from the elements we had come to dwell among. The storm could not frighten us, for we loved it and heard no malice in its voice.

In a few moments, we were at work again. We built a roaring fire in the fireplace, hung the hammock across the room, put a gay-colored blanket over the table for a spread, drove nails for the kettles, built racks for the dishes, and made the whole place as bright and cozy as a ship's cabin.

For three days and nights the storm raged, and we did not weary of it. I have never had enough of a storm. The wind has always hailed me with a wild halloo and fled before I could find my wings to join it. The rain has beat upon the street I followed, or fallen with a multitude of sounds through the trees over me, or lured me to the loft where I might sit dry and hear its serenade, but it has always ceased before its song was finished, and left me dangling at the broken ends of its melody. On this island, I may get my fill of weather. Storms on land are strolling minstrels, or, at best, but little more than street bands, and on the open sea, they are not much better, for there, though the wind may wipe out cities and dismantle ships, it plays too much alone. Here in this harbor of the Sound, opening upon the ocean, in the midst of islands, exposed reefs and hidden rocks, where the tide races through the channel and human effort comes in contact with the elements on every hand, a storm is a full orchestra, with a great chorus of man's devising.

From the northeast, if it keeps its wind, it may come from Europe without obstruction. On the southwest, there is nothing but the bridges of the East River to check its course up the Sound from New York to me. On the south, I am sheltered by Fishers Island; on the north, by Connecticut, but as one of these wind-breaks is three miles and the other a mile away, they do not smother me. I am set in the midst of a watery highway. Three hundred feet west is a bush buoy, marking the edge of my shoal. On a line with this, a little to the north, is a pole buoy, that swings with the tide. Just outside of these is the channel between Noank and Stonington. A mile and a half to the south is the main channel of the Sound, running between New York, New Haven, New Bedford, New London, Stonington, Watch Hill and the ocean. I can see eight of the lighthouses marking this way. Four of them form a straight line southwest. They are the Noank, North Dumpling, Race Rock and Gull Island lights. Just abreast of me, in the centre of the channel, a light-ship rides at anchor. Three miles further east rises the rock and round tower of Latimer's Reef, standing boldly against an horizon of air and water. Northeast of this, forming the other two points of a triangle, are the Stonington and Watch Hill lights. With a steady wind, on a fine, clear day, or on a starry night, this channel is an open, gleaming pathway. The tide for twenty hours of the day is racing through it with a deadly force to the helpless, but the course is marked and when all is fair, a bark canoe might skim it safely. But when the wind is strong and the sea high, when rain or fog conceals the lights and buoys, it becomes at once a narrow, tortuous runway between a thousand impending deaths. Then you have your orchestra at play. The wind alone has many voices here. It rushes across the surface of the water with a prolonged hissing, it shrieks about the dormer windows of my cabin, it whistles and moans down the chimney, it whips the green bushes and sings through the stripped branches of the dead wood; it passes overhead and through the unimpeded ways abroad, with the roar of an invisible avalanche. My cabin, anchored to the rocks, trembles in its clutching, tugging arms like a wild bird in its captor's hand.

And the water, in a tempest from the north, thunders against the rocks until the island quivers. It washes the ledges, sucks at the holes it has made, gurgles in the crevices, and slips, hissing, back to meet the next billow, as it comes rolling and crashing in.

The roll, the beating, the wash and gurgle of the water, is constant, while the storm lasts. The wind is variable—a moment's violence, a moment's lull. The rain comes with the rush of wind against the windows and sides of the cabin, and when the wind retreats, it falls with a steady downpour upon the roof and water. These are the parts the elements play. But in all this storm, sailing craft and steam vessels are threading the channel with its rushing tide, its rocks and reefs, and through the sounds of water, wind and rain, come the hoarse calls of boat whistles, far and near, the constant warning of the light-ship's bell, the distant bellow of the fog trumpet at Race Rock, nine miles away.

To describe these individual voices or the marvellous effect of their combination, would take a lifetime. Of them all, the most important to me has been the light-ship's bell, for it has given me a sound to the quality of mercy; it has made my ear familiar with the spirit of tender, watchful benevolence. For a day and a night I have sat in the midst of a fog so thick I could not see through my window and greedily listened to its tolling. As if rung by a clock, it sounds every minute with three notes, the first two in close succession, the third after a moment's interval. When it is still and the fog lies dense and motionless, these three musical notes steal from it softly, sounding far away through the muffled air. The unseen boats, creeping slowly, feeling their way, call and call again with anxious toots and prolonged whistles, but the bell, neither hastened nor delayed, regular as the throbbing of a steady, wise and tender heart, sounds its mellow notes for all or none. And when the storm is raging and the rain or driving mist obscures the light, its kindly voice flies with the wind or penetrates against it, faithful, sweet and undisturbed. The maker of this bell, by chance or design, fashioned a masterpiece. It is the true voice of Providence. What the shepherds heard on the hills near Bethlehem is repeated for the crew of a coal barge or the belated fisherman, beating against the wind, through the fog or rain, where the tide races through Fishers Island Sound.

On the fourth morning, we awoke to the sunlight. The storm had swept the atmosphere clean and the air was cool and clear. We walked the shores of the island in amazement, the world about us no longer lost in fog or vaguely outlined through the gray of rain and mist. The water was a brilliant blue, rippling and sparkling, like an inland lake. The little houses among the trees on the hills of Noank, the white church, with its spire and golden weather-vane, rose so close to us that we could see the people moving like toys in a cardboard town. A speck of a woman, no larger than a lady-bug, was shaking the bedclothes from an attic window.

The Connecticut shore was a long, low line of green. Stonington and Watch Hill, white and gleaming, were set between the blue sky and water like painted cities in a fanciful, fairy-like, unreal world.

All day, the sounds of tools upon the oak timber came to us from the shipyard, softened by the distance, and distinct because of its unobstructed way. We heard a snatch of song, a fragment of laughter, the call of a voice. We saw the sea gulls preening their feathers on the rocks of a little island a quarter of a mile to the east. Along the channel of the Sound passed a steady line of ships, and far out to sea were white sails leaning from the wind.

Since that morning, most of the days have been mild and fair. Every moment of the day or night there is a new wonder unfolding before me, if I choose to look.

You may have an island if you will take one, but to enjoy it, you must love the wind and the rain, the water and the fog, the sunlight and the tasks of the day.

I have found, in fact, that to be happy and comfortable here, beyond the first few days of novelty, one must possess the spirit to be so anywhere. The requirements are the same, the facilities, of different outward form, are still the same. I loved these surroundings first because they were new and beautiful. I love them more now because they are familiar.

Familiar things are never the same to us. They have a different aspect, a new meaning for every moment. The man who is intimate with his surroundings is never idle. There is no monotony for him. His soul and mind and body must be on the jump. All things shift and change with a swiftness of itself unlimited, and limited to each of us by the measure of our perception. A landscape, an occupation, the routine of a day, becomes most monotonous to him who is most aloof from it, who looks most often at it and sees it less.

I have been on my island for a month alone. I have had my friends here. To me it is always wonderful. I live on two dollars a week and what I gather from the sea. When I am alone, I must be up at sunrise and move briskly to do my necessary manual work and get two hours in which to read or write. When my friends come up, the labor is divided, and I may busy myself with neglected things—I may loaf longer, dream more, discuss the world and my neighbors, dispute a bit, take voyages of exploration up and down the Sound, or among the islands, or along the coast. I may some time get beyond Watch Hill and into the ocean. My sharpie is twelve feet long and has a centreboard and mutton-leg sail. It cost me twenty-two dollars.

When I came here in May, I was ignorant of the sea, above and below. I was landed on an island, as barren of the comforts of civilization as a reef in mid-ocean. The problems of food and fresh water, of cleanliness and comfort, were for me to solve. In meeting the necessities of existence here, and doing, with my own hands, the things that must be done if I would live in comfort and plenty, I have crept into an intimate and friendly understanding with the life about me and found my happiness in the common details of my days.

CHAPTER II

THREE days of storm had left us on our island with little food and no water. The fourth morning, as I came out early to watch the dawn of a fair day, I saw Captain Green in a row-boat, making for our beach. The water was without a ripple, and the sound of the oar-locks and dipping oars came to me mellow and clear. The Captain threw a net full of live lobsters on the shore and pushed away. I called to him to come in, but he would not.

"No, no," he said brusquely, "I smell of fish. Been hauling up my lobster-pots and thought you'd like some."

I wanted him to come in and talk with me, for to such a man seventy years of life must have brought many events. I knew this much of him,— he had loved his wife and given up the sea for her sake. Rum and tobacco had once been his boon companions, but he had tossed them from him on his wedding day. His wife was dead and when he spoke of her now, it was with a hushed and tender voice, a softening of the eye. He had also spoken once or twice of a wrong he had suffered. I could see that it was a bitter thing to him, constantly present in his mind. But it was difficult to break through his rugged personality. He escaped me, as he did this morning, with an act of kindness and a brusque departure. I stood on the beach, the net of lobsters at my feet, until he and his boat, like a speck on the water, slipped into the shelter of his shop on shore. Then, as I stooped for the lobsters, I saw a sail making for the island. It was Ashbey's catboat. He brought her about and came ashore, bringing a jug of fresh water, two loaves of bread, a ginger cake and a morning paper.

"I see you're still here," he said cheerily.

"Oh, yes, we weathered the storm."

"My women folks were worried about you."

"I am sorry for that, for we enjoyed every moment of it."

"You don't say so. Well, if you liked those three days, you ought to be happy here. You won't get a spell as bad as that this season."

He spoke so pleasantly that I hated to mention the chimney, but he had built the house for me and it must be done. So, even as I took the water, the bread, the cake and the newspaper, I said:

"The only trouble here is with the fireplace. It smokes."

"It does, eh?"

"Yes, it fills the house with smoke."

His face fell at once and he looked at me anxiously, his eyes filling with the hesitating, helpless distress of a sensitive child when it is scolded.

"The house itself," I hastened to say, "is perfection. I never saw so strong and warm a cabin."

Instantly, his face brightened and he hastened up the path with me, explaining as we went, just how he had figured on the best location, how he had selected the lumber and used only the best nails, how he had finished off the doors and windows so the wind and rain could not penetrate.

"I thought," said he, "you would want one porch to face Noank, so I set the house for that. I tell you, it's a grand view of Noank from here."

The view I had wished for most was the one across the Sound and out to sea. Noank seemed much too near and I looked upon the porch we now stood on as practically useless. The other side of the house was where I expected to sit. There I could utterly forget, for a season, the world of men, groping, greedily reaching, toiling and contending, and rest my soul in the limitless spaces of sky and water. But I could not tell him this, and it was not necessary, for the porch upon the other side gave me what I wanted, and there were the wide ledges of rock, beside.

"Yes," I said, as he left me, "the cabin is warm and strong. The storm did not shake it."

"I did for you as I would for myself," he answered heartily.

Glancing at the net I held, he added:

"Captain Green brought you those? You will want to set some pots of your own. You can catch all the lobsters and fish you can eat.

"When I entered the house with my booty, Nancy and Elizabeth were descending the stairs, wrapt in their dressing gowns, on their way for their morning bath. I told them of our visitors and showed them the gifts. The lobsters, great green and black creatures, were struggling in the net, clutching at and crushing each other with their strong claws.

"I thought lobsters were red," said Elizabeth, eyeing them askance.

"They are, when they are boiled," said Nancy, cautiously poking one with her finger. "How do you handle them?" she asked.

"I don't know. We must find out. Ashbey says we can catch all we want if we get some pots. I don't know what a lobster-pot is, nor how to set one, nor what kind of fish are to be caught here, nor how to catch them."

Here we were, in the midst of an unknown world, with plenty about us and everything to learn. From that moment, an eager spirit of industry possessed us.

The girls hurried down to the beach for their bath, and I, taking my towel, went to the other side of the island, where the water was deep. I spread my clothes on the rocks in the sun and plunged in. Compared to this bath-room of sky, salt water and great granite border, how poor and little seemed the porcelain tub, not quite my own length, where I had taken my cold bath all winter. A plunge, a stroke or two, and I was out again in the sun, on the warm rocks, tingling and aglow. My clothes seemed never so sweet and wholesome to me as when I put them on after their sunning.

"That beach," said Elizabeth, "will be perfect when a few stones have been removed."

"Yes, that is one of the things we must do."

"How long do we boil the lobsters?" asked Nancy, "and how can we ever get them into the kettle?"

"If it takes very long," said I, "let us have our coffee, bread and butter and potatoes now. I can't wait."

"We have no more butter, and the lobsters ought to be ready as soon as the potatoes are. Come on now, let us try them. We must put them alive in boiling water. I know that much."

When the time came, we untied the net and shook the lobsters on the floor. They immediately backed toward the corner of the room, reaching out with their menacing claws. We picked them up between two sticks and dropped them in the kettle. They did not seem to notice the hot water. I was surprised by this, for it had seemed a cruel thing to do, and I had dreaded the moment of their fall into the kettle. But lobsters seem to have no sense of pain. Their one desire is for food. They reach for whatever comes near them and close upon it, if they can. If it be good to eat, they hold fast; if not, they drop it. A broken claw or the loss of their eyes, boiling water, a crushed body, do not cause them a start or quiver.

We allowed the lobsters to cook until the potatoes were done and the rest of the meal was served, about forty minutes in all, and found that we had guessed close enough. It was a grand breakfast, but soon finished, for we now saw a multitude of important things waiting for us to do.

All the driftwood I had gathered was gone, and I went about our shore line to find what the storm had brought us. High upon the rocks was about thirty feet of the railing of a steamer, with its nets of rope clinging to it. A little further was a panel from a state-room and a piece of gilt scroll work. The tide was low, and I hauled this wood well out of the reach of its return. I wondered if these evidences of disaster were from a recent wreck, and scanned the water for further signs. It stretched around me, smooth, still and glossy, like a vast cloth of lilac and lavender satin. The little island, a quarter of a mile to the east, that I have named

"Ahoy," stood clearly forth, its shore of gleaming sand and rocks like a silver ring, its mound of earth and sod like an emerald setting. Here and there were pieces of driftwood afloat, but almost motionless, for it was the time of slack water, just before the turning of the tide. It was difficult to realize that this placid element had been so wild and terrible but the day before. Here at my feet were the fragments of a strong ship, and the water that had tossed them up would now float a maple leaf without moistening its upper surface.

I found a barrel resting between two rocks at the water's edge, and a little further, a piece of oak and a mass of small sticks and chips. By degrees, I worked around the island and came to the beach. Here I found Nancy and Elizabeth, in their bathing-suits and rubber boots, washing the dishes with sand and salt water.

"Look," said Nancy, "I found it in the sand."

She held up a baby's shoe, a little white kid, soiled and streaked with yellow.

"And here," said Elizabeth, "is the blade of an oar. It must have snapped in the hand of some one struggling with the storm."

She stood up and waved the frying-pan she held toward the water.

"You beautiful, sleek creature," she exclaimed. "I hear your soft purring among the pebbles. I see your innocent repose and seductive tints, but what of this baby's shoe and this broken oar?"

"Your pose is very dramatic," said Nancy, scooping a handful of sand for the kettle she was scrubbing, "but the sentiment is too worn to move me. I don't believe there is any malice in the sea. We seem to think it should run with our desires and when it don't, it's a mean, old thing. It seems to me that the sea is a great and noble force, attending to its grand duties in a grand way."

"Elizabeth lowered her extended arm, and squatting in the water, renewed her work upon the frying-pan.

"This sand," said she, "is a fine thing to scour with, but salt water don't seem to take the grease off."

"We really ought to have a little more fresh water for washing purposes," said Nancy. "Do you suppose," she added, looking up at me, "that we could have a well?"

"We can't afford that now," said I, "but that was a fine idea of yours about the sea. Men have called the sea treacherous, just as they revile any force they don't understand, and that doesn't always work in their favor. A few thousand years ago there was some excuse for this; then, for men to think about the sea at all was a step in advance. What was then, however, the inspiration of a searching mind becomes now but a thoughtless repetition. For thousands of years we have seen the sea calm and beautiful when the air is still, and we have seen it rough when the wind blows. For six hours the tide flows out, and for six hours it comes in, with such exact regularity that its course can be predicted for years in advance. There is surely nothing underhanded in all that. If it were less to be counted on under conditions as we learn to know them; if it turned, for instance, every time you turned your boat; if it occasionally lay quiet in a tempest and rose in furious white-caps when the air was still, or there was no eruption of the earth to cause a tidal wave, we might suspect it of treachery. Take this broken oar—"

"Yes," said Elizabeth, "take it and reach me my dish-pan; the tide is carrying it away.

"And where is my water-pail?" exclaimed Nancy. "It was here a moment ago."

"I see something off there."

"That's it, half-way to Noank."

"Well," said I, "we must do some marketing this morning and if we start now, the tide that carried the pail away will help us over."

I had not yet bought my boat with a centre-board and sail, but was using the sharpie Ashbey had left with me. This was our first trip to Noank, and we were surprised at the ease of our voyage. I rowed without once stopping for breath and with no sense of weariness. The girls lolled in the stern seat and I pulled leisurely, even feathering my oars. I watched the receding island with its cabin perched like a bird among the brush, and the glowing, peaceful world of water through which we moved. I was filled with a great contentment and smiled upon the girls, who smiled in answer to my spirit. Following my eye as it glanced beyond her, Nancy turned and looked lovingly at the tranquil scene.

"A dream come true," she said. "I can't quite feel its reality yet."

"And to me, too," I said, "it has a peculiar, dream-like quality. It has always seemed so far away and now it is here. To think that so great a treasure may be so easily possessed. And now to enjoy it, we have only to enjoy the details of life here, supplying such necessities as we may, and forgetting what we must lack in what we can delight in. I have only two dollars a week for myself. That is my limit just now, if I would stay here. What have we to buy to-day?"

"A dozen eggs," said Elizabeth; "a pound of butter, a pound of coffee, a quart of milk, two loaves of bread and a quart of molasses. We all like molasses, and it can take the place of fruit and desserts for us. It is cheap, satisfying and full of food."

"Good," said I. "When we have learned about the lobsters and the fishing, we will need fewer eggs. In fact, we can live on fish, potatoes and bread, if we have to."

"Look out!" cried Nancy.

The boat stopped short with a bump, and I was thrown upon my back in the bottom of it, my feet in the air.

"You'll find it handier to go around those things," said a gruff voice close to me.

I got to my seat, rescued the oar that had flown overboard, and glanced at the obstacle in our way. It was a large square box, perforated with auger holes, floating at anchor about a hundred feet from the dock. I turned toward the man who had counselled me. He was a short, thick-set, smooth-shaved, rugged man, standing on the deck of his catboat, a coil of rope in his hand, a number of strange looking objects piled about him.

"What did I run into?" I asked, pushing away from the box.

"That's a fish car," he said. "I keep my lobsters in it till I have enough to sell."

"And what are those things on deck—lobster-pots?"

"Yes; I am going out to the channel to set them."

"How far do you go?"

"My ranges are off Race Rock—about nine miles southwest."

"Must you go so far to get lobsters?"

"To get enough to sell, we do."

"Well, I only want enough to eat."

"You can drop a couple just off your island near the pole buoy and catch all you'll want."

"Have you got any pots to sell?"

"I might spare you a couple."

"How much?"

All rigged up with nets, warp and floats—a dollar apiece."

"All right, I'll take them."

"That's my shop by the dock there. Come in when you're ready. I sha'n't start for an hour yet."

The marketing was now of small interest, for I was to plunge at once into the mysteries of lobstering. We postponed our ramble through the village, made our purchases at one store and hurried back to Captain Peterson's shop.

My pots were standing by the door. They were about two feet wide and three feet long, and made of lath, almost the shape of a half-barrel, split lengthwise.

"You throw this back," said the Captain, showing me an opening on the side, "and hang your bait on this hook in the middle."

"The lobsters come through this hole in the end?"

"Yes. Your pot sinks to the bottom. You must set it where there are rocks, for the lobsters come there to feed. They smell your bait and crawl through this hole after it."

I now understood the arrangement of the pot. It was divided into two sections. The lobster, entering the open end, would crawl through a funnel-shaped net toward the top and drop through the small end into the bottom of the pot. The bait would then hang just above him, at the opening of a second net funnel. Crawling up this, he would reach the bait. When he had eaten, and was ready to leave, he would find his readiest progress, for the moment, through the funnel, into the second compartment. Here he would remain a prisoner, groping at the bottom and remembering no more the little hole at the top by which he had entered.

"You fasten your warp here," said the Captain, showing me where he had tied the rope to the pot."

"I have given you a hundred feet of warp. We use seventy-five fathoms in the channel, but this will do for you. You fasten this small float about ten feet from the pot to keep the bight of the warp from catching in the rocks, and this large float we fasten to the loose end, so you can pick it up from your boat when you haul the pots."

When I haul the pots! With these words in my ear, I hastened to load the boat and push away. I was puffed with knowledge. The mystery of an hour ago was now made clear. I held the life of many lobsters in my hand, and by another morning I would haul my pots.

It had taken me twenty minutes to row over. I expected to return in fifteen, by keeping a strong, steady stroke.

We were scarcely under way when Elizabeth said, in a voice of deep reflection:

"It is hard on the lobster."

"I have thought a good deal about that," I replied. "Should we catch a lobster, throw it alive in boiling water and eat it? To answer that, we must solve the whole problem of life. The same questions are involved wherever we turn. Our daily life is one great slaughter. Cows, sheep, hogs and hens fall by the hatchet or the knife. We draw in fresh air and consume it, casting out the stale remains. We ruthlessly haul water from the well and feed our veins. We plant living seed and coax them forth, guarding their life from all else that would devour it until it is ready for our use, when we haul it forth by the roots or mow it from the fields. We devour ourselves. Every pull on these oars destroys a portion of my being, and I cast the refuse from me into the crucible of life, where all things go, from whence all things come. And in all our labor, we destroy before we create."

"Here are the shipyards," I continued, as the great, ribbed hulls of barges and floats came into view, and the sounds of mallets, planes and whirling saws, the voices of workmen and the loud call of the bosses, filled my ears. As I looked and listened, I saw the forests that had fallen with their multitudes of insects, flowers, and birds, destroyed or driven forth, and I leaned upon my oars, the better to give expression to the thoughts that rushed upon me.

"Here are the shipyards—"

"But the island is over there," said Elizabeth, pointing. "We seem to be going away from it."

I saw at once that we were, and that, though I had been rowing constantly, we were still close to shore.

"Why didn't you tell me before?" I asked, pulling the boat about, surprised at my difficulty in doing so.

"We were lost in the discourse," said Nancy. "Really, now, I'm not sarcastic. I want to catch, kill and eat lobsters, and I was waiting to be justified."

"This boat seems to weigh a ton."

"Perhaps, it's the tide," said Elizabeth.

"It is." Her tone and glance caused me to add: "But that proves nothing. We knew that it would flow this way six hours from the time we started. We don't choose to wait for it, and must take our chances. Are the elements treacherous because our shifting desires take us upon the sea? What nonsense."

But I was through with argument, for, row as I would, we made slow progress. There was a wind now, blowing quite fresh from the east, and this, with the tide, so turned and twisted me that I was compelled to keep my boat several points from its true course and to row with all my strength to prevent its drifting past the lighthouse to the Sound. I tugged and puffed, until my face was purple and the sweat ran from me. An hour after leaving Noank, we made our beach.

I hurried around to the rocks and plunged into the water. When I was dressed again, my body rejoiced in the labor it had undergone.

I brought the lobster-pots from the boats and discovered that I had no bait. I did not know what to use nor where to get it. All my boasted knowledge was still of little use, for I had not yet learned enough. I stood for some time, with the empty pots at my feet, lost in reverie.

"And this is why," I thought, "there can be no final conclusion. Any theory of life is necessarily false in so far as it professes a complete solution. There must always be something more to learn. Every seal of finality that we affix is but the arbitrary closing of a path of thought against further perception."

I know that this is an old idea, but it now became my own, and for the sake of it, I was glad to have forgotten my bait.

When our dinner was ready, we spread the table on a wide ledge by the water-side, in the shade of a huge rock. And here we remained for the afternoon, in the cool east wind, sitting now in the shade, now in the warmth of the sun, watching the white sails upon the water, and the white clouds in the sky, for it was our first calm, fair day, and the vision was like a thing of magic, holding us irresistibly. And this was not idleness. All the world's activity is prompted by its search for delight, and he who finds it, sitting at his ease, achieves as much as he who opens a new diamond mine.

At sunset, we strolled to the beach, and watched the trembling colors on the water—the crimson and orange glow above the town of Noank. The wind had died away. Row-boats were moving from the shore. The sound of voices came clearly to us.

We looked across the narrow run between us and Mystic Island, and saw a man and a dog standing quietly on the grassy point, watching us. Their figures were vague in the twilight, but I saw the dog's bushy tail move slightly, and there was something decidedly amiable in the man's pose, and in the droop of his wide hat brim.

"Hello, neighbor," I called. He lifted one hand to his head and remained silent. An evil being would have made a sinister picture, standing as he stood in this lonely place; but so truly does the mind and body cast its import abroad that I felt the reason of his presence. He had come to show himself a good neighbor.

"Have you a well?" I asked.

"Oh, yes," came the answer in a soft, full voice, "we have a good well. Come over."

We got our pails and rowed across.

His name, I learned, was Gibbie Wilcox. With his wife, he kept the island for its owner. They had lived there eleven years. It was a half-mile walk from the point where we beached our boat to his house at the other end, overlooking the Sound. The path followed the ridge of a grassy field, sloping to the water on either side. In the soft twilight, the way was full of a tender beauty. We walked through wide beds of marguerites, and down through a hollow filled with tall, swamp grass. Here was a wild rose-bush, and there a vine-covered boulder.

"I see dandelions," I said. "Can we dig some up for greens on our way back?"

"Now, I'll tell you," answered Gibbie, with the unctuous good-will ever present in his voice and willing eye, "I can show you something better.

"He led the way to the edge of the island, and, stooping over, showed us a wild form of sweet pea.

"Just pick the tops," he said, "they make a tender green."

He took off his hat and filled it to its ample brim.

"Gibbie," I said, "I have some lobster-pots. What shall I bait them with?"

"Why, now, anything will do. You can buy bony fish in Noank, or you can use the blackfish and cunners you catch yourself."

"What sort of fish do you catch about here?"

"Mostly blackfish and cunners now."

"No flounders?"

"It's early for flounders. A little later you can get them right off your island."

"What kind of tackle shall I get?"

"Well, now, I'll fix you all out with tackle—I've plenty of it."

"And the bait, Gibbie?"

"Crabs make good bait. You can get all you want when the tide goes out, under the stones on your beach."

He took us to the well and pumped our water for us. Mrs. Wilcox came out with a loaf of bread and some baked beans.

"Well, this is good for you," said Nancy. "We can't bake in our fireplace, and we have to get our bread in Noank. And the beans do smell good."

Mrs. Wilcox beamed upon us with the friendliest good-will and took Nancy and Elizabeth into the house.

Gibbie got me the fish lines, fastened lead and hooks to them and answered my constant questions with a never-ceasing goodwill, seizing every opening for an offer of service.

"Now, you come past here in the morning," he said, "and I'll show you a good place to fish. It's all right, too, out by your pole buoy. There are rocks out there."

"What have the rocks to do with it?"

"The mussels cling to the rocks, and the fish come there to feed on the mussels.

"And the lobsters to feed on the fish?"

Yes—that's the way," he replied genially.

He helped me carry the water to the boat, and waved his hand as we landed on our own beach.

"Mrs. Wilcox told me to get her a sack of flour," said Nancy, "and she will bake our bread for us."

My head was dizzy with the impressions of the day.

The stars were out. Under them lay the still sea. The lovers of Noank were abroad in their boats. Deep under the water was the battle for food being fought. What a world of slaughter and good-will, of throat-cutting and kindly deeds!

"What a wonderful night," said Nancy. "It is beautiful," I replied, "but I am off for bed. In the morning I must hunt for crabs and catch some fish and set my lobster-pots. I, too, will go where the mussel clings."

CHAPTER III

NO one more ignorant of boats and the water, than I, ever went to live by the sea. I had sailed in many sorts of boats when I had nothing to do but move about as I was told. I knew that there were schooners and barges, and steamboats, and sloops and catboats and punts, and launches, and dories afloat. I could distinguish between a steamer, a sailboat and a row-boat. Beyond this my knowledge was not accurate. I knew that a small boat with one mast and one mainsail was not a schooner or a barge. If I saw a trim-shaped craft, newly painted, with clean ropes, white sails, easy chairs upon its deck, its crew in clean jumpers, its officers in blue uniforms with gold buttons and braid, its passengers in white duck, I ventured to speak of it as a yacht.

After my arrival on the island, I felt a keener interest in such things. I must have a boat of my own, and I did not know what kind to get. I followed every sail that passed with a speculative eye. What kind of a thing was it? How much did it cost? Could I afford it? It is often hard for me to choose between a calico and a silk. I have seen expensive orchids that delighted me as much as does a sprig of sorrel grass.

I have two bowls for my bread and milk. One is of delft, ornamented with round-limbed cherubs, young rabbits and listening fawns. It cost quite a sum. I have forgotten how much, for it was bought three years ago. The other one is of common clay. Its body tint is a pale greenish yellow. At the top is a border of impossible terra-cotta daisies. The lower three-fourths is covered with a scrawl in purple and crimson. It cost me ten cents at a Noank store the other day. Compelled to part with one of these, I could not know which to choose. I know that each was fashioned by one who loved his labor and found a beauty in the thing he made. The material of each moved with sympathetic willingness in the potter's hands. The one is small and dainty, the other large and fat and comfortable. On the whole, I think I like the cheap one better. Its gaudy colors, blended by a nature at once tender and jovial, have given the choicest qualities a form in chinaware, and any man, for ten cents, may have it on his cupboard shelf.

Not every boat I saw allured me. The laws of man are his perception of the commercial laws. He reads from the statutes of life, and transcribing what he finds, puts it in his libraries, and is governed by it. All things are subject to the same influences. A boat is as much a created thing as is a man. It has as much to do with its own character as he. I believe that the same qualities are found in men and trees, in iron, in cotton and in hemp. The man who fells a forest and takes it to his shipyard, has to deal with as great a variety of dispositions as if he had carted a city full of people there. Were he to build all his boats upon the same model, each would still possess a personality of its own. The wholesome, happy tree, in sympathy with the sunlight, the soil and the air, friendly with its neighbors, eager to meet and to conform to the changes of a progressive destiny, makes willing timber. If such wood as this be joined by one whose hands are willing, whose eye is fixed upon his purpose, the result must be a willing body for a boat. And if, like this, the sails and rigging have been created from cotton and hemp, you will have as true and fair a creature on the sea as is a tender woman in the world of men.

Boats, both large and small, sailed past my island and affected me as do the cross-grained natures I encounter on the street. And others, large and small, caressed by the waters that bore them, and the winds that blew them on, skirted my island daily, assuring me that the spirit of the air and sea was kindly to the kindly soul.

I had said to Mr. Ashbey when he first brought me over, "I shall want a small boat of my own—one that I can sail or row. I can't pay much for it, either."

"I have a sharpie with a centreboard," he replied. "If that will do, you can have it for twenty-two dollars, sail, oars and all. It is twelve feet long."

"How much would a new one cost?"

"They charge a dollar and a half a foot for sharpies, and if a centreboard is put in, about five dollars extra. The mast and sail and oars would be something besides."

A few days later I saw the boat at his dock. A sharpie is flat-bottomed, square at the stern, and pointed at the prow. It is the prevailing form of row-boat around these waters.

"It will sail very well with a centreboard," said Mr. Ashbey.

It was long and narrow, and not so deep as others I had seen. Its lines were graceful and easy to my eye. It was well worn and scarred in places, a weatherbeaten boat, in fact, but it seemed a friendly, trusting and trustworthy thing to me.

"I think I'll take it," I said, "but I will let you know."

I did not have twenty-two dollars, and I could not buy it then. And that was fortunate, for, in the interval of waiting, I was the possible possessor of every boat that pleased me.

"What kind of a boat is that?" I would ask of a fisherman putting his pots aboard, or of an idler on the dock. For all my asking I have learned little that is definite. The prevailing craft among the lobstermen are from eighteen to twenty-five feet long, and from a foot and a half to two feet under water. Some have cabins and some have not. Some have but one sail, and others carry a jib or two. Those with jibs are called just sailboats, those with only the large mainsail are catboats. Fishing smacks seem to be two and three-masted vessels used only for fishing. They bring their catch home alive, in wells constructed so the sea circulates through them. In these coast towns, a boat is to men what a horse is in the country, a bicycle in the town. Every aspiring youth possesses one or hopes to. If he is of a solitary disposition, he makes a companion of it. If he is adventurous, a leader of aping daredevils, it is his means of sport. If he covets a lady, it becomes the excuse that lovers seem to need.

There are the boats of those who love them, and the sea, and the boats of those who have money, and chance to spend it in that way. There are multitudes who wander to the water-side in summer, in search of the comfort they never find. Since they are here, they go a-sailing, as just a thing to do, and there are boats to carry them.

There is a small, blue, round-bottomed boat with a little square sail, that comes out of Mystic River. Its owner sails alone. It could hardly carry another in any sort of breeze. It moves like a thistledown over a meadow, when the sea is still. It bobs merrily in rough water, bowing and curving with the waves and gusts of wind.

I wished to hail the owner and ask the price of such a boat, but I needed one that would carry more and stand a rougher usage. I would watch it come dancing from the mouth of the river two miles away, and circle about the island and return, following every move with wistful eyes, and concluding at the last that Mr. Ashbey's sharpie would serve me better.

A certain catboat I fancied cost five hundred dollars. I asked the price of a long, low-lying yacht that lay by the town dock one day. It was three thousand. I was told that a boat like Captain Green's could be built for eight hundred. It is after a model of his own, and smacks of the ships the Vikings sailed. There is nothing just like it afloat, and never will be. It rides the water with scarce a sound in the roughest seas. The Captain chose every stick of its timber, selected every nail and screw, put every part together, and no hand but his has touched its helm when away from its moorings.

He came about one day in the deep water off the ledge of my island to put me ashore.

"Are there any rocks close in there?" he asked.

"I think not," said I.

He was in the stern, and I was looking into the water from the prow.

The boat, headed to the wind, moved slowly to the shore. Before I could jump, the Captain had passed me, and leaping to the ledge, caught the boom and pushed the boat gently back. I now saw, a few feet from the prow, a great rock just under the water.

"She has never put her nose to the ground," said the Captain.

"How did you know it was there?" I asked. "You couldn't see it."

"I felt her quiver," he replied, with something like a challenge in his eye.

No, I could not buy a boat like Captain Green's at any price. If I knew as much as he, and would take the pains, if I had sprung from a race of sailors and spent fifty years upon the sea, I might make me one as good.

During most of the month of June, in passing Mr. Potter's house, going to and from a nearby dock, I had seen a good-sized sail-boat, bereft of canvas and rigging, reposing in his dooryard, its mast rising to a level with the eaves.

There are boats that, in such a place, would look like pigs in a parlor, but this one seemed as much at home as did the old yellow cat asleep by the door. One day I saw Mr. Potter painting her.

"What kind of a boat is this?" I asked, laying my hand upon her side.

"She is a catboat."

"Is she a good boat?"

"Yes; she is a good boat."

With paint-brush suspended, he held his head a little to one side, contemplating her with an affectionate eye.

"What is she worth?"

"Charley Smith built her for $180 twenty-five years ago. She might not be worth twenty in the market now, but I would not sell her."

"Charley Smith seems to make good boats."

"Yes," said Mr. Potter, with a nod," he does.

Later in the season, I frequently saw Mr. and Mrs. Potter sailing past the island, and it was very evident that their family was composed of three.

I was sitting on my porch one sunny morning. It was a day of unusual calm and radiance. In the city it might be piping hot, but here where the blaze of sunlight was tempered by the moving air, it was bright and mild and tranquil. The sky and water were of a light, clear blue. A few white clouds moving overhead were reflected in the sea. As I followed the dimpling paths where the breeze passed down the Sound, half-dozing in my chair, a sail crept slowly through the run between Mystic Island and my own. It was a little, weather-beaten sharpie, like the one at Ashbey's dock. The prow was out of the water. The stern was sunk within a few inches of its surface, by the weight of a man. He was very old. A white beard fell almost to his lap. Thick, gray hair hung below the brim of a high-peaked straw hat with a hole in it. One suspender was over his shoulder. He wore a calico shirt. He was settled far down in the boat, propped comfortably against its back, one elbow leaning upon the tiller that was clasped lightly in his long yellow hand. One leg was crooked upward toward his chin—the overall that covered it rolled above his knee. There was scarce wind enough to fill the sail, but the boat was moving with the tide. As he passed slowly, the old man turned and looked at me.

"Hello, neighbor," I called.

He lifted an arm above his head, and waved it lazily without otherwise disturbing his indolent repose. He was about eighty years old. He had, perhaps, never possessed a boat more expensive than this sharpie, with its patched sail. Or, if once a captain of a three-masted vessel, the shifts of fortune had left him only this. Whatever his history or his worldly state, he was surely one whom neither man nor circumstance could rob. "I hope," thought I, "that I shall sit whatever bark carries me with as much serenity as he." Long after he disappeared, I practised waving my hand above my head, but I missed the seasoned, wise and roguish abandon of his gesture.

"I think," said I to Nancy, "that as soon as I have enough, I will get that sharpie."

"Please get it now," she urged for the hundredth time. "I have the money."

A few days later, as we were standing on the beach, we saw Mr. Ashbey leave his dock and sail our way, the sharpie with its mutton leg in tow.

"It's a pretty small sail," said he; "but you want it safe at first, and my old one is too large."

He threw me the painter and took his row-boat in exchange. I pulled the nose of my ship to shore and, stepping on board, shoved off.

The mast was about twelve feet high, tapering from two and a half inches in diameter at the foot to an inch at the top. It passed through a round hole at the point of the boat, and rested in a socket on the bottom. It was easy to lift it out and put it in place. The sail was three-cornered, fastened along one side to the mast from the top to a point just clearing the boat, where it was put in place. It came to a point just above the stern, by a long, straight slant down and a slight slant up. There was a small noose fastened to the mast about eighteen inches above the boat. A light pole, pointed at each end, kept the canvas stretched. In making the sail ready after the mast is up, you slip the noose of the flapping point over one end of the pole and push it out until the other end may be fastened at the mast. A long rope was tied near one end of the pole for the skipper to hold his sail by. The boat had three seats, a wide one in the stern, another just aft of the centre, and a third one forward. The centreboard was built between the second and third seats. It was a board an inch thick and a foot wide, hung on a hinge in a casing of inch boards. The whole affair was, therefore, a three-inch partition a foot high, dividing the boat in the centre between the two forward seats. The centreboard was lifted and lowered by a wire rod with a wooden handle. The rod was fastened by a loop through a staple on the top edge of the board. When the centreboard was up, a nail put through the staple across the casing, held it so. The rod would then fall back along the top out of the way. To lower the centreboard, you remove the nail, and, holding the rod up straight, push it down until the handle rests across upon the casing. Then you take the sail rope in one hand, avoid entangling your feet in it, and sitting in the stern seat put your other hand on the tiller.

"Now," said Mr. Ashbey, "let's see you beat against the wind."

A light breeze was blowing up the Sound from the south, and I turned the boat in that direction. Presently the sail fell back straight behind the mast and hung over the boat, lengthwise, flapping slightly. I saw that no progress could be made that way. The wind to propel a boat must meet a resistance in the sail. I turned the boat a little toward the west, the sail acting like a weathervane, remained north and south. I pulled it toward me so that one side was exposed to the wind. It filled and pulled steadily. It began to move diagonally across the path of the breeze, southwestward. I turned the boat more and more from the wind, experimenting. When the wind was directly behind me and we were moving northward, the sail hung at right angles with the mast. "I will try all the directions," I thought, "and see what happens." Suddenly, as I turned toward the east, the wind hit the sail from behind and threw it over the boat. The rope jerked in my hand, and we tipped a little to one side. I knew that something was wrong. If such a thing happened in a gale, the boat might easily be yanked over. We now moved steadily with the sail to the left of the boat. As we headed more to the south, I had to pull it toward me, so the wind might continue to strike its side and keep it full. When we pointed south again, the sail hung idly for a moment directly over the boat, but as we continued to turn, it caught the wind upon its left side and, filling gently, bore us onward without a jerk. I saw then that the wind cuts the compass in two. You may make all the points of one of its hemispheres with the wind on one side of your sail and all the points of the other with the wind on the other side. Again I brought the boat to the west and to the south. Now I saw that if I kept turning, the sail, at right angles with me, would point north and south when the boat was east and west. The free edge of the sail would be southward and, as the wind, ceasing to press it forward, would catch it from behind, it must throw it over suddenly with what force it had. If I wished to go to the east then, I must come about the other way, so the wind would change from one side of the sail to the other, striking it at the mast line first and bearing it over gradually as the boat turned.

"Very good," called Mr. Ashbey. "You must always come about toward the wind. This is the sort of weather for you to practise in.

"Nancy was watching me from the beach. I headed my boat her way and came proudly into port.

"And now," said I, "I will take you for a sail."

As I spoke, there was a sharp sound of grating under me, the boat tipped and lurched and stopped a few feet from shore. I had forgotten to raise the centreboard.

"I notice," said Mr. Ashbey, "that this boat you have been using is pretty well worn. You must keep your boat in the water. It won't do to leave it on the beach where the water can rub it in the sand and against the stones. You should fasten it with a long rope to the beach, and then take it out beyond low water mark and anchor it with a stern line."

That was a simple and very evident fact, and yet I had not thought of it.

"Is the one you loaned me damaged much?"

"Oh, I can fix it all right," he answered cheerfully; "I just told you, so you'd know."

I heard the soft voice of Elizabeth. Looking up over the rocks and between the bushes that partly hid the cabin, I saw her by a window, singing and sewing.

"Come down," I called, "we are going for a sail."

She looked down at us and smiled and shook her head. When Elizabeth declines to do a thing there is an appealing softness in her dark eyes as if she felt herself a culprit.

"Did you see me with the boat?"

"Yes—you made a pretty picture out there, but you did look very small and the sea so big. I thought you did splendidly."

"And yet you will not come?"

"You and Nancy go."

"You are not afraid for us?"

"I shall be glad when you are back, and I shall be less afraid for you if I am here. If anything should happen, with me aboard, I should only be another danger. I cannot help myself like you and Nancy."

I went up the path and came to the window where she sat.

"What makes you afraid?"

She smiled cheerily and shook her head.

"I don't know."

"It must make you unhappy then for us to go?"

"Indeed, it doesn't. I want you to go. I know that you enjoy it. I am happier at home with my sewing."

"And you will not be anxious and distressed?"

"If you were gone a long time I might, but I ought not to and so we must not act on that."

"You ought not to?"

"I am happier here. Perhaps that is selfish of me. Shall I come?"

"Not much. What are you making?"

"Sunbonnets. This blue one is for Nancy."

She put a half-finished one of lavender and crimson over her black hair and drew it down under her chin. Her eyes questioned me earnestly, and I could assure her truly that the effect was fine."

"I got the pattern from that sweet old lady where we got the last dozen eggs. I shall finish them this afternoon."

As Nancy and I put off alone she came to the door and watched us round the island and head toward Stonington.

"I hate to leave her there alone," said Nancy, "but it would be a real hardship for her to come. She would never leave the house and dooryard, even at home, except to please me."

"We can serve the happiness of others best," I answered, "by being happy ourselves." In a moment more, I should have been lost to my surroundings, hot on the heels of that idea, but I put it aside for another time."

"Teach me to sail," said Nancy.

"I don't know much, but enough for this kind of weather." I gave her the rope and she took the seat in the stern.

"I know the rudder is to steer by, but how do you do it?"

"You move the helm in a direction opposite from the one your boat should go."

"So?"

"Yes. Now fix your eye on a point to make for and keep the prow of the boat pointed toward it. An inch to the right or to the left, is an inch too much. It would mean a mile or more off the course at the other end. We can sail easily in this direction, for the wind comes over our shoulders from behind, athwart the boat and fills the sail pretty full."

"This is certainly a pleasant change from rowing."

"Indeed, it is."

We looked complacently at each other, made ourselves comfortable, peered deep into the smooth water, watched the shore line of woods, and fields, and farmhouses, looked back at the slowly receding cabin, and forward passed Latimer's Reef Lighthouse to the ocean.

We were going very slowly, but we were sailing our own boat, and the strangeness of our situation, the little we knew, gave us a sense of adventure and far travel. When we came abreast of Ahoy, the small island a quarter of a mile from our own, we felt like old salts. When this was passed and nothing but water and the lighthouse lay before us, it became from moment to moment a question of how far we would dare to go. The breeze remained light and steady. I did not consider the tide then, but I know now that it must have been with us and when, two hours later, we turned about, it must also have turned, or we would have had trouble in so light a breeze. As it was, we sailed out between Stonington and Latimer's reef, within sight of the ocean swells and returned in love with our little boat, surprised by our seamanship, and ready to assure Elizabeth that, with any care at all, there was really no danger on the sea.

Lobstering off the east side in the skiff Captain Ashbey built. The rounded top woooden pots were in use up to the mid-20th Century. Henry seems to have set his trap on the edge of the fast moving water of the eastern entrance to Noank harbor. As the Quirk Islanders only had the one boat, the photo seems to have been taken from Ahoy where Henry must have set one (or both) of the women ashore. Much further out to the left, he would have risked losing the lobster pot to the current, especially on spring tides. Note fedora, jacket and high boots. (Photo from Second Edition)

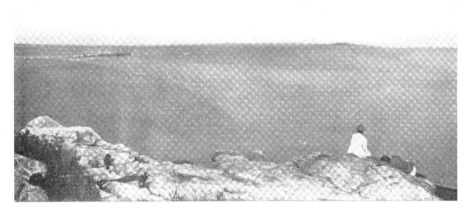

A meditative moment facing east toward the Watch Hill Passage and the open sea. Gates Island, to the left, was larger and shaggier before the 1938 hurricane. Fishers Island is on the horizon to the right. A simple painting based on this photograph was used on the cover of the first edition. (Photo from Second Edition)

CHAPTER IV

O F course, I knew that our little boat might encounter winds and seas too heavy for it, with the best management, and that I must learn much more than I knew to carry it safely, even in brisk sailing weather. But what its limitations were, and how to handle it, I could discover only by adventure and watchfulness.

We had been here two weeks, going often to Noank, to the pole buoy, to Mystic Island, and occasionally to Ahoy, but there were a hundred places in our circle of vision that tempted us. There was the valley of the Mystic River, leading westward between wooded hills. There were dark recesses in the forest on Mason's Island, three quarters of a mile away. To the north of this was Dodge's Island, its broad, green surface divided into fields by stone fences, its centre crowned with a clump of high bushes. Six miles northeast, on a point of land, lay Stonington, its cluster of buildings lost to us in misty weather, but so clear on clear days that we could see the windows and doors of the houses. Beyond this was a dim coast line, curving away and out, and coming to a point nine miles to the east of us. Here was Watch Hill, the last of land that we could see. Lying between the sea and water, so far away, it was a ghostly city through the haze. It gleamed and sparkled in the strong light of fair weather. There have been moments, just before sunset, when a blaze of reflected glory flashed from it. After this came a wide reach of water between Watch Hill and the north end of Fishers Island. In the centre of this gateway to the ocean, rose Latimer's Reef Lighthouse, a round tower set upon a rock. Whoever looks at this conspicuous object rising from the sea feels some emotion. To one it is beautiful; to one it is austere; for most it possesses a nameless fascination. It is at once a sign of danger and protection; a thing to avoid, if may be; to run to, if you must. In the daytime, it is a strong arm for warning or rescue, raised in a place of solitude. At night, it casts a revolving white light, flashing my way at regular intervals. I have watched it in the darkness for hours, and every moment as it breaks anew upon my sight, gleaming like a planet near the horizon, its reflection, like a string of jewels reaching to my shore, I experience a new emotion, as keen and fresh as all that have preceded it. I am as a man in a strange wilderness, who hears a far call, but knows not whence it comes, from whom, nor what the message is. Perhaps the inhabitants of Mars are sending us repeated signals. But let the wise men read me first this earth of mine. We have not yet answered its patient summons. Few of us can speak with all our kind—not one has learned the language of the cricket.

Fishers Island, forming our horizon to the south, stretches for five miles, its nearest shore three miles away. And all down the Sound are rocky reefs and green islands—points of land by day and their lights by night.

The soul of Nancy is a nomad. Her curiosity is stronger than her fears. Her love of the air, the water, her exploring instinct, are passions. I would have sailed my boat alone until I knew it better, before taking long voyages with her, but she would not let me.

"Where shall we sail to-morrow?" asked Nancy.

We were on the beach, the girls were washing the dishes, and I was standing in the water, near them, holding my bait pail and stooping now and then for a crab that scuttled past me over the sandy bottom, decoyed by the remains of our supper.

I stood up at the question, and looked down the Sound.

"We might explore those rock reefs. Or we might go farther, and visit North and South Dumpling."

"Where the lighthouse stands?" asked Elizabeth.

"That's North Dumpling. South Dumpling you can see close beside it. They must have a surface of several acres."

"But they seem pretty far away."

"About four miles."

"Why don't you go to the nearer places first?"

"We might go up Mystic River, or over to Mason's. Will you go with us if we don't go far?"

"No, but I can watch you."

But how about Noank? Will you want me to row when we go there?"

"Of course not. I like to do the shopping, and I wouldn't hear of your rowing when you can sail."

But it's farther than Mason's, and as far as those reefs."

"I know, but it's different."

"Safer?"

Elizabeth looked at me reproachfully.

"You know I can't reason about such things as you do," she said softly. "I just feel that way about it, and I don't want you to care."

"I don't care. I would give a good deal, though, to follow your thoughts for one day. I would like to understand how your mind works."

"I don't think it works very much," she said, with a merry snap in her eyes. "If it does, it's mighty sly about it."

I gave her up, as usual, and returned to Nancy.

"Why not just go with the wind?" I said. "There will be something to see wherever it blows."

"We'll just do that. But we must go to Noank first for some groceries."

"And we will need some fish," said Elizabeth. "I took the last one out of the car for dinner."

"We might have some lobsters."

"There are none."

"There were three left when I put the blackfish in."

"I guess they ate each other up. There are some pieces there, but that's all."

I waded out to the fish box, anchored to a stone about five feet from low-water mark, and looked in. I saw five claws and three empty shells.

"That's queer," I said. "I know they eat each other, but there ought to be one left."

I heard a familiar sound on the shore of Mystic Island. Sam, the helper, was making his evening's tour, turning over the large stones, looking for crabs. It was he who had made my fish-car and given it to me. I called to him now and told him what I saw.

"The blackfish ate 'em," he hallooed.

"The blackfish!" I exclaimed. "How could they?"

You mustn't keep 'em together. *God!* They pick the lobsters' eyes out and then they've got 'em. You must have separate cars. I'll make you another. Say—there was a picnic here to-day—some damned Sunday-school from New London. They tore a door off one of the bath-houses. A young woman come up to the well by the house and washed her feet in the water pail and poured it out by the well. *God!* but they make me tired."

"I must come over and see you with one of your picnics, Sam."

"I could tell you enough about these people that go on picnics to fill a book. Mr. Osgood lets 'em come here for nothing, gives 'em everything free—bath-houses, pavilion. *God!* You'd think they'd been coaxed to come, and were mad because they'd done it.

"I caught fourteen blackfish off the dock this morning in an hour and a half. Do you want some? Why don't you come over?"

It grew dark as we talked, and long after his form was lost in the shadow of the hill behind him, his voice came distinctly to me, over the water between us. It would require a good many thousand words to portray Sam's character. Since I have quoted him so far, however, I must add that his "Gods" and his "damns" mean nothing at all. They are what a more careful man's "hems" and "haws" might be.

Sam was once a brick-layer. One day he was on a swinging board, seventy feet above a sidewalk of Providence. His comrade, at the other end, was worried because the rope above was frayed.

"You trade with me," said Sam.

A few moments after the exchange was made, the rope broke.

"Look out below!" called Sam, and the next he knew, he was in a bed at the hospital, three weeks later. After four months, he was discharged, a man with a weak back. Since then, he has roamed from place to place, earning what he can pick up during the summer, tramping it occasionally, living in the cheap lodging-houses of New York and mixing in the best society of the Bowery during the winter. For three seasons he has been on Mystic Island from May to October, earning twenty dollars a month as helper. He is there to clean up after visitors, and to prevent them from injuring the premises.

"How do you like it here?" I asked him.

It's all right for the summer," he said. "I like it fine, except for the picnics. The other day a preacher had his church along, and he asked me to cart the things to the pavilion. I hauled seventeen wheelbarrowsful from the pier.

"'How much,' sez he. 'A quarter,' sez I. He offered me fifteen cents, and I told him to put it in the contribution box. I'm a Catholic myself. When I come to at the hospital, the priest was there and he sez to me, 'The nurse reports,' he sez, 'that you cussed and damned all the time you've been lying here. I hope,' he sez, 'that you're sorry for that.'

"'To hell,' sez I. 'I'm glad I'm alive,'

"'You had a big fall,' sez he.

"'I did,' sez I.

"When the rope broke,' sez he, 'did you bless yourself?'

God! Did I bless myself? I was looking for something to grab to, I was. And what time did I have? If I talked as fast as a priest saying mass, I'd hit the sidewalk first."

"Why did you call 'Look out below?'" I asked.

"So I wouldn't hit anybody. If you're working above, and something falls, that's what you sing out."

"What made you change places with the other fellow?"

"I didn't think it would break and he was nervous about it and I sez to myself, anyhow, if it did, he had a family. *God!* If I died, they'd have to buy beer to coax enough mourners for a wake."

It will be a great thing to commune with Mars. I hope its people have their eyes our way, and their instruments at work. If excursions land there in my time, I should like to throw my eggshells on its grounds with the rest, but, meanwhile, I am in a world that produces Sam and his pick-nickers, and I don't as yet know enough of either. And if I went to another planet now, I would leave all these islands and waters and coast lines unexplored, and the mysteries of my own dooryard unsolved.

In the morning, early, we set sail for Noank. Our days were always full. I find that I am giving a poor impression of our activity. We were busy then, so busy that we had no time for anything. But in writing of those days, memory takes her ease, idling and dreaming by the way, as one is apt to do when returning to familiar haunts.

"It will take an hour to do our shopping and get back," I said. "If we fish after that, the morning will be gone. Suppose we haul a lobster-pot and see what we get. It might save time."

I spoke the words, although in my heart I did not mean them, for I have learned, and learned it well, that Time is for no man's saving. If any one thinks he has some of yesterday's in his strong box, he is mistaken. He may fill his warehouse and turn the key, but when he returns, the present moment, and no more, is there. But when I talk, I sometimes gabble, helping to keep these empty phrases in use. They serve a purpose in the world, for, without them, there are multitudes who could not speak. Were there no statements ready-made, to be learned by rote, how many of us would be at a loss for an opinion? But, as it is, the world is old, and there are phrases enough coined by now to cover all subjects. One has but to commit those accepted by the society he seeks to be admitted as a proper member of it.

If Sam had chosen the right set, he would not be looked upon as an uncouth ruffian by his picnickers, nor would the priest and the nurses have considered him profane, for he is of a kindly, generous spirit, though his thoughts do ramble some. There are many like him on the Bowery—courteous souls, sent into the world with the wrong labels on them, lacking the wit to change them, buffeted and shoved through life third-class, picking up the customs, the language, the manners of their way.

Noank lay directly before us. One of my lobster-floats was visible about a hundred fathoms to the right. The wind was blowing from the north. I had to point close to it to make the float.

"Now, I will show you," I said to Nancy, "how to sail against the wind. By drawing the sheet in, you can keep the boat headed almost to the point it blows from."

"That is strange," said Elizabeth. "I should think it would blow you back."

"No. You see, the sail, fast at the mast, slants a little away from the boat. Now, you come toward the wind just as far as you can, and keep the wind on this side your sail. As it passes over its resisting surface, it must drive it ahead."

While the girls were marveling at this disclosure, I looked about me and saw the island still abreast of my elbow. I watched it narrowly, and discovered that we were leaving it sidewise. A moment later, we reached the channel, and began to move steadily backward. For a moment I was perplexed and annoyed, and my face must have revealed it

"What's the matter?" asked Elizabeth.

"We are drifting. The tide is stronger than the wind, or our sail is too small for this sort of thing. I will have to row."

"Don't you think we'd better go back?"

There was an incipient panic in Elizabeth's eyes, and the sight of it stirred me to angry amazement.

"Why should we go back?" I exclaimed. "Does the mere sight of a sail deprive you of your senses? I must row, but what of it?"

"I didn't know. But you seemed nervous, and it frightened me. "Are you sure there is no danger?"

"Good heavens—can't you see? Don't look at me—look at the water. There is hardly a ripple on it. Look at the sky, just a few thin, white clouds. There is not wind enough to move us against the tide. Now, what danger can there be?"

"Don't be so cross."

"But, Elizabeth, why don't you think? Here you are, the victim of a causeless, foolish terror that the faculties of a child might protect you against. It is absurd for you, with eyes to see and a mind to reason with, to abandon yourself to panic without a thought or an effort. *Why don't you think?*"

She was silent and grieved, and I calmed myself. Now, I knew very well that at such times Elizabeth did not think—perhaps, could not. I knew this as well as I knew that we would drift with the tide, if I did not row. Why, then, should I be surprised and upset by the occurrence? Why did I scold her for doing what I could expect her to do? Because *I did not think*.

"Come, Bess," I said, "let's be good."

"I will. I was foolish, but it's all right now."

"Just reach it, will you?"

Nancy leaned over the side of the boat and picked the lobster float from the water as we passed it. I shipped the oars, and taking the float from her, caught the rope fastened to one end and hauled it in, hand over hand, pulling the boat forward as I did so, until the hundred feet was in, and we were directly over the pot. Now I hauled more slowly, for it was a heavy pull. Presently the little float that keeps the rope from catching in the rocks appeared, and then the pot itself came to the surface. I reached over, caught it between the laths, and drew it up half-way, until its centre rested on the edge of the boat. Tipping it toward me, I got it in with one good pull. As its lower end left the water, we heard a mighty splashing, and Elizabeth screamed.

"What's in it? What's in it?" she called, scrambling hurriedly over the seat to the prow.

"Sit still!" said I. "You will fall overboard. There is nothing worse than we came for here. It's full of 'em. Lobsters and—look at the black-fish! My lord, what a mess."

It was the best haul I had made. There were eleven blackfish, not one less than three pounds, eight lobsters, a great sea eel, and one blue-shelled crab. I took them all out, catching the fish by the gills, the lobsters by the back just behind the shoulders, and the crab by the hind leg, close to the shell. The eel snapped at me viciously, and I had to poke him out with an oar. As I dropped each creature into the boat, Elizabeth, clasping the mast and looking backward, wild-eyed, gasped and lifted her feet nervously. Nancy, her skirt to her knees, was squatted quietly in the stern seat, watching with keen interest and talking soothingly to Elizabeth to calm her fears.

"There," said I, "we won't have to fish for a few days now. That's settled."

We turned about and sailed back to the island quickly, for wind and tide were with us. The fish flopped now and then, but were exceedingly helpless. The lobsters crawled to the shade under the seats and were still. The eel lay on his back and gasped. Elizabeth, seeing that our cargo was so well-behaved, released her hold of the mast and sat down demurely.

"You ought to have your other car," she said, speaking sweetly, but keeping a bright eye on the eel.

"I think I'll sell the lobsters," I said. "We don't seem to care for any more just now."

I put the fish in the car, and getting two pails, filled them with sea water and dropped my lobsters in them for the market. I suspected that they must be alive to sell. Then I scrubbed out the boat, and we pushed off again for Noank.

I gave the rope to Nancy, and told her to sit beside me, and sail us over.

"Steer for the church steeple," I said, "and it will guide us straight to the town dock."

She brought the boat to its course and held it there for a moment.

"That's good," said I. "You will make a good skipper."

While I was speaking, she took her hand from the tiller, got up and going to the seat she had left, rummaged in a basket until she found her market list. The boat, left to itself, swung around with the wind and tide, the sail flew over, and catching Nancy's sunbonnet, knocked it into the water. She scrambled back to her seat, pulling at the sail with a senseless jerk and snatching at the helm.

"What happened?" she asked in bewilderment.

"As I remember it," I replied, "you abandoned the rudder, pulled the sail in, and went wandering about the boat. If you are going to sail it, you must attend to it. If there had been a stronger wind—"

"My sunbonnet!"

"I shall have to row for it. We can't sail in that direction."

I spoke severely, and seizing the oars, brought the boat around and pulled back, making considerably more fuss about it than was necessary. I wanted Nancy to learn to sail well, because I knew she would venture out alone, and I wanted to feel reasonably sure for her. We caught the bonnet as it was sinking, and Nancy once more took the helm. She headed for the church steeple and kept her eye on it until Elizabeth said:

"We ought to have brought some blackfish over for the postmaster and Mrs. Loewey."

"I wish we had remembered it," said Nancy. "She would have been so thankful."

I have a suspicion that we will get a cake from her daughter to-day. She asked me what kind we liked, and when we would be over again. We must take them some fish to-morrow."

It's singular that there is no fish for sale in Noank. Every one there seems crazy for it, and they all tell me they can't get any. Why don't they go fishing?"

"Nancy," said I coldly, "why don't you steer for the church steeple?"

She gave the sail a quick pull and looked frantically before her.

"You steer with the rudder," I prompted. She turned it the wrong way. "Let the sail out and push the helm from you."

"You take it seriously," she said, looking at me in some astonishment, her clear blue eyes fully opened and questioning.

"It is serious. When you can talk and sail at the same time, you may do so, but you must sail correctly first. You were pointing a good quarter of a mile off the course. We cannot afford to lose an inch. I have been watching the shore line and I see that the tide and wind, going in the same direction, cause us to drift some. We evidently cannot keep a true, straight course when we cut them at all diagonally. We ought to make the town dock without rowing if we head for it steadily, and don't keep pointing away. Now, I would like to see if you can do it."

There was silence in the boat, but we came neatly into port, and as we landed, I looked at Nancy. She laughed and answered my appeal with a free and sincere assurance that she was glad I had insisted.

"I want to sail," she said, "and I mean to learn quickly. Don't you think I did well to-day?"

"You could not have done worse with your chances."

"Isn't he hard on me, Elizabeth?"

"He is a stern master," she replied.

But, of course, you must know that while we talked, our hearts were warm and friendly. I was the most serious, for I was determined that Nancy should not rest until she sailed, and while she looked at me with an affectionate, half-rebellious mockery in her eyes, she really expected me to hold her to her task.

I lifted the water pails from the boat, and we walked to the lobster market, a small building on a dock of its own. The buyer looked at my pails and smiled.

"I suppose," he said, "that you fetched 'em that way to keep 'em alive."

"That was my idea."

"Well, you couldn't find a way to kill 'em quicker."

He emptied the pails on the dock and looked at the lobsters.

"Two have gone up already," he said, pushing them one side. "They smother in a pail like that. With no water at all, in a shady place, they would live a long time, but put them in water that has no circulation and it kills them quick."

"That must be why our crabs die so soon in the bait pail," I said, as we came away. "I remember now that Gibbie told me to put a little wet sand in the pail, but I thought sand and water would be better."

At the store, I left the girls to worry the clerk, and going to the rear, got a large soap box and an auger. If I had made me a fish-car the day before, I would have been content with a hole or two in the side, to let the water in. Now I knew what the holes were for, and I bored it full of them, on the ends, sides and bottom. I had seen a hundred or more cars afloat since coming here, and I always wondered, as I looked at them, why any one should bother to punch them so generously. I am daily astonished at the stupidity of my gaze. I sometimes fancy I must have the eye of an ox. Things I have stared at for years, and that have remained vague and meaningless, are suddenly revealed to me, marvelous, full of far-leading significance, by a chance word or a chance perception.

While I worked, I heard the clerk say something about a well and a murmur of rapid questions came to my ears. As we left the store, the girls seemed excited. They hurried on ahead, forgetting, in fact, to give me the things to carry. They talked rapidly, both at once. I made no effort to overtake them nor to understand what they said, for I knew I would learn the whole matter presently.

"Isn't it great?" asked Nancy, as we were again in the boat.

"What?"

"Why, the well."

"I heard the clerk say something. Where is it?"

"On Dodge's Island," said the girls together, and then between them: "There is a well on Dodge's Island."

"And nobody lives there." "Not a house on it." "No one near." "And it's splendid water." "We can do our washing there."

"Whoop!" I exclaimed. "That is great."

We looked at each other in silent delight.

"Will you have to row going back?" asked Elizabeth, in real solicitude.

"I think not; the wind has changed a little and is freshening. We can tack toward Mystic and come about for home, I guess."

"If you will take us over there this morning," said Nancy, "Elizabeth and I will have a grand old washing."

"We will take all our things, both washed and unwashed, for even the clean ones need a good, fresh bath. Anything washed in salt water will get damp in damp weather. I have found signs of mould lately, in spite of all our sunning."

The breeze continued to freshen, and we cut across it at a good gait, the rope steady and eager in my hand, the water lapping at the boat with a merry sound. Elizabeth seemed unconscious of her voyage, but I caught a covert expression of appreciation from Nancy now and then.

As soon as we landed, we hurried to the cabin. The girls threw the bedding from the attic windows and I carried it to the boat. Then came great bundles tied in bath robes. We brought pails, a wash-tub that had drifted in one day, soap and ammonia. With a boat heaping full, we set sail for our distant laundry. We were in such good spirits that I hated to speak of disturbing things, but I thought it wise to warn Elizabeth of what might come.

"It will be a quiet trip over there," I said, "but if this wind continues, it may be a little rough in the channel coming back. Are you willing to stand it, Elizabeth?"

There was a shade of trouble in her eyes, followed by a quiet glance of courage.

"The clothes need washing," she replied, smiling serenely.

After a thoughtful silence, she asked:

"If there were really any danger, you would wait, wouldn't you?"

"With you in the boat, I will not risk any danger I can foresee."

"Then I will not think about it again, and just take what comes."

Will you go to Fishers Island tomorrow?"

"No, indeed. I'm off on duty now. I go where the washing goes, come wind, come waves. It is easier to take the clothes there than for you to carry such quantities of water."

We passed the pole buoy. The island was falling behind us rapidly. The wide stretch of water ahead was deep blue. The ripples had increased to little waves, flashing the sunlight from their restless points.

"I have never seen the sky so clear," said Elizabeth.

"Listen to the tern," exclaimed Nancy. "There is one just taking a bath."

"It is diving for fish," I said.

The alert, swift-winged creatures were all about us, and the air was filled with their clamor.

"Do you see that group, dodging and screaming just over Ahoy? If you watch, you will see that four of them are chasing the fifth. He has caught a fish, and they are after it. Poor fellow, he may have been on a hungry hunt for hours, and now that he has got his dinner, he must escape those pirates or lose it."

"And he would pursue another, just as relentlessly," commented Nancy.

"True, true," I answered hastily. "I was not thinking then, but drifting—gliding in a sentimental pose along beaten ways. He is the victim of his disposition, as every creature is."

But I could not speculate with ease while the sail was tugging at me, and the boat was bowing and scraping to the waves. I felt that the wind, the water and my boat were at play, and the thrill of their delight stirred in me.

A sigh came from the forward seat. I looked at Elizabeth, surrounded by her pails, her tub and her bundles, and I saw by her serene eyes and dimpled cheeks that it was a sigh of contentment. She caught my glance and laughed outright.

"It's fine," she said. "I never thought I could be so happy in a boat."

"Good for Bess," said Nancy.

The sea slapped our boat jovially, and slapped some water in, but we did not mind it.

As we passed the fish nets near Dodge's Island, I saw an old stone pier, and just this side of it, a narrow, circling beach of clear, white sand. I ran the boat on this, and Nancy, jumping out, tied the painter to a stone.

An overgrown path led us to the well on the edge of the bushes, not a hundred feet from the beach. It was an open well, walled with stone and curbed with thick granite slabs. Its mouth was closed by a lid of long green ferns, growing from the inner edge, about a foot from the top. On the ground near by was a long pole, with a piece of rope at one end. I fastened a pail to this, and dropping it through the ferns, let it fall some twenty feet until it struck the water. A pleasant sound of dripping accompanied its return. The first drink was an important event. I put the pail on the curb, and we all stooped over it. As we stood up again, and wiped our chins, we looked at each other shrewdly and smacked our lips. Here was a fine fat cellar for you. The water was cold and sweet.

I brought up the things, the tub and the pails, and as the girls fell to work, retired to the shade of a sumac bush to reflect and smoke.

Far out over the water, I saw the flashing white wings and breasts of innumerable tern, and the full, white sails of the boats of men.

"Those smacks," I thought, "are hurrying to New York. Anxiety is at the helm. They must compete with the fast freight from the fish markets of Boston."

I could hear the far-off rumble of a train speeding south, along the coast.

"The engineer," I thought, "is, perhaps, wondering if it pays to strike. I wonder if ever a tern has said, 'Give to him that asketh,' and if so, was he crucified? Who can blame the tern? They have had no example. Who can blame men? They have had too few."

It is not through cowardice, for men die by the thousands for what they believe. It is not through unwillingness, for they have ventured most for the Holy Grail, and even through cruelty and avarice and cunning and desperate endurance, they are still pursuing or defending it.

"We receive what we inspire, Mr. Tern. If you would have your fellows kind and generous and just, show them the way."

CHAPTER V

WHEN we returned from Dodge's Island with the washing, there was not a breath of wind. We waited for the tide and drifted home, keeping to our course with a lazy dip of the oars now and then. The weather during these June weeks had been mild and fair. None but light winds blew, and they were quickly spent. We had forgotten the storm that had greeted us in May and had not yet experienced the sudden squalls that sometimes break through here, lifting the water into waves, darkening the heavens, and driving the staunchest boats before them helpless. I have been told that we ventured too much in our little boat. Perhaps we do owe our safety to the even weather that attended our first experiments, but we surely owe the delight and fullness of our days to fearlessness. If a tempest had overtaken us, we might have learned more rapidly, or we might have drowned. Whatever death awaits me, it shall come but once. I think too well of life to hamper and discolor it with nameless fears.

We busied ourselves in doing what we wished to do, and in preparing for our ventures with all the wit we had.

"Perhaps," said Elizabeth, "I shall not be afraid to go sailing with you after this."

We were spreading the wet clothes on the rocks to dry.

"As soon as we are through with our work," I said, "we will go bathing, and I will teach you to swim."

Elizabeth stood up suddenly, holding an end of a sheet suspended, and looked at me curiously. Her face was dimpled, her mouth smiling, but in her eyes was a wavering shade of alarm.

"Why must I learn to swim?"

I wish to be frank and direct with every one, and I strive to be so, in spite of the fact that a veiled purpose often wins its way more rapidly because it is unseen.

"If you are around the water, you ought to swim. If you go much in a boat, it is necessary."

"You hear that, Nancy? He admits that it is dangerous. I guess I'll stay at home."

"Oh, come, Elizabeth. He only wants you to make the thing more safe. I should think you would like to learn. I am going to keep at it every day from now until I can swim a mile."

"You could do that now," I said, "if you would only think so. It's your fear that undoes you. As soon as your feet are off the bottom, you begin to worry. You wonder how deep it is now. You fancy yourself drowning. Your mind is struggling with imaginary conditions, and you involuntarily put forth all your effort, when a very little would be better. Your nerves are taut; your whole being strained and apprehensive. This is what exhausts you.

"I will try," said Nancy, "to take it easy."

I looked at Elizabeth, and saw that my harangue had only increased her uneasiness. The picture was very real to her. She saw the frightened creature I had drawn, and her large, dark eyes were fixed upon herself straining and struggling and sinking in the sea. Nancy saw her expression, and reaching out quickly, caught her by the arm. "Saved!" she cried. "Here you are, safe on land." We all laughed together, and the spell was broken.

There is something in me that protests at subterfuge. I would not gain my point with anyone by deceiving him, or by calling in irrelevant influences. I love a sane and reasonable mind, and seek to address myself to that. To win another to my ways by artifice is no comfort to me. It is not "my way" that delights me, but the beauty of it. If another knows a lovelier one, I am eager to exchange. If my own is to be followed, let us see the true reason for it and walk with open eyes.

Nancy is not so particular in this. Were she to find a magician's wand, she would hide it up her sleeve and with its aid set the world a-dancing to her will, without a qualm of conscience. It is true that could she do this, it would be a merry, wholesome, generous world, as merry as a poet's May day, as wholesome as air and water and sunlight could make it; as generous as the love we wish for.

But how pitiful the relapse would be if Nancy lost the stick!

Before I could speak again, Nancy, looking placidly before her, said softly:

"How still and beautiful it is to-day."

Elizabeth followed her gaze across the water, and her face grew tranquil.

"It seems foolish to be afraid," she said. "It does look harmless."

I left the girls together and went to the beach to clean the fish for dinner. My spirits were disturbed and I was ashamed of them. Presently Nancy came down with a pail which she filled with sand.

"Elizabeth is all right," she said cheerily. "She is going in with us off the rocks today."

"She is not all right," I replied seriously. "You have induced her to follow us with her eyes shut. It will bring trouble."

"No—I just soothed her alarms by getting her to look at the quiet water. You know that she takes things very calmly as a rule. I am sure she will be all right."

"She is learning to swim because the sea is tranquil, and she can overlook, for the moment, all necessity for swimming. How illogical! It makes me shiver. If she learns in that spirit, she will only tempt disaster. We will rely on her and venture too far on an illusion. If we were capsized out there in the Sound, when the waves were rolling and the wind howling, the terror she has not destroyed, but just turned her back upon, would have her by the heart, and all she has learned would be useless."

"Now, you know that Bess keeps her head better than most people."

"She is not frightened by many things. But what would she do when frightened? The test lies there."

"She is going into the deep water off the rocks to-day. I think that is pretty brave."

"It is the folly that would naturally spring from her false attitude. Those who won't look frankly at a danger are often inclined, on an impulse, to jump blindly into it. She should go into the shoal water here on the beach until she can swim a little."

"Please don't have her do that," said Nancy coaxingly. "She is anxious to go in off the rocks, and if you won't let her, she might never learn at all. Be good now. Leave your old reasoning alone and be good."

"All right," I said, made light-hearted and reckless by her bright eyes and coaxing voice. "Off the rocks she goes."

Nancy took her pail of sand up the hill and returned for more. She was making a path around the house. I heard the sound of the hatchet as she chopped away the brush, and of the spade as she filled her pail with sand. She came and went, her active, sturdy body warming the atmosphere about me, enlivening it with her own superfluous vitality. I suppose that Nancy, when she sings, has a queer, little, squawky voice. She says so, and I guess she has, but I love to hear it. Her only song consists of two lines. It is a fragment of the Punch and Judy show:

> "'Tis the law, 'tis the law,
> And the duty of the old turn-kee."

Whenever I hear this fragment borne to me from the beach, the bushes, the kitchen, from off among the rocks, or from wherever Nancy is busy, there is a soft echo in my heart. The sentiment of the song is the one most repugnant to me, but I only smile at that, amused and charmed by the incongruity. These lines upon her lips are a signal of happiness and liberty. They are the mis-begotten offspring of a spirit as tender and lawless as they are austere and terrible. You should hear her piping voice proclaim them, and smile with me at "The law, the law, and the duty of the old turn-kee."

I carried the fish to the house, going the long way around, at Nancy's request, to walk upon her sandy path. She watched me proudly.

"This is great," I said.

"Isn't it glorious? How I love to do it!"

She held the hatchet in her small, strong hand, scratched sunburned and dirty. She wore a bathing suit that had cost a good deal in her stylish days. Her plump, bare arms were brown and brawny. Nancy is only four feet ten and one-half, and weighs a hundred and ten pounds. Her shapely, buxom legs were thrust into rubber boots. Her freckled face and fine blue eyes were aglow with enjoyment.

"I want you to look at the things that grow here," she said. "In cutting this path, I have come upon laurel and barberry bushes, wild raspberries, wild rose and all sorts of grasses and shrubs I don't know. You can't see through the jungle around me, it is so thick and tangled."

The house was enclosed by a forest of sumac and a network of grasses, vines and bushes. Through it all, rose the tall stalks of a flowering weed with a flat bloom, as large as my hat and as white and delicate as the elderberry.

"It seems to me," I said, "that I see poison ivy in there."

Nancy's eyes sought mine for sympathy.

"Yes," she murmured pathetically, "the place is full of it. It is everywhere. I found signs of it all over me this morning. I will be one burning blotch in a day or two."

"That's what's the matter with my hands. They prick me."

"I didn't want to mention it," she said apologetically, "but what can we do?"

"Tear it out by the roots and pour salt water on the ground."

"It seems too bad to do that. It is very beautiful."

"Here is a vine by the porch."

"Here is one at my feet."

"Here is one—and another. It is springing up all over the dooryard."

"It is everywhere."

"We would have to strip the island bare and spade its entire surface to get rid of it."

"Never! I would not remove our jungle or mar its beauty if it killed me. We seem so sheltered and alone in here. It smells so good. And look at those great blossoms."

"And our birds would leave us."

"We will keep the ivy. Elizabeth and I have put bread on the roof and the rocks and among the bushes. I think the birds will stay."

A number of song-sparrows and two blackbirds with red epaulets had been our daily visitors. They came in sunshine, wind or rain, and sang to us constantly. We had seen them swaying on the tops of the bushes in the driving storm. Through the night, at intervals, we heard the sweet, clear carol of the song-sparrows. We had been careful not to frighten them at first. We had fed them, and they had at last accepted us and our huge nest in good faith.

"That is settled," said Nancy. "We will not disturb the jungle."

She picked up her pail and went for more sand, unconsciously piping:

"'Tis the law, 'tis the law,
And the duty of the old turn-kee."

I stood and listened until she had reached the beach. Another voice, humming very softly, came to me from the cabin. I went inside and gave my fish to Elizabeth.

She was squatting before the fireplace, frying the potatoes with a fork. Her face was red from the heat of the flames. The smoke came out in puffs and enveloped her. Between gasps, she was humming a tuneless melody, now and then putting in a word or two. I heard something about "Boys and Girls of the Emerald Isle" and "Dancing on the Green." She took the blackfish, dipped them in flour, and put them in a frying-pan with a piece of salt pork. She raked out a heap of coals and set the pan on them.

"You can cook very well by a fireplace," she said, wiping the mist from her eyes.

"I must get the chimney fixed."

"It would be nice."

She put five heaping teaspoonfuls of tea in the pot and placed it near the fire to heat. Then she took the tea-kettle from the embers and poured in the boiling water. Going to the window, she leaned out and sent forth a musical summons, three notes, such as we use these days for a call. There was an answer like an echo, from the beach, and up the path, and around the house, came the plaintive piping sound of,

"'Tis the law, 'tis the law,
And the duty of the old turn-kee."

Nancy came in, kicked off her boots, put on a pair of gay red slippers, and pulling the table from the corner, carried it to the door. I helped her through with it, and we placed it on the grass in the shade. I stood near by, while she brought the seven-cent knives and the five-cent spoons and forks, the agate-ware plates and cups, the fifteen-cent sugar-bowl, the butter on a wooden dish. I heard the fish sputtering. A delicate odor filled my nostrils. I sniffed and looked greedily inside at Elizabeth by the fireplace. My whole being yelped for food and my soul laughed and licked its lips over the sauce of good cheer in which the feast was served.

When the meal was over, we worked for an hour that it might digest before the bath. Nancy combed the beach and Elizabeth helped me make a raft of planks and logs that had drifted in. When this was finished, I tied a long rope to it, fastened it to the boat, and towed it around the island to the deep water, and throwing the line onto the ledge of rocks, fastened it to a small boulder.

I got a rock weighing about fifty pounds and tying twenty feet of rope to it, dropped it overboard thirty feet from shore and anchored the raft to it.

"Now, Nancy," I said, when we were ready to swim, "you first."

Nancy knew how to swim, but not easily. She could take ten or twenty good strokes and was through. The girls had never been in on this side, and they stood staring at the deep water, as if it were a new, strange sight to them.

"How deep is it?" asked Nancy.

"I will talk about that some other time," I replied. "It is not to the point now."

"Shall I jump right in?"

"Dive."

She stepped to the base of the ledge and stood on a ridge near the water.

"So?" she asked, lifting her arms above her head.

"Yes. Be sure and go in head first. As soon as you are under water, point your hands up and that will bring you to the surface."

She shut her eyes and mouth very tight and fell forward, striking on her face and stomach with a loud splash. She came about and made hurriedly for shore, sputtering and gasping, her eyes very wide."

"It took all my breath," she panted as I helped her out.

"You knocked it out of you. You must give a little jump and throw your head down. Get your head in first. Just think of that."

"How deep is it?"

"Nancy!"

"Are you sure I will come up?"

"Now, you jump in there, head first. Get your head in. Think of nothing but that."

She leaned over and jumped, and I shouted: "Get your head in there."
She made a good dive this time and came up smiling.
"How was that?" she called, turning for the shore.
"Fine. Don't come back. Swim out to the raft."
She turned about and began to work hard to make it.
"Take it easy," I called. "Go slow. Breathe naturally. You have all day to get there. Just loll along. Have a good time with the water. It will do all the work if you will let it."
I could see that she relaxed and that her strokes became slow and effective. She reached the raft and climbed on it.
"I guess I'll strike out and see how far I can go," she said, with shining eyes. "That was easy."
"Just swim back and forth until you can go and return ten times without stopping."
Then I turned to Elizabeth.
"Shall I dive?" she asked quietly, getting close to the edge.
"Not to-day. You must swim a little first."
"How deep is it?"
"That has nothing to do with it. If you will lie quietly on your back, your arms stretched out, your chin up, you will float indefinitely. Wait a minute and I will get you a board. You can fool round with that until you have learned to kick and float."
I got a plank eight feet long and a foot wide, fastened it to the rocks by a long rope, and threw it in the water. I led Elizabeth to the edge, let her down, and brought the board in to her.
"Now, hang to that and thrash around. You will soon get acquainted with the water."
"Oh," she called, clutching the board and struggling to lift herself from the water, "Oh, dear, what has happened?"
"Your feet are coming to the surface on the other side of the board. Don't lift yourself up. Lie back quietly; lie back! There you are. Now, just touch the board lightly. You see how easy it is to float."

But I can't get my feet back. I can't do anything."

"But you can't drown if you lie still. I want you to realize that."

She smiled up at me sheepishly.

"You seem to be afraid because you aren't sinking."

"I'm not afraid."

"All right. Now, kick your feet. Kick them hard and bring them under you."

She kicked and laughed gleefully, as they came under and then up behind her.

"Now keep on kicking and push the board along. Let yourself down in the water. Throw your head back. Nothing but your face out of water."

She kicked and pushed, and presently the board was at the end of the rope, near the raft.

"That's fine. Now, come back."

"What's the use?" she asked. "I'm attached to the place."

She laughed and wiggled her feet at me as they came above water on the other side of the board.

"This is my fourth trip," called Nancy. "I'm not tired at all."

"Turn over on your back."

There was a scream from Elizabeth. I looked with a start and jumped to my feet. She had put her arm over the board, and catching its edge, drawn it toward her, turning it over. She began at once to clutch and struggle and scream. Her face was turned toward me, very beautiful in its terror, but very wild and frantic also.

"Keep still," I shouted.

As the board turned on edge, she lost her hold and snatching it again, lifted herself up and screamed. As it came over on its flat side, she reached across it, and seizing the far edge, pulled it over again. She was working like mad and the board turned swiftly.

"Don't throw your arm over it," I called. "Be quiet and listen to me."

She paid no attention. It seemed that she would surely let go and in her wild thrashing, she would choke in the water and go under. I knew that if I could not get her attention, it would be impossible, perhaps, to rescue her, for she would snatch at me and struggle until I might go with her. If she would become sane again, she was safe with her board. I made ready to plunge in, and as a last resort, I shouted again to her.

"Be still, Bess. Be still. *Be still, you damned fool.*"

She stopped in the act of a lunge and scream. Her mouth remained open, but no sound came forth. A look of surprise and resentment replaced the wild panic in her eyes. The board lay quiet, on its broad surface.

"Now, just hold it lightly, your hands on the edge nearest you. I will pull you in."

I took the rope and drew her slowly to the rocks. She came out and went to the house without a word.

"She is not angry, is she?"

"Well," said Nancy, climbing out, "you know that *was* a hard thing to say to her."

"Good heavens, Nancy!"

"I know you meant it all right."

"Never mind," said Elizabeth softly. She had returned at once, and as I looked around, I met her eyes, warm and forgiving.

"If I could have thought of anything to shock you more, I would not have shouted what I did."

"Come in again," said Nancy.

"I am afraid."

"Well, come in on the beach, then," I urged. "Don't stop with this experience. If you will only think of the water in a friendly way; if you will trust yourself with it and just do your part for the simple thing it is, you will be as safe in the water as out of it."

We went to the beach, and I got her to lie on her back and float by holding my hand under her shoulders. I stepped away and left her alone.

"Just keep your head back and breathe naturally. Hold your arms out straight. You see, you cannot sink unless you do something to make you."

For a few moments she floated quietly, laughing like a tickled child.

"Now, Nancy, swim out as far as you can go and I will rescue you."

I could rely on Nancy to keep outwardly cool and to do as I told her, and I could venture a long ways with her.

Suddenly Elizabeth cast a frightened glance my way and called out:

"Where am I floating to? How deep is it here?"

In a moment, she lifted her head. This, of course, threw her body under. She made a great lunge and began to splash and cry out, swallowing water and gasping. As she turned over, she hit the bottom with her hands and knees. It was not two feet deep, but in her excitement, she fell forward, and head and shoulders disappeared. She got to her feet, choking.

"If you tried hard enough," I said, "you could drown yourself in your dish-pan."

"I thought it was deep."

"And so you did your best to sink? Do your thrashing and screaming in shoal water. If it is deep, you should do the little that is required of you to keep on top."

"If you are going to be so cross all the time, I'm going home."

"You are going to swim first," I replied severely.

"Come on, Bess," coaxed Nancy.

"Walk out up to your shoulder with me and swim in. I'll hold you up."

She came unwillingly, but I was determined now.

"You see you can hardly walk here. You could float more easily than you can hold yourself down. The whole thing is this: If all the rest of your body is under, and you keep it full of air by breathing, it will become very light and your mouth, eyes and nose will remain out. If you are afraid to let yourself down and try to keep too much of you above water, you just douse up and down, and your whole head goes under. Then you gasp and scream and choke and drown. Now, relax. Put your arms out and lie forward. Get under water. Let yourself down. Throw your head back and turn your face to the sky. Let the water come over your neck to your ears and chin."

I held her by the shoulders until nothing but her mouth and nose were above water. Then her feet left the bottom of their own accord.

"Kick!"

She did so, and they came to the surface.

"Keep on kicking and move your arms. Bring your hands together at your chin; palms out, so. Then, reach forward, keeping them just under the surface. Reach way out. Look at the church spire at Noank, give a kick, and try to grab it with your hands. You see that takes you forward. As soon as your arms are straight before you, your hands back to back, bring them around in a strong, circling sweep and in to your chin; then, straight before you again, with a reach and a kick."

As she did this, I took my hands from her shoulder and placed one of them under her chin. She took ten strokes correctly, and I stepped away. She took five more alone, and stood up.

Nancy was a hundred feet from shore, swimming steadily toward the bush buoy. It suddenly occurred to me that she would reach the channel soon, and I was not sure what the tide would do with her.

"Don't go any farther," I called.

She did not hear me, and I swam out to her. The drift of the current was apparent before I reached her.

"Better turn around and come back," I said quietly. "This is far enough to-day."

"How easy it is if you take it so," she said, taking a mouthful of water and spouting it out again. She came around and I watched her covertly. She made no progress against the tide.

"I will show you how to be rescued," I said.

"I know."

She put her hands lightly on my shoulder and I began to tow her in.

"Take a firmer hold," I said. "I want to give a stronger stroke and you might slip off."

It was all I could do to breast the tide.

"Better kick a little," I said. "The current is strong here."

"I see it is," she answered pleasantly.

"You are all right," I said, as we made the beach. "You can swim well enough to get onto the bottom of the boat if we capsized and Elizabeth would be able now to keep afloat while I got to her. In a few days, she will swim well. When you can take five strokes right, you can take five hundred, if you will go easy."

"I'm glad you kept at me," said Elizabeth, with dancing eyes. "I will surely learn to swim." She waded out as far as she could go, and came back successfully, with good, even strokes. "Let's go off the rocks again. I'm not afraid."

"To-morrow."

"Isn't it fine when you're not afraid?"

"There can, at least, be no terrors for us if we are not afraid."

"Another day gone," said Nancy. "Just think of it!"

"How fast they go."

"The city is coming too near. Next week I must mix in the crowd and listen to the din and wear long skirts again. How I hate it!"

"You look it," I said reproachfully. "You are not pleasant to see just now."

"I know. But there are no mirrors here, and I forget. But I do hate it." She smiled, and her words, spoken softly, lost their sting."

"You are not thinking of it now, but of yourself and me, and the kind of spirit you prefer. If you hate the city, it will hurt you. If you don't think of it at all, it is four days from you. Don't bring it to you now."

We sat upon the beach, when the girls were dressed, and watched the boats of the lobstermen sail up the Sound, past Long Point and into the harbor of Noank. They came home as the sun was setting. We returned to the cabin in a tranquil mood. As we walked up the path, I reached among the bushes and smiling to myself, patted the leaf of a vine. We sat upon the porch for a long time, silently listening to the murmur of the jungle.

"Do you know, Nancy," I said, at last, "I think we might make friends with the ivy and it would not harm us."

"Do you really think so?"

"I do. I shall talk to the poison that is in me when it itches and it will go away. I believe that these vines, if they could understand that no harm was intended them, if they could feel that we loved them and wished them around us for their beauty's sake, would, of their own act, restrain their poison. This is probably impossible, but I am sure that if we do not fear it, nor look upon it with malice, if we think of it always in a frank and friendly way, we will render it harmless. A sane mind, fearless and friendly, is a preserver of health. We are inclined to smile at each new application of this old truth, for it is easier to be sceptical than to experiment; to O.K. a sentiment than to apply it."

"I hope," said Nancy, "the ivy has ears and will remember my sentiments to-day. It was I who spared it."

"You forgot the boat again," said Elizabeth suddenly. "The stern line, do you call it?"

I got a rope from the cabin, and going to the beach, found a great stone that would suit me. It was square and the rope would not slip off. It was so heavy that I had to pry it, foot by foot, to the water, but I knew that a boat anchored to this would not drift, and the hard tug now would bring me an easy mind when the wind and sea were high. When it was well in the water, I could move it with my hands. I worked it fifteen feet beyond low water mark, and went for my boat. It was held to the beach by a long rope, but unless I pulled it high on shore, the full tide washed it about, wearing it against the rocks and sand. If I did, it was hard to push it to the water when the tide was out.

I brought the stern to where I thought the stone was sunk. I groped about in the water for the rope, but could not find it. "This will be a wet job," I thought. "On a stormy night it would be hard to do." I found the stone at last, and picked up the rope. I had to put my head and shoulders under water to reach it. "If the rope would only float!" And then it occurred to me to fasten its end to a stick that would float. I got a lobster float from a pile of driftwood on the beach, and carrying it out, ran the rope through a hole in the end, pulled it through for about two feet and tied it. The float was large and white, and I saw I could find it in the dark and pick it up easily. The loose end of the rope I fastened to a ring in the stern and came ashore. The boat seemed very comfortable as it rode the water safe and clear of land.

"Now," I said, as I looked back upon my job, "I shall rest easier for that."

CHAPTER VI

WHEN we say we shall rest easier because of this or that, we speak foolishly, for we do not know. Most of us pass through life missing its significance, because we do not seek it. We look upon it in a greedy spirit, fretting at the moment if it brings us something to do, and if we are hopeful, anticipating the future only because we fancy it will somehow shape itself to our vague and selfish whims. The value of to-day, and in the thing we do, lies in itself, not in what it may bring to us. If we work now that we may rest some time, we will find a fitful pleasure in our work, and in our time of rest. In toil and idleness alike, we must form our beings to joy or misery. If to-day brings us labor, and we delight in it, we may delight in rest if to-morrow brings us that.

In the night, a wind from the south blew up the Sound and tossed the waves upon my beach. When I am awakened by wind and water, I am glad to listen, in a partial doze, until lost in sleep again. But now, with the gust and splashing, there came a dull pounding that disturbed and fretted me. It was the voice of a thing gone wrong. I tossed and listened, until wide awake, and I understood at last that the lobster float, from which I had expected so much, was beating against the boat. As the waves increased, the violence of the blows redoubled. I passed the night in restless tossing, now wondering if it could batter a hole, now trying to force myself to go down and unfasten it, now vainly seeking for some way to correct the faults in my device. If I used a small stick, it would be hard to find in the dark. I left my bed in the morning with heavy eyes, and went to the beach to solve my problem. The wind had moderated, but the waves were still restless. The boat had a badgered look. It was scarred about the stern, but not injured much. The violent pounding had softened to a dull rapping. I had no particular plan, but I threw off my bath gown, and wading out, picked up the float and held it for a moment idly.

"I will get more rope," I thought, "and see how that works."

As I dropped the float, it occurred to me to place it in the boat. I did so with a thrill of amazement. I looked at it reposing quietly on the stern seat. If I put it there when I fastened the boat, there would be no trouble. I returned to the cabin, chagrined and pleased.

"Why are you astir so early?" Elizabeth called from the attic.

"Did you hear that thumping through the night?"

"What thumping?"

"*I* did," said Nancy. "What was it?"

"Come down and I will show you."

"I hurried to the boat again, and put the float in the water. When the girls came down, I pointed to it.

"The waves were beating it against the boat."

"It was pretty bad," said Nancy. "Can't we fix it?"

"That's what I was wondering all night. How would you do it?"

"You might nail a stick to it and have some way to fasten it to the boat and hold it off."

"What do you think, Elizabeth?"

"Won't that way do?"

"I don't know how you would fasten the other end of the stick to the boat so it would hold and come off easily. Do you?"

"I suppose we could get used to it in time," said Nancy cheerfully.

"It will hurt the boat, I'm afraid."

"Would a smaller stick do?"

"That's as near as I got last night," said I, "but if you will look the other way, I'll go in and fix it while you wait."

They turned their backs, and I waded out, put the float in the seat and returned to my wrapper. They faced about again and looked. We laughed in glee and marveled at our simplicity.

"And yet," said Nancy, "just think how long men saw the apples fall and the steam lift the lids of kettles."

"And," I added, "we have not yet ceased to grumble at our difficulties as if they had a will to spite us. That is the greater blindness."

"There is a good wind to-day," said Nancy. "Where shall we go?"

"We might make those rocky islands and from there go down to the fish hawks' nest off Long Point."

"Way down there?" asked Elizabeth.

"Then we could cut across the Sound. There is a little island, I am told, near South Dumpling where all the tern around here go to breed. I would like to see that."

"Good!" said Elizabeth, with genuine pleasure. "This will be a fine day for me to kill bugs. I shall have the house to myself, and I will spare nothing that crawls or spins webs."

We had been surprised by the great variety of familiar insects on our island. When we first came to the empty cabin, in May, we saw nothing but the birds to welcome us. "It will be a comfort," Elizabeth had said, "to be rid of ants and cockroaches. In the city, you must guard against them constantly." A few days later, she found the sugar-bowl full of ants that had crawled in under the lid. In walking through the jungle, we discovered hundreds of spider's webs, and one morning we awoke to find them sparkling in dew and sunshine on every bush about the cabin. A number had found their way inside, and occupied the corners and the spaces between the rafters. We swept them away, but by night there were twice as many. It became our custom before retiring to hold our candles under the spiders above our beds, burning them in the flames. It was not a pleasant deed with which to end the day, and I finally ceased to slaughter them.

"We know nothing of these spiders," I said to the girls, "and if they do us no harm, why should we pursue them? Because they are here, the birds come. I cannot judge between them and the birds—that is beyond my province, but since my slaughter of them serves nothing but my ignorant prejudice, I will stop it." And I slept more peacefully afterwards.

It was now the last of June, and we had ants and flies and potato-bugs and moths in plenty. Elizabeth looked upon them with a restless eye, but she refrained from open onslaughts in deference to my peculiar views. I could see that she enjoyed the prospect of a day alone with her enemies as much as Nancy and I enjoyed the thought of a cruise.

"All right," I said, as I left the girls to their bath, "it is not for me to say how long a bug shall live."

As I walked up the path, I saw a file of ants crossing it. Near the cabin, I stepped on a worm, by accident.

"It is evident," I thought, "that the results of my conduct are beyond me. Wherever I go, I leave a trail of fate I know nothing of. I am responsible only for the spirit of my deeds."

While the girls were getting breakfast, I made the daily tour for driftwood, bringing it in armfuls to the pile near the house. As I dropped a load, Nancy came out to get some for the fire. She rummaged about for the sticks she wanted.

"Look here," she exclaimed. "I have made a discovery."

She held up a damp board, swarming with little, grayish-blue bugs, fat and soft. "These things are beginning to infest the house," she said. "We find them in the bed-clothes, the wardrobes, under the food boxes and wherever it is dark and a little dampness gathers. They must come from this wood."

We worked through the pile and found them by the thousands.

"After breakfast," I said, "I will spread this wood in the sun. We must keep it dry, I guess."

I had caught a whiff of food and could work no more until I had eaten. I sat on the porch, all my thoughts hovering about the fireplace. We had bread toasted over the coals, fine amber coffee, brewed from Mocha and Java, mixed with an egg, not allowed to boil, and served with

Borden's evaporated cream. We ate but two meals a day, had no meat, no pastry, cake or rich puddings, and could, therefore, afford this luxury of fine coffee and cream, with an omelet, besides. It is food I want, good, wholesome food and twice a day, but bread and butter and potatoes, or a plate of beans, or a bowl of bread and milk, with cheese, is a feast for me. I can draw up to the same old meal with a new and eager zest every day. It is food I want, not indulgence. When I have eaten my beans, I look about me for my dessert, finding it in what I see and hear, for my senses have been fed and are at work again.

Not far from me on the porch was a piece of bread we had put there to decoy the birds, if possible. As my eye chanced to fall upon it, I saw a number of large bugs at work. I went toward it, and they scurried away. I picked it up, and two bugs dropped from its under surface. I managed to capture one of these. It was certainly a cockroach, but of enormous size,—nearly an inch long.

"We've got 'em," I shouted. "You're all right now, Elizabeth."

She came to the door and looked curiously at my captive.

"A cockroach," she murmured. "Well, did you ever!"

And Nancy came and wondered.

"Where do you suppose they came from? Did you ever hear of wild cockroaches?"

"I never did; but how do the flies get here?"

"I can understand that better. They can use their wings."

"But we are a mile from the mainland."

"They could come to us from boats that pass close by. But these cockroaches can neither fly nor swim, and, besides, they are larger and cleaner looking than the town variety."

Elizabeth took the bread and threw it far into the bushes.

"I will leave nothing to eat around the cabin," she said quietly.

"I don't know as we ought to throw things anywhere on the island," said Nancy. "We will be drawing rats here next. I can stand anything but snakes and rats."

"What's that in the water there?" cried Elizabeth, pointing.

"Where? What is it?"

"That's a little block of wood," said I.

"Rats can swim, can't they?"

"Yes."

Nancy got the bread from the bushes and from the rocks where it had been left for the birds, and threw it in the sea.

"Before we go sailing," she said, "I will give this cabin a thorough scrubbing."

"I thought you scrubbed it every day."

"I just run a mop over it. I will take everything out, and go over it thoroughly with a brush and sand. I will shake all our things, and sun them good, and pick up all the paper and scraps about. It pays, I guess, to keep mighty clean, even on an island by yourself."

"It's too bad for you to miss this good breeze," said Elizabeth. "If you two will pick up around, I'll do the rest while you are gone."

"Do you know," said Nancy smiling, but with a note of sadness in her voice, "I don't care so much about sailing? We only have a few more days here, now, and I hate to leave the island for a moment when it comes to going."

We were at the table inside, and through the open south windows we could see far down the Sound.

"Look at that sparkling stretch of water," I said. "And how about the fish hawks' nest and the island where the tern breed?"

"Yes," said Nancy, with a wistful gaze, "we will go. What a fine thing life is when you are free."

"You are never free," I said gently, for the happiness of Nancy is dear to me, and it hurts me to see her let it go when she might so easily keep it always.

"I am free here," she said, with a question in her eyes.

"Not more so here than there. You are bound to us and to all the things about you. You plan this and do that, because the elements or the insects or some new necessity interferes. But you love us and this place, and you find your fetters pleasing."

"There you are. That's what I say. I love it here and find life good. I hate the city, and life is a wearing, dreadful grind to me there."

There is little fault to be found with Nancy, even in the town. She has a copying-office on the top floor of one of the highest buildings in New York, and her windows, always open, summer and winter, overlook the city to the heights and the North River and New Jersey, to the Palisades. It is a clean, sweet-smelling office, full of fresh air and sunlight and good spirits. Her girls call Nancy "Ma," and they love her dearly. She is really like an older sister to them, wiser and more experienced than they, and giving to them freely of the best she has. I have known her for years in her home and in her business life. I have found her at all hours of the night, working briskly in her office alone, bright-eyed and cheery, too busy with her task to think of her aching back and fingers. And whether these late hours are kept for a customer who pays well for them, or in the free service of friendship, it is all one to her. All sorts of girls have passed through her office, and if they could be benefited by a shrewd and generous spirit, fresh air, a frank, unaffected view of the world, and its ways, the ideals of poets and philosophers, long, sisterly talks, on their own concerns, a clear setting-forth of their follies, their incapacity, their good traits and their bad—if these could benefit them, with the example of Nancy's own cheerful activity thrown in, they left her better than they came. I will recount none of her generous deeds, for her life has been full of them. They filled my mind as I looked down the Sound, past Long Point and North Dumpling light, and the open waterway beyond.

"Nancy," I said, "your nature in a nutshell is this: Your first impulse is superbly generous. You open your breast to the world, and if it bites you, you seek to hide the wound, you turn at bay and bite back when you would rather hide and weep. You become as resentful as you were generous before. You are very sensitive, and since you have not realized the true uses of that fine quality, it only renders you too easily hurt. You believe your friend is beautiful, and you find him full of faults. Your love of beauty is outraged ; you are filled with resentment, and, behold, you are no longer beautiful yourself, but ugly and unhappy. You do not love a quarrel, as do some, but though you wage it bitterly when once begun, it makes you miserable.

"Let your sensitiveness make you sympathetic. When you are bit, or you see those around you who might nibble some, remember that the sneer of man is cousin to the snarl of the wolf, his brother. Do you see these two pointed teeth of mine,—a shade longer than the rest? They are what remain of the fangs of my ancestors.

"When you think of the world, be gentle with its faults and sing its virtues loudly, for it has found them all by groping in the dark. Remember how blind and ignorant the wisest are."

"Am I so terrible as all that?" asked Nancy, with a gasp.

"You are a proper theme," I said; "and what's more, it's true."

"But I loathe the city. I cannot help it. I wish I might never see it again. You came here yourself to escape it, and you were glad—you said so."

"I did, but I know that is not the proper spirit for you or me. I do not hate it, though. I love it, in a way, but not enough. You are better than I and may help me win. It seems a long way off, as we look toward it, down the glittering Sound, and all the world seems far away to us now, but you see the flies and the cockroaches have found us out, and all the rest will follow in good time. Go back to the city, Nancy, and be glad you can, for you need it yet. So long as you can be stirred to resentment or disgust, you are so much the worse for it, even if there is less occasion for them here. And in time, these impulses remaining, will cease to lie dormant for lack of a probing, and will find vents of their own. You plan to remain in business three years longer. You are working for an independence, that you may shake the world from your feet. But the world will not be shaken. Go to where you will, you will not be rid of it, but you may gain something more precious than an independence. Three years in the city will bring you opportunities enough to ripen your virtues and correct the impulses that destroy them.

"Love the city and it will help you. When you leave it, bring with you a wise and tender attitude toward its follies and its meaner faults, and you will be ready for the same old world in your seclusion, when its fragments drift to you, now and then."

"Well," said Nancy, "that would be a fine thing to do if I could, but I wish—I wish I need not go."

I turned to my toast and omelet, and finished them with a will, for they were good, and there was a fine, warm light in Nancy's eyes that my harangue had not dimmed or hardened. The girls waited for me with the best nature in the world. They certainly do bear with me.

We carried the dishes to the beach, and as the tide was out and I could reach my boat without wading for it, I pulled it to the shore and unfastened the stern line. I washed it out and put up the sail.

"Now," said I, "when you are ready, we'll be off."

"Come here," said Nancy, "and see these things. They look like snail-shells but see how fast they go."

As far as we could see under the water, the sandy bottom was covered with moving shells.

"You are right," I said. "They are snail-shells, but the things that are in them now are called hermit crabs. They have eaten the snails and crawled into their shells."

I picked one from the water and two lobster-like claws and a queer little head, all eyes and whiskers, shot out and back again, with a sharp, snapping sound. I seized a disappearing claw and pulled, but I could not get him out. I cracked the shell, as I had seen them do at Wood's Hole, and we found the long body of the crab wound about in its spiral cavity. I got him out, and threw him in the water. He seized at once upon a passing comrade and began to pick at him. If he could induce him to reach out and fight, he might pull him to pieces and possess his shell.

While he poked and pinched at the opening, two others came, and finding him soft and houseless, ate him up.

"What horrible creatures," groaned Elizabeth. "Get another out and let's see how he acts."

"They are monsters of selfishness," said Nancy.

"Perhaps"; I said, "but who knows? They had no hand in their making. It's the way of their race. They have no shells of their own and must get some or be eaten. 'Tis the law, 'tis the law, and the duty of the old turn-kee.'"

Nancy looked at me reproachfully, and I fear I did attempt an imitation of her voice, but a few moments later, as I was spreading the wood to dry, I heard her unconsciously piping her refrain, and I blessed her again for her disposition.

"May she grow in grace," I thought, "for the sake of her own peace and contentment. But what more could I ask in a friend of mine? No more."

The island resounded with the noise of our labor for six swift hours. Three o'clock came, and dinner-time before we knew it. I had chopped wood, and hauled water from the sea to Nancy and brought up sand and gravel for her path, and cleared the jungle of its dead brush until I was ravenous again. In spite of the cool, strong wind, I was warm from my work in the sun. I cleaned two three-pound blackfish and gave them to Elizabeth to fry with onions for our dinner. She put the potatoes on to boil, and we went for our swim off the rocks. Nancy made the raft and back ten times without stopping, and Elizabeth, plunging boldly in, took a few strokes in the deep water and returned.

It was four o'clock when Nancy and I pushed the boat from shore. The wind was still fresh from the south. To make the points we had planned to reach, we must beat against it, tacking between Noank and Mystic Island, until we reached the channel, then down the Sound. We could not put the rudder in, until the boat was a little ways from the beach, because it hit against the bottom and came off again, nor could we lower the centreboard until we were some ten feet from shore. I pushed away with an oar and told Nancy, who was on the centre seat, to put the rudder in. Her lap was filled with the odds and ends she always carries. I know there was a handkerchief, a pad and pencil, a pastille box, a package of gum, two small bottles, one of them containing perfume. What else there was, I do not know, but I saw these in the anxious glance I cast her way, as she carefully gathered them up and carried them to the stern with her. She picked up the rudder and dropped her pastille box. While stooping for this, the boat swung around my oar and was blown to the beach again. I pried it off and said sharply:

"Now, get the rudder in quick. Never mind those traps of yours until we are safely off."

Nancy is clever with her hands, and the rudder was deftly slipped in its staples.

"Put the centreboard down."

She gathered up her load again, fumbling it in her haste, but delayed, nevertheless, until we were on shore again. The rudder flew off. Nancy laughed, but I could not join her. I gave her a glance that brought a cold glint to her eyes. She put her things on one end of the seat and picked up the rudder in silence. Again I pushed off, and we got safely away. Before I could bring the boat around, we were carried close to the rocks, near the end of our island. I pushed hard on the helm and we swept past them and went scurrying through the run to the north of Mystic Island. This was the wrong side for the course we had planned.

"It don't matter," said Nancy. "Let's go this way."

She spoke cheerfully, but I could see that she was hurt.

"Nancy," I said, "most boys learn to do things because they are taught with a club. They are thrown in the water until they swim. They are hammered with marline spikes and sworn at until they jump at the sail when they are told and keep a boat to its course. They are fired from this job and that until they must sell goods or lay bricks true or starve.

"Of all things, I know sailing requires the closest attention. I can see that much now. The wind and the tide are not thinking of pastille boxes and handkerchiefs. If you are to deal successfully with them, you must keep your will as concentrated as theirs. Girls don't learn to sail because when they do things wrong, the helm is taken from them with a smile and a compliment, and they feel very proud of their seamanship since they did not sink the ship."

"I know that is so," she said, with the warm light in her eyes again, "and I'll try and not mind your blows. Let me sail."

We were in the lee of Mystic Island, and not much of a breeze reached us.

"That looks as though it might be a wood on Fishers Island just ahead of us. And there is a streak of white that might be a sandy beach. Shall we make for that?"

I turned and looked. It was three miles across the Sound, and I could see whitecaps ahead, but they looked harmless and the wood and the beach were surely there. Near them rose a high hill, its sharp peak overlooking the whole island, the ocean upon one side and the length of the Sound upon the other. There would be a wide view from there.

For half a mile we moved easily in the lea, with Nancy, attentive, at the helm. We reached the end of Mystic Island, and the wind, sweeping past its nose, struck our sail and tipped the boat far over.

"Let the sail out," I called; "let it out."

She first jerked it in and then dropped the rope. I caught it quickly, and letting it out, changed places with her. The boat had come about to the wind, and the sail was flapping loudly over it. I turned it a little away, and as we moved ahead, brought the sail in slowly, easing it as the boat tipped, but keeping it filled with wind and the boat in motion.

"I think we could stand a hurricane with this sail," I said, "if we kept going, and the sail just taut enough. You see how quickly the boat rights itself when I let the sail out."

We slapped along swiftly, came abreast of the lightship and passed it with, I think, a somewhat wistful look. The waves were now huge, foam-crested creatures, rising much higher than the boat and tossing us with a sidelong lurch as they rose over us, lifted us up and passed under. I found, however, that by watching their advance, I could balance my body to meet them and help to keep the boat on its keel. I watched every wave as if it were the whole sea and no water came over us. Nancy, to assure me that she was not nervous or afraid, began to talk briskly about irrelevant things, calling my attention, at intervals, to indistinct objects on the far-off coast.

"I will attend to the view when we get out of this," I said grimly, easing the sail and pointing the boat toward an enormous billow I thought would engulf us.

"There is no danger, is there?"

"Not if I heed what I am doing."

Of a sudden, the nature of the water changed. It no longer swept past us in long billows, but rose in great peaks, leaping and dancing and splashing about us, tossing the boat lengthwise, and sidewise, and dashing over the sides and stern by the pailful. I have since learned that this patch of water is called the tide rip, and may be expected where the race is against the wind. I did not know what it was then. I thought we might be doomed, but I kept my eye on the sail and the boat in motion. All my life I have heard of men fighting with the elements, but this did not seem like a battle to me. The wind was a strong and friendly force, and if I worked alertly with it, it would help me through. We left the rip and came again to the comparatively easy billows. I winked at Nancy. Her eyes were snapping with delight. We sailed in silence into the lee of Fishers Island, and approached the beach slowly, through quiet water. The boat touched bottom some fifty feet from shore. I threw the stone anchor overboard. We took off our shoes and stockings and waded in. The bottom was of smooth, white sand. There were no pebbles, but a number of hermits moved over it in their stolen shells. We found an egg in the water, as large as a bottled pear. Its shell was a pure, transparent white. I don't know who laid it, but we found it fresh and good.

We passed through a wooded hollow, kneeled by a brook to drink, and climbed the hill, stopping to eat wild strawberries and sorrel grass. At the summit, we looked silently over the lonely ocean, until our hearts ached. We turned our backs upon it, and faced the Sound. We stretched upon the grass in the shade of a boulder and marveled at the view. More than twenty miles of the coast lay before us, with the water between. We looked and said nothing. We had our fill of beauty and when the sky and shore and water were aglow with the sunset at its brightest, we crept down the hillside like sluggish gormands returning from a feast.

The wind had ceased. We waded to the boat and began the long row home. There were little waves in mid-channel, but except for this narrow strip, the water was a mirror, reflecting the colors of the sky.

A dark bank of clouds rose over Watch Hill and came our way. I turned the boat toward the north, that it might face the storm, and giving the oars to Nancy, took my place in the stern. We heard the wind and the rain when it was still some distance. We felt its cold, wet breath. The sail flapped, the boat turned and moved steadily forward, as I pulled the sail in slowly. There was more rain than wind. The clouds spread and swept the colors from the canvas. It became very dark in a moment. Then Elizabeth lit the lamp, and I turned the boat toward the cabin windows. We came to our beach cold and drenched. Nancy ran ahead to start a fire. I lifted the mast out and carried it beyond high tide, threw the anchor stone on the beach, pushed the boat off, found the loose end of my stern line easily, and fastening it to the ring, *put the float on the stern seat*, and walked with a quiet satisfaction to the cabin.

Elizabeth was making a hot milk punch. The fire cast a grateful heat through the room. It is a fine thing to enjoy a fire in June. I clothed myself in pink pajamas, worth ninety-eight cents in New York, but, dry and clean and gay-colored, worth millions here. Nancy came down in a blue gingham wrapper, freshly starched and ironed, a head-dress of red ribbon, blue stockings and red slippers. These colors were becoming, for her face was brown and glowing, her eyes are blue, and her head is a little top-heavy with a thick, dark mass of hair.

We did not sail during the next three days, except to Noank and to Dodge's Island for water. To both of these places Nancy sailed alone. Sometimes she made the voyage well, but again I watched her curious manoeuvres restlessly.

"When she returns," I thought, "I will hold her to it rigidly. She must learn to sail."

I knew the difficulties of my task, for Nancy is something of a brigand and much of a woman. She is as bold and active as a tomboy, as feminine as the maids in your grandmother's time. Her tender heart is so near the surface always that it is wounded by a look or word.

We passed three busy, tranquil days. Sunday night, I took the girls to the train, watched it whirl them away, and returning alone to the dock, pushed off in the dark and rowed slowly across the mile of still water. The island seemed very quiet as I walked up the path.

The only beach on Quirk is this stony section facing southwest. The little pier is fairly substantial given the low technology employed. The question is, why didn't Henry tie the skiff to the pier rather than beaching it on such rough ground? A magnifying glass fails to reveal the name on the skiff's transom, but the dog is lying on the aft seat. The voluminous garmet of the woman sitting on the bow of the skiff is typical of the period. It is hard to imagine that this is the sort of ensemble Quirk's ladies sported on a daily basis. Surely this is not the stuff that would feed the oglers on the mainland. Perhaps she is dressed for going ashore. (Photo from Second Edition)

In the second edition of *An Island Cabin* this photograph is identified as "An Island Eyrie." The text has us remembering Dreiser and Henry doing their heavy mental lifting from the top. Dreiser in his rocking chair which he bought from the reluctant Elihu Potter. It is good to know that the women were permitted their moments as well. It is interesting to speculate which woman is which and wonder what each was reading. The stepping stones in the background lead to Ahoy which is obscured behind the foliage. The land on the horizon is the southern tip of Masons Island before it was developed. (Photo from Second Edition)

CHAPTER VII

WITH the passing of the summer on my island, I have found that the despised porch overlooking Noank has become the one most frequented; that absolute solitude is not the best thing for me.

For two weeks I was here alone. A plunge in the sea, a breakfast cooked on the coals in the fireplace, the bed-clothes spread upon the roof, the cabin swept, a tour of the island for driftwood, and I was ready for the morning's fishing. If I wanted mussels for dinner, I would wade among the rocks, finding them in great clusters. In a little cove I discovered an area of mud and sand, where clams burrowed. If I wished for lobsters or blackfish, I would take a pail and hunt the beach for bait. At first, it was difficult to find the little crabs I was seeking. But when I became acquainted with them, it was possible to capture fifty or a hundred in a few moments. If the tide were out, it was only necessary to overturn the large stones, where they had crawled for shade and moisture until the water should return. If the tide were coming in, I found them everywhere along its edge, carried back and forth with the wash of the water, or scrambling over the pebbles in search of a shelter or under the small stones, where they had found a temporary rest. I learned that many of them take their color from their surroundings, becoming an almost transparent white in the white sand, brown and green where the seaweed hangs to the rocks, or speckled where the pebbles are of many tints. To catch them, you must move quickly, for they see you from a distance, and dart away sideways on their eight legs, with the swiftness of water-bugs. And they can dodge your descending hand with incredible skill. They seem to possess, to a great degree, that instinct which, in birds, avoids the flying missile, in hell-divers, the rifle bullet, and makes it possible for a man to hit a curved ball or parry a thrust too swift to see. Noticing this sign of kinship, I hated to hunt them for the hook. But what was I to eat—a grain that had been ground in the mill, a piece of flesh from the slaughter pen?

"So long," I thought, "as I can see no other way of living than in the destruction of some form of life, I may as well bait my own hook as to eat of another's fish, or to turn my nose away while another hand sticks the knife or swings the sickle for me."

So I filled my pail with crabs and put out to the pole buoy. At first, it was all a matter of chance with me. I might have found reason for smiling at my good fortune, or for railing at the elements and my bad luck. There were days when I rowed to my post under a clear sky, through limpid, opalescent water, and lay quietly at anchor, dropping in my line and pulling out three and four-pound blackfish.

There were fine days, also, when I caught nothing, and still others when my hook would not fall to the bottom, nor my anchor hold. I learned in time that I must hit upon the hour of slack water, that the fish swim against the tide, going out as it is coming in and returning with the ebb. Accommodating my needs to these conditions, I could supply them easily.

For two weeks, my constant companions were fish, lobsters, crabs and the elements. When I went to Noank for groceries and mail, I found my heart warming more and more toward such people as I met, and in my idle moments on the island, I found myself most often on the Noank side. The sounds of toil from the shipyards, the faraway voices from the village, the smoke from the chimneys, the white houses, half hidden by the trees, became constantly more alluring. The endless path of water, leading out to sea, was as changeable and as full of beauty as before—

why then, was my face turned back toward land? I asked this question until the answer came.

The destiny of every atom of the universe is equally associated with our own. It is not with men alone that we need to adjust ourselves in sympathy, but with the earth and air and water and all the innumerable forms of life that these contain. They, too, are our fellows. We cannot escape this necessity by flying from the city. We but change our associates. If we seek for rest and peace in a tranquil contemplation of nature, as a thing apart from ourselves, we will not find it. For, though we may look at it with a far-off, impersonal vision, we cannot alter our actual and intimate relationship. Our fate, our moods and all our movements are bound to those of the stars and the pebbles, the wind, the rain and the sunlight. All that concerns men and crabs, concerns us whether we will or no. It remains for us to determine how great shall be the discord or how complete the harmony of this relationship. It is true that our knowledge must always be incomplete, but a sympathetic willingness to know will keep sweet our fellowship with men and things.

I had watched the crabs devouring each other. I had lived a life of constant murder for a week. I had struggled with wind and tide. I had listened and watched and felt emotion; but these companions around me now were still too distant. I heard the voices of the wind and water, the bells, the fog-horn and the boat whistles, but their words were lost to me. I had left the city to escape the greedy contentions of men, only to find that I must join with the fish, the lobsters and crabs in the pursuit of life.

And now, with my eyes on Noank, the world of men appeared to me in a new light. I remembered the hands I had touched in affection, the eyes that sought to comfort those who suffered, the voices I had heard pleading for the beauty of love and service. I had seen no evidence of a Christ among the crabs, but in Noank there were old sea captains who had risked their lives to save their crews; in New York there were ditch-diggers who had helped their comrades to safety before seeking their own.

Grim and barbarous as the struggle is, there are, in the mass of contending men, multitudes of lonely, tender hearts patiently seeking in the darkness and storm for what will satisfy the longing of the world. Their voices are of the quality of my light-ship's bell.

Every day at noon, I went across the water to the town. Just off the shore, there is a line of posts where the fishermen moor their boats. Sometimes the boats were gone, and again they were riding lazily at anchor, with here and there an owner aboard, mending his reef points, touching a scar with paint, or arranging his lobster-pots. Here was the first picket line of a friendly camp, where, so far, no password has been required of me but a smile, a nod, a word of greeting.

If I made a certain landing, I might see Mrs. Potter standing in her doorway or sitting by the open window, sewing. She would smile at me over her glasses and, seeing the pails I carried, offer me the water of her well. If I made a landing higher up, I would sometimes find a fishing smack at the dock, and the men on board, busy with their cargo, would ask me how I liked the island, if I had good luck with my lobster-pots. They would tell me when I might expect the blue-shelled crabs, and how to fish for flounders.

Once, a two-masted smack was unloading and, as I watched the men sorting the catch and packing it in barrels, I noticed that each one had selected a few small fish, putting them one side. When the work was done, they cleaned these, cut them into strips and carried them away, strung upon a loop of fish line.

"What are those for?" I asked the captain as he picked up his string.

"The cat," he answered. "My old Tom," he added affectionately, "would be mad at me if I didn't bring him some fish."

If I met Mr. Ashbey on the street, he would say, with always the same kindly light in his eyes:

"I hope everything is all right now on the island"; and I would have to answer that it was, except for the chimney.

"The fireplace still smokes," I would say, as gently as I could, and the light would pass from his eyes. Then one day, he came over with cement and trowel, and, as he was patching up the holes, I suggested that a mason should have done the job"

"Do you know why I built this myself?" he asked, looking squarely at me like an animal brought to bay. "It was not from meanness. There ain't no mason in Noank, and the only one in Mystic wouldn't stop to do it, so I just had to build it myself as best I could."

I suddenly realized that it was no small task to build a house in the winter on this exposed and remote island; that he had made little or nothing by it, and that he had borne my implied blame with a wonderfully sweet patience.

I spoke my thoughts to him, and asked him how he had lost the fingers of his left hand.

"That happened more than thirty years ago," he said, holding out the almost useless stump. I knew that he owned a good hotel, built by himself, and that he worked as a carpenter and boatbuilder. He had kept his family in comfort and his reputation clean.

"Did you have any money at that time?"

"No," he replied quietly. "I was a young fellow, and unmarried then, just working by the day. I've made all I've got since I was pruned."

One day, as I was sitting on the steps of the barber shop, Mr. McDonald, the superintendent of the shipyard took a place beside me.

"Now, you are a writer," he said, laying a great, strong hand on my knee; "and I want to ask something of you. I want you to get the sentiment in. I tell you, we fellows who like to read want more sentiment than we get. Life is just full of it, but it is hard for a man to always see it. Now, take the shipyards, for instance. I know there is sentiment enough around me every day. And I wish I could feel it more and not do anything contrary. But I've over three hundred men at work, and I must see that there is no waste in time or labor. If I don't keep everything moving just so, they wouldn't get their wages when the month came around, and there would be nothing for the company, and the whole concern would go. I have to keep things going, and sometimes I am just forced contrary to sentiment. Now, you come down there some day, and get it all out for me, and write it down where I can have it to read when things don't go right, will you?"

That afternoon, as I returned to my boat, I heard a woman and her daughter quarreling over the position of a flower-bed, and I saw two boys fighting in the street; but all the way to my island, the sounds from the shipyard followed me across the water, and I felt Mr. McDonald's hand, heavy and warm, upon my knee.

Considering what I have heard of angels, what I have observed of crabs and what I know of men, I should say that we have reached in our progress a state midway between the devouring instincts that move the creatures of the sea and the ideals that shape our dreams of Heaven.

For a week I did not hear a human sound on the island. Its unbroken silence became oppressive. If I attempted to sing or talk aloud to myself, my voice died on my lips, and my heart swelled with homesickness. When I went to Noank, I began to inquire if any one had a pup or a kitten to spare. A good dog is the best of company for me. The dearest friend of my childhood was a dog, and I have never forgotten him. Since then, I have not been able to have one, for I have lived too much in cities and in houses where they were not welcomed at all hours and in all kinds of weather. This island would be a fine home for such a friend. But I could not find a pup in Noank that would suit me. I heard of a litter of Irish setters, but the mother was said to be of an uncertain character, stubborn and suspicious, and I did not want one of her brood.

The town was full of cats, but it was some time before I found a kitten. I had spread my inquiries abroad, and one morning, Mr. Potter informed me of a family of Maltese kittens lately weaned. I hurried to the house he mentioned. It was under the hill, near the water-side, and possessed a comfortable, domestic appearance that pleased me.

I was met at the kitchen door by a young woman, perhaps nineteen, who invited me in before she knew my errand, and stood near me, listening with an amiable expression in her eyes while I told it. I have not seen her again, but I shall not forget her. If I were an artist, she would appear on some canvas of mine, for her face and pose as she stood before me gave a perfect expression to Simplicity, Innocence and Sympathy, and were beautiful because of these. She might easily stand for the world's domestic ideal.

"I am glad you have come," she said. "We have some kittens, and Papa was about to drown them. He won't let me keep all of them."

She went to the door and called, and a dozen or more cats and kittens came scampering around the corner to her feet. They jostled each other as they jumped and crowded about her, looking up, rubbing against her ankles, mewing. A tiny gold heart hung from blue baby ribbon about the neck of one of the Maltese kittens. She picked this one up, and held it to her breast while she stooped for another. The first one climbed to her shoulders, and turning about, cuddled close to her throat, its head under her chin, its paws dabbing at the second button of her dress. The top one had been left unfastened, for it was a warm morning. The second kitten was a fat little thing, with a thick fur of good color, but its eyes and nose were stopped up as with a bad cold. I saw that all the family of young ones, except the one at her throat, were badly affected with distemper.

"What do you feed them?" I asked.

"Mostly milk."

They look as if they had been eating too much fish."

"I guess they do get a good deal. Their mother and all the other old cats bring them fish. Jerry—the old tomcat there,—is their father, and their grandfather, and their greatgrandfather, too, I guess, and he is busy bringing them things all the time. He came up with a live eel yesterday, and it crawled under the house."

"I will take this one, if I may. It will get well on a diet of milk."

She gave me the second kitten, and said a little appealingly:

"If you would take another, it would be less lonesome for this one."

"The one at your throat?" I asked.

She hesitated a moment and agreed.

"You may have this one," she said freely. "I can keep another one, and we will then save three of them."

The one at her throat had pushed its head into her dress, and as she drew it forth, the second button came undone and I caught a glimpse of her white bosom, swelling to a graceful fullness. She did not notice the revelation, and I tried not to. I glanced away, and still wished to look. Who can read me truly the riddle of these impulses?

She got me a covered basket for the kittens. As she was putting them in, I said:

"You will want the locket. Let us take it off."

"No," she answered simply. "You may have that, too."

"Are they both girls?"

"Yes, but you won't mind. You are very good."

She stood behind me, smiling and silent, looking pleasantly into my eyes. And that was our adieu.

I carried the basket to my boat and pushed off. A stiff wind was blowing, and the water was rough. The boat slapped up and down sharply as it crossed the uneven waves, and I was afraid the kittens would be frightened. It was necessary to tack over a long course, and almost an hour passed before we reached the island. I beached the boat and took the basket to the cabin. I shut the doors and windows, and placed the basket on the floor and removed the cover, wondering if they were dead from fright or if they would leap out and dash about the cabin, as cats will sometimes do in strange surroundings. I found them curled about each other on the bottom, fast asleep. I sat back in my chair and watched them carefully. Their presence, the sight of their quiet repose, brought me a sense of home and affection, and tempered the silent loneliness of the island.

I watched them till they awoke. The one with the ribbon stood up first and stretched herself. She licked her right paw and rubbed her eyes

In a few moments, the other one stood up and stretched, and rubbed her eyes, and looked quietly over the edge of the basket. She made no attempt to get out, but followed the movements of her sister with a tranquil gaze. I named her Betty.

I went outside and left the door open, that they might be free to acquaint themselves with their home, in their own way.

I put a saucer of milk on the porch and went to the beach. As I was at the far end of the island, turning over the stones for crabs, I felt something against my leg. It was Yannie. She was a little thing then, only a few weeks old, and it must have been a long journey for her down the path through the jungle, along the beach, and over the rocks and pebbles at this end. It was wet where I stood, for the tide had recently fallen, and because of this, I was the more surprised, for cats are opposed to wet places and are careful where they step. She followed me closely. When I turned over the rocks, she jumped at my fingers as I scratched among the sand and pebbles. If a crab ran out, she ran after him, stopping and stirring him up again with her paws. When I waded into the water, she came to its edge, sniffed at the ripples, stretched her head toward me and mewed in her anxiety to follow.

It was the most cheerful half-hour I had spent since the girls left me. Returning, we found Betty watching for us at the foot of the path. The milk was not touched. They were evidently waiting for fish.

They sat by the fireplace while I cooked my dinner, watching me with moist, half-closed, affectionate eyes, and purring loudly. When I was seated at the table, they climbed up my legs to my lap and reached up to my plate. I snapped their noses smartly and carried them to their saucer on the porch.

"Now, girls," I said, and it was pleasant to talk without a sense of greater loneliness for the sound, "you cannot eat at the table. Here is your dinner."

They turned away and, following me closely, climbed into my lap.

"You may lie there, if you want to, but keep your noses down."

If they lifted their heads toward the plate, I rebuked them. Before the meal was over, to raise my finger was enough.

In the evening, I lit the candles and sat by the table to read. Betty climbed to one arm of my chair, and Yannie to the other. The cabin was filled with their purring. But Yannie was not long quiet. The candle attracted her. She jumped to the table and thrust her nose into the flame. With a cry of pain and a great spit of anger, she sprang away, returning instantly, to hit it with her paw. Then she moved to the other end of the table, to nurse her burns, casting curious glances at the candle now and then. Of a sudden, she fell upon her side, kicking and struggling. I picked her up and found that the ribbon collar was caught in her teeth. I removed it and hung it with its golden heart on a nail in the wall. Such things have little meaning for me, but this trinket does, at least, no harm, and while I do not need it to recall the one who gave it to me, I should miss it now.

In the morning, I gave the kittens fresh condensed milk, and they ate it willingly. A few days of this diet cured Betty, and she began to develop a brighter spirit. She never became as adventurous as Yannie, for she is not of so restless a spirit, but there is nothing cowardly or mean in her. I was never alone now. The kittens followed me everywhere, or, if they disappeared for a time in the jungle, they would come out upon me unexpectedly, seeming to know where I was, as if they had watched me constantly. When I left them on the island, they watched me from the beach as long as I could see them, and when I returned, they were there to welcome me.

One morning, as I pushed away, Yannie seemed unusually distressed. She came to the edge of the water and mewed piteously. I turned to speak to her, and saw her jump to a rock some four feet from the shore. There was a good breeze and the boat was moving swiftly. I was a hundred feet from the island when she leaped from the rock into the water and swam after me. I brought the boat about quickly, and made for her tiny head, just visible. Her eyes were very wide and somewhat terrified, but she swam steadily toward me until I picked her up. Betty was close to the water, craning her neck and watching in great anxiety. After this, when I went fishing, or to Dodge's Island after water, I took them with me.

They were a great comfort to me, each in her own way, showing an affection entirely free from the selfish indolence I had previously attributed to all cats. But they could not supply all my need. Most of the day I was busy and contented, but at night I tossed on my tick, for the very beauty of my surroundings and the conceptions they fostered, increased my longing for a kindred being to see and think and speak with me.

CHAPTER VIII

I HAVE also found that any one who will, may go to an island as beautiful as this and take his miseries with him, setting them up as he would his bric-a-brac, busying himself with them and converting all that he sees into a setting for them.

One morning early, after a night of lonely wakefulness, I heard voices near the island, and hurrying to the window, saw a Noank sailboat making for the beach, with a long-expected friend on board. It had been previously arranged that Tom and his wife should spend a month with me, and that Nancy should come up with them. We four had passed many days together in occasional tramps about New York, and the complete harmony of our relations and the delight we found in our comradeship was a thing to gloat over. Between Tom and myself, there was such perfect accord that we met after weeks of separation and silence as if but an hour had passed.

"Where are the girls?" I asked as he came on shore, with his grip, and paid the boatman for his passage.

"They will be here in a few days," he said. "I came up in advance to help you get things arranged. I want Ruth to like it here so we can stay for the summer."

He stood by his grip on the sand, and as I turned from the sky and water and distant shore line, radiant and sparkling with the hues of a fair morning, I saw a cloud of uncertainty and trouble in his face.

"Well," said I, eager to have him enter with me into the joy of the place, "what do you think of it?"

"Beautiful," he said, coming for a moment out of his abstraction and looking about him with glowing eyes; "I can see great things for us here. The life of the sea is profound and grim. It gets me with a terrific grip."

We climbed the path leading from the beach to the house, and the warm breath of the earth, the sweet odors of shrubs and vines and wild roses, caused him to stop and exclaim:

"That's a fine thing to get out here in the sea. It smells like a patch of woods."

I ushered him into my cabin, confident of his delight. Before he had put down his grip, he said : "Let's scrub the floor." I had swept it thoroughly every day and it was clean, but his eyes were shocked by the contrast between unpainted boards, spotted by use, and the rugs of his cozy flat. And the walls, I could see, seemed rough and bare to him. I was surprised and grieved, for I had looked upon him as another self, and it had not once occurred to me that he would think of what might be lacking where there was so much to delight in.

I moved the scant furniture out, and the floor was scrubbed. I built the fire, and got the breakfast and was glad to see Tom in the hammock on the porch, because I was anxious that the beauty of our surroundings should delight him. As I was setting the table, he came in, and picking up a plate, rubbed his finger over it and said:

"Why, these dishes are greasy."

"That is the moisture that gathers on everything around salt water," I said.

"It's grease," he insisted, with a wry face. "I can't eat off such dishes."

He picked up a knife and exclaimed over the rust.

"Can't you get these clean?" he asked in helpless distress.

"Suppose you try it while I am getting the breakfast ready," I replied.

He gathered up the dishes and held them disconsolately until I found the dishpan for him.

"Now," said I, "if you will take this pail and get some sea water, you can wash them on this box on the porch. Here is the sapolio."

Now, there are at least two ways of going to the edge of the rocks for a pail of water. You may keep your mind fixed on the necessity that drives you there, grumbling and fretting with yourself and getting nothing from your errand but the drudgery of it, or you may lift your eyes to the far-reaching sky and sea, taking your pail empty and returning with it full, as a simple incident of a stroll to the water-side and back. Tom went and returned, taking the images of the rusty knives and the moist dishes with him. He had great difficulty in finding a rag for the sapolio. He finally tore a piece from a towel and began to dab and scrub, sighing and groaning at his work.

"This sea water won't get the grease off," he complained. "Just look!"

"Tom," said I, "those dishes are clean. I scrubbed them with sand and washed them afterwards with hot water and sapolio. We can't have fresh water on this island for washing purposes without devoting all our time to getting it. Come and eat, for the breakfast it getting cold."

I cleared the table and washed the dishes while Tom examined the premises.

He asked me how much the house had cost and thought it was too much. He found that the stones could be knocked from under one corner of the porch and suggested that we clear the island of its wild tangle of sweet-smelling shrubs and replace it with a smooth lawn. I listened and looked at him from the corner of my eye. I could not believe that this was the Tom I had known.

When the dishes were done, we went to the beach and captured the crabs for bait. As we picked them from their hiding-places, Tom's wonder and interest grew. He cursed them for elusive devils, sighed over their fate, wondered at their intelligence, their trick of assuming the colors of the weeds and pebbles. He held them up to examine them ; he watched them eat and fight, and discovered as much in a few moments as I had learned in weeks. But he continued to shake his head dubiously as we dropped them in the bait pail, and when, anchored by the pole buoy, we put them on the hooks and cast them overboard, he seemed to see only the wretched nature of their end. If the fish did not bite, he grew restless; if they did, he hauled them in with a grim zest, and struggled to unhook them, now pitying their state, now damning them for the trouble they made.

For two hours, while the water was slack, we fished in mid-channel, and when the tide became too strong, we moved out of the race and anchored where our hooks could fall to the bottom. I needed fresh bait for my lobster-pots and my car was empty, so we fished all day. It was a clear, calm morning, and our boat rode tranquilly at its anchor. There were long intervals when the fish did not bite and when Tom, forgetting them, looked with appreciation across the gleaming, quiet water and along the distant, far-stretching shore line. Then my haggard spirits would revive, in the hope that he would see and enjoy and complain no more.

In the afternoon, a breeze came to us from the southwest, and freshened to a gale. As the waves rose about us, rocking the boat, Tom watched them with a restless eye.

"You think it's safe here?" he inquired.

"It will be a stiff pull home," I replied, "but it's safe enough."

"All right," he said courageously; "if you want to stay, I'm with you."

At five o'clock, we pulled up the anchor and the boat began to drift swiftly with the wind and tide. The pole buoy was passed in a flash, and we were racing along in mid-channel. Before I could get to my seat, a bucket of water dashed over the rocking boat, and Tom exclaimed:

"My God! Look at that."

I seized the oars and began to row, keeping the boat steady and in motion.

"Let me help," said Tom. "Give me an oar."

I was glad to do so, for it was a hard pull. I untied the cord that held the oarlock in position and passed it back to him with an oar. He slipped the lock in its hole, but did not tie it. He worked with feverish haste, gave a mighty stroke with his oar, and fell back in the boat. The lock had been yanked out and had fallen overboard. We were driving out to sea with the rushing tide. The wind was whistling past us, lashing the water into white-caps. And we could no longer row!

"We are in for it now," I exclaimed.

"We can paddle," cried Tom, his face set grimly, his eyes now gleaming with determination, now dull with despair.

"You row and I'll paddle," he said, standing up in the prow and sweeping the water with a strong stroke. I saw that we held our own by this method, and that if we could once get out of the tide race, we could make the island in time. Tom paddled until he was exhausted, and we exchanged places. We worked our way, inch by inch, and pushed our boat on shore. When it was all over, and we sat before the fire to dry, Tom admitted that it was a fine adventure.

"It's all in the day's work," I said. "Let's have our dinner."

I took him to the beach and showed him how to skin the blackfish.

"See," I said, "you hit him on the head with a stone to stun him. You leave the head on until the last, to hold it by. Now, I fasten my fingers in his gills, stick the point of the knife in his throat, and rip him open down the belly to the tail. Now, I cut through the skin down his back, first on one side the fin, and then on the other. I cut his skin across the top, just beneath the gills, and loosen it from the flesh along this line. When you have an inch or two free, you can grip it with your fingers and tear it off."

As I illustrated this, the half-skinned fish jerked from my hand and slapped convulsively in the sand.

"My God!" exclaimed Tom. "It's still alive."

I caught my victim, cut off his head, and scooping out his entrails with my thumb, washed him in the sea.

"Now," said I, "you clean another one while I build the fire and get the dinner."

Half an hour later, I went to the beach and found him washing the fish, picking and scrubbing them, his face set with lines of disgust.

"I guess I can eat them now," he said.

At his table in New York, I have eaten fish perhaps two days dead, and that some one else had caught and killed and cleaned in the same relentless manner. We talked of this at the table, and he agreed that we cannot judge as to the value of life, sparing the animal and slaying the vegetable, and that if we eat what another kills, it is sheer cowardice to avoid the act of slaughter for ourselves. And yet he ate his meal with a poor relish, and from that time on, I was expected to clean the fish, *because I did not mind.* I am glad of this, for each time I did so, this phase of the problem of life came forcibly before me, and I have had many a long and profitable think as I skinned and gutted our dinner on the sand.

After dinner, Tom suggested that we get some fresh water, as he did not like to drink it two days old.

"You go," I said, "while I wash the dishes."

"I don't know the people," he replied, "and I'd rather not go alone."

"But I didn't know them at first. I had to get acquainted with them. They are as friendly as they can be, and it is understood that we are to get water there. If you want to wash the dishes, though, I'll go for the water."

"Oh, no. I'll go for the water."

He took two pails and rowed to Mystic Island. I watched him walking along the grassy path, over the gentle rise, and saw with delight that he was looking at the brilliant sunset back of Noank, and I knew that none of the beauty of the graceful dark line of land and the glowing sky and water would be lost to him, for there is no one more sensitive to the world about him, more deeply sympathetic with it, than is Tom, at most times. A little later, I saw him at the crest of the hill, returning. He stopped twice to rest between there and the beach. When he reached the boat, he put the pails in at once and I called to him to push off first, so the lurch would not slop the water. There is nothing more exasperating than to be told how to do things. Tom, however, did not heed me. By careful management, he got away successfully and thumbed his nose at me in triumph. When he brought the pails in, he said, with an air of weariness:

"That's a long way to go for water. We ought to have a well here."

"I can't afford one. It would cost a good deal to drill through these rocks."

"Gibbie says the well on Mystic Island rises and falls with the tide. It's just sea water filtered through. Why can't we get a barrel and sink it in the beach?"

"I have tried that, but there is a ledge of rocks about two feet below the surface of the sand. That is a beautiful path across Mystic Island."

His face brightened, and his eyes glowed with the soft hues of pleasure.

"Yes," he said warmly, "it was a fine walk over. That long point of land between the sky and water assumes a mysterious and appealing shape in the twilight. The colors were brilliant and exhilarating. As I climbed the hill, I felt like shouting."

There is a huge rock rising twenty feet above the water at the edge of the island, about forty feet from my cabin door. Its flat top is as large as a good-sized room. We climbed to this comfortable observatory to watch the night fall. Tom took with him a square platform of boards and his rocking-chair, and I, a blanket and pillow. If I may throw myself flat, with my head up enough to see, I am most at my ease. What this is to me, Tom finds in a rocking-chair.

A great sea-bird, enlarged to our perception by the darkness, flew swiftly over us. We could hear an occasional shrill note from the gulls, perched for the night upon the fish nets staked near the island. The incoming tide washed the rocks under us. The moon would not rise for an hour, but the night was bright with the light of such a multitude of stars as I have seldom seen; and they were unusually full and luminous.

"How little we know," said Tom, as he rocked and gazed. "It is pitiful. Here we sit with our eyes cocked on the universe like two wise frogs croaking by their pond. If we toppled over this rock, while craning our necks at the stars, we would sink, gurgling, into the sea. We look and speculate, but what can we say after it all, except to exclaim in meaningless phrases over its varying aspects? Why all this marvelous beauty? Surely, it is not simply for us to gape at. Just look at this night—listen and look! I could sing or weep. No one can avoid the emotion, but why do we feel it?"

"There must be some significance for us beyond the mere tickling of our senses," I replied. "The beauty, the mystery, the magic of the earth and heavens has not fulfilled its mission when it has caused us to sing or weep."

I have always been able to talk with Tom as with no one else. No other companionship has been so profitable to me. We grow in wisdom as we learn to understand our emotions. To feel and to understand; these are the requisites. Tom has been for me as a deep shaft. His emotions reach further than mine. We are two sympathetic prospectors. He, with the groans and straining of the delver, brings up the hidden quartz, and I fashion it into exchangeable coin.

Tom perceives the world as it is, more clearly than I, but the world, as it is, is a riddle without head or tail, unless we also recall what it has been and conceive what it is to be.

"The universe," I said, "is seeking to know itself. Its good is the order, its evil the disorder of its parts. As its various forms of life learn to know each other and to form a sympathetic relationship, good ensues. There is no real separation between the various forms. Because of their close connection, the friction and discord that comes from their ignorant, crisscross activity produces all that we call evil.

"The good of our universe is revealed to us by the senses. It appears in beauty to the eye.

"Here we are, little individuals in a greater one, composed of his elements, bound up in him, fated to share his destiny. And as we share it, we shape it, also. A part of the universe without, we are creating a miniature universe within, drawing into ourselves the elements and shaping them to our ways. If the universe displeases any one, let him make a better one within himself. In this way, only, may we lend a hand to fate.

"Again, this universe of ours is an individual among others, a little thing in yet another universe. Is it a man, a leaf, a crab, an atom of the air, a grain of sand? That would be an interesting question to pursue. The answer would be found by discovering what form of life is really dominant here. But we are after the significance of beauty now, and that is the same for every form alike. What, then, is the moral quality of our universe? Is it good or evil? If it be a man, is he ignorant and malicious; does he skulk in the darkness; is he sullen; is he a coward? Is he bold and unscrupulous; is he polite and cunning; is he honest and greedy, or is he wise and generous and tender?

"Our universe is good. I know this, because in its larger aspects, it is beautiful. You and I may hear discordant sounds and see ugly sights when we detach them from the whole. A bad man is an affair between him and me. I may live at outs with my village and it is ugly, but if I forget my quarrels and climb to the crest of a distant hill, the town, reposing in the sheltered valley, becomes at once a place of fine dreams and prospects. My bad man, my sharp-tongued neighbors, are lost in the beauty of a harmonious whole.

"Men rob and murder and deceive, and yet the sum total of their conduct, from the beginning until now, is progress toward a loving fellowship.

"Is there a bog in your meadow? Is there a barren waste? Extend your vision, include a wider reach of earth and heaven, and your eye will rest upon a scene of beauty. Varying degrees of discord still prevail between the parts, but the universe, as a whole, is wise and generous and tender. Its trend is toward harmony, beauty and order. Its spirit woos us toward this end. We cannot behold its beauty without emotion, for its spirit is our spirit, and the elements within us, seeing the larger harmony without, recognize in it an ideal that may be attained. Its spirit woos us, and as we see and shape ourselves into accord with it, we increase the harmony of the whole. We are at once creatures and creators. We are subject to a destiny we partly shape. We help to fashion the countenance of our God, inspired by the beauty it has already attained."

"For my part," said Tom, "I think the universe is an individual very much like McKinley or King Edward. It might be a Bismarck, a Gladstone, a Morgan or a Rockefeller, but I question if it possesses, as a whole, the singleness of purpose and the strength of will of these men. It is certainly not a malicious brute, but it might very well be a John L. Sullivan, good-natured enough when sober, mellowed by a little liquor, made maudlin by more, and ugly by too much. I think, however, it is just an average, rather phlegmatic sort of fellow, preserving a formal, well-balanced poise in mediocrity; or, as you suggest, it might be a crab or a leaf or an atom of the air, and man but a minor subdivision in its make-up."

"But the significance of its beauty would be the same."

"Yes, that is true. Whatever it is, its larger trend is toward harmony and beauty."

We remained on the rock until the moon rose, and its widening pathway of light led from us, past Latimer's Reef, to the ocean. In my own mind, the argument did not end where we had left it. I saw the ships of man passing over the water around me. Some time his vehicles will be as freely riding the air. Surely he, more than any other form of life, is an active agent in the effort of the universe to know itself. He is bringing the elements into a closer and closer acquaintance. Through him, the forces of the earth and air are joining hands, and the sea, the forests, the mines, the fields of cotton and hemp, have become related in purposeful activity. And man himself is becoming more sympathetic and friendly with a greater variety of conditions. Harmony is produced by tuning to a single string, and it may be that the race of man is the keynote of universal accord.

"I shall be content," I said, "if I maintain, through every moment of my days, an attitude in harmony with the colors of this evening's sunset ; if no mood of mine does violence to the spirit of this starry night. If I can always enter Noank and take with me the sentiment its distant aspect awakens ; if I can dwell in New York, and in my life give expression to what the city seems to be as I view it from the Palisades; if I can sail the sea and walk the fields, noting as I go the conflicting details, but keeping my own being in tune with the beauty that shapes their larger forms, I shall be satisfied."

"And when you die?"

"And when I die, I hope that my broken vessel will return a well-seasoned mess to the parent brew."

"Any conception of life is good," said Tom, "if held in reverence. Reverence is man's salvation. The world has outgrown its old beliefs, and it has not yet gained enough of the knowledge it is seeking to inspire a reverent attitude."

"Shall we stop our croaking for the night?"

"Yes. It is eleven o'clock. There goes the Stonington boat."

The boat, six miles away, gliding from its harbor into the channel of the Sound, appeared to us as a narrow thread of light about a foot long. We could hear the dull throbbing of its engines.

"There are, perhaps, fifty people on board," I said. "I would like to write a romance, opening it with a picture of this scene, and dealing with a boatload of people, whose every impulse would be in keeping with its beauty. What a fine voyage they would have, down the moon-lit Sound."

"Listen!" said Tom, turning his head quickly, and lifting his hand in a gesture of suspense. There is an island about the size of mine a few hundred feet to the north. It rises from the water in receding ledges. Its surface was now quite clear in the moonlight, but the side toward us was lost in darkness. As Tom spoke, a loud flopping came from the shadows. We could see nothing, but we knew that a flounder or sea eel or a large blackfish had been left upon a ledge by the falling tide, and was struggling desperately, as it smothered in the air.

"Horrible," said Tom, his eyes staring, his great mouth twisted in distress. "There is not much beauty in the scene for that poor devil. I've had enough for one day. Let's go to bed."

As we were spreading our blankets on the ticks, Tom grew depressed. I could see discomfort of spirit clouding his face. He sighed and closed a window. He held up a quilt, felt of it, threw it down, and said in a mournful tone:

"Everything is damp. We ought to have closed the windows before we came in."

I like to get into a dry bed. I think I would prefer it so, as a rule, but a damp one does not distress me, and I have had many a sweet sleep in the rain. On this occasion, I had noticed no dampness, but had slipped under the clothes, my mind still dwelling on the theme of our discussion. Tom's manner and comment entered my mood like a branch of thorns. "If you must have dry clothes," I thought, "why don't you arrange to keep them so, and if you neglect to do so and find them damp, will a distressed and complaining spirit dry them? Confound it, Tom, how can you reconcile your philosophy with your conduct now?" And I did not see that I was committing the fault I condemned. Material things irritated him, and his fault-finding irritated me. The good or the evil lies in our attitude ; the cause is never an excuse. Whoever feels irritation, is in fault, whatever his reason may be. Whatever disturbs us is our opportunity. Tom's complaining was mine, but I did not recognize it, and I allowed myself to be rankled and upset.

"How can you sleep on these narrow ticks?" asked Tom. "They are full of lumps. I don't believe Ruth can stand it."

"I will venture to say that Ruth doesn't make as much fuss as you do," I replied.

"Perhaps not," said Tom frankly. "Perhaps that's so."

In the morning, we went for a plunge off the rocks. Before this, I had gone in my wrapper and returned to the house to dress. Tom showed me a better way. He taught me to take my clothes with me and spread them out in the sun, sitting for a while, myself, in a warm corner of the rocks before the bath.

A form of seaweed grows on the rocks to the line of high water. It is green and strong and pleasant to the touch. I have found it one of the conveniences of my bath-tub, for it protects me from contact with the hard, rough surface of the rocks, and offers something to cling to as I climb from the water. I was surprised to see Tom pulling it up.

"We ought to make a place clear of this for our bath," said he. "Here is a succession of ledges, leading like wide steps into deep water. If we get this seaweed off, we can walk down and see where we are going."

He worked away for some time and seemed put out because I did not help him. I could not sympathize with his purpose, but I wish I had sympathized with *him* and lent a hand. A happy fellowship is not for those who stand aloof. We may think that we know more than our neighbor, but real wisdom is that which takes us closer to him.

When Tom had cleared a ledge, we dove from it, and climbing out again, cut our hands and knees on the barnacles the clearing had left exposed.

"We can knock those off with a hammer," said he, but this was never done.

As we were dressing, Tom said:

"I have thought of a way to get fresh water. We could take a barrel, fill it half-full of dirt, pour in sea water, and let it filter through."

Had this been proposed to me as an experiment, I would have entered upon it with interest, but I got from Tom's suggestion only the lingering concern he felt. I protested to myself against this bringing of bugaboos and anxieties to my island, and so taking resentment for a companion, I lost another pleasure. It would surely be interesting to know if one could get fresh water from the sea by so simple a means, but as I left Tom to follow his own suggestion, the test was not made.

I built the fire and got breakfast, and cleared the table. Then, seeing that Tom had taken his rocking-chair to the porch, I asked him to wash the dishes while I cleared the cabin. This was another prompting of ill-nature in me, for had I preserved a serene and wholesome spirit, I would have found my interest and happiness in doing what needed to be done. All labor is in itself a means of knowledge, and a source from which the truest happiness flows. If another man leaves me his work to do, he is bestowing upon me his choicest gift. My only concern should be for him in his loss, and I should seek the wisdom with which to induce him to share it with me for the blessing it is.

Tom came to his task as if all the drudgery of life had been thrust upon him. It was a wretched morning for us both.

"I'll tell you what we could do," said Tom suddenly. "We might get a barrel, fill it seven-eighths full of water, and tow it here. A barrel seven-eighths full will float."

"All right," I said, "we'll get the barrel."

It was about noon when we started for Noank.

The water was rippling pleasantly under a light breeze that would just carry us before it. I put up the sail and we made the trip as easily as one might lie in a hammock. We were in a pleasant humor as we got on shore, and strolled leisurely through the town. We spoke of the grassy streets, the fine, old trees, the fragrant yards, the friendly faces of those we met, and the old-time relations of sympathetic reflection and converse were restored between us.

Our search for a barrel led us at last to the shipyard, and Mr. Mc-Donald. We met him as he was leaving a half-finished barge, and told him our want.

"I can give you an empty whisky barrel," he said. "We place one in every boat we build. They are used to carry water, and I never heard any complaint of the whisky, except that the flavor was too mild."

He selected the barrel and helped us roll it to the water-side, and when we asked him the price, he said genially:

"I've forgotten what we pay. If I think of it some time, I'll look at the bills, and if I forget it, there'll be small loss."

With the barrel in the boat, we set sail for Dodge's Island.

"Let me sail," said Tom. "I want to learn how."

He took the rope and rudder and squatted comfortably in the stern seat. The wind was dying away, and the boat moved through the smooth water as peacefully as a cloud floats through a tranquil sky.

"This is wonderfully fine," said Tom. "I'm beginning to see the delicate charm of the place. It's not the house that we're here for, but the world of open air and water about us."

"I'm glad of that," I said, "for I was afraid you were seeing nothing but discomforts."

"It's strange," he answered thoughtfully, "how a man's habits will get hold of him. A few years ago, I would have slept on a bare floor and not noticed it, and I thought nothing of my food. Ruth has certainly spoiled me for all that. She makes me so comfortable in a thousand ways that I'm lost now when I must take care of myself or where my personal surroundings are not just so."

"Yes, we groan over the stress of life and the need for constant toil. We look with terror upon the reaching hands of want, and all because we are not content with what the earth offers us for a fair return of labor. We are not slaves to necessity, but to our palates, our vanity, our love of power."

"We seem to be standing still," said Tom.

"It's worse than that—we are drifting back. The wind is gone. We must row."

Tom took the oars, and I told him what McDonald had said on the barber's steps."

"That's fine," he exclaimed. "You can bet the ones who are looking for sentiment are those who carry it with them."

We passed half a mile to the west of my island, but its reflection in the glossy water almost touched our boat.

"I can understand now," said Tom, resting on his oars and turning toward the Sound and sea, "what you feel about the absence of the police."

"Look, Tom, you can see the vegetation that clings to the rocks below us. It is ten feet deep here. That must be a big boulder down there, covered with ferns."

"Don't you think that the creatures of the sea, moving among their beautiful groves, take the same delight in them that we do in ours?"

"Yes, I do. No beauty is thrown away. All forms of life perceive it, and are being modified by it more or less rapidly, according to their perception."

"But this is not filling the barrel," said Tom, taking up the oars again.

"Do you see those ripples coming this way? We won't have to row, I guess."

In a moment, we felt the breeze on our faces, the sail filled, and the boat glided forward.

"It's like a dream," said Tom, with a sigh of content, as he shipped the oars and took his place at the rudder. "I didn't know it was so easy to sail."

By almost imperceptible degrees, the ripples grew to waves, and the breeze freshened. The boat leaned from the wind. A seething sound came from its wake. As the waves grew, they lifted the prow and slapped against it in its descent.

As we neared our port, we were scudding before a strong wind, in the midst of swiftly moving white-caps.

"A little to the right!" I said, as we neared the opening between Mason's and Dodge's Islands. "Steer to the right!"

We were moving swiftly, and it was necessary to clear a long reach of nets set directly in our path.

"To the right—to the right!" I shouted.

Tom muttered to himself, and the boat turned just in time. As we shot past the nets, toward the beach, I pulled up the centreboard, and a moment later, we were landed, with the nose of the boat three feet on shore.

You should have let go the sail. We might have struck a stone."

"Now, that it's over," said Tom, "I don't mind telling you that I had troubles enough. The rudder came off out there, and I was holding it in the water with one hand."

We found that one of the brads in which the rudder swings was gone.

"That's bad for us," I said.

"Do you think we can get back? It looks pretty wild out there in the channel now."

The wind would be against us on the return, and our rudder was useless.

"I can steer with an oar," I said, "but with a barrel of water to tow, we would have some difficulty."

"I don't think we'd better try it," said Tom dolefully.

"We might go back around behind these islands. It would be a longer way, but we would be in comparatively smooth water."

"All right, if you think we can."

We got the barrel from the boat, set it on the sand, tied our tow line to it, and filled it two thirds full. Tom hauled the water from a deep well, by means of a pole, and I carried it down to the barrel. It was a half hour of hard work, and I could see by his sweaty, disturbed face, that my friend was no longer contemplating the joy and sentiment in man and nature, for he could not see it in his own toil and danger.

But the barrel was filled and rolled into the water, and fastened to the stern of the boat. Tom was to hold the sail, while I steered with an oar. It was difficult to leave the shore, for the wind and waves worried us back to it as often as we pushed away. Several attempts failed, because Tom and I were working at cross purposes. At last I said:

"Look here, Tom, two minds can't run a boat. Now, you do as I tell you, and we'll get out of here."

I was not conscious of my tone or manner, but they must have been exceedingly irritating. Tom submitted in silence, and we eventually got clear of land and began to move steadily with the wind and tide, up the inlet. I was not sure of our way, for I had never sailed this course ; but I believed we could pass around Mason's Island and reach the channel between Mystic and Noank. We had no trouble moving in this direction, but I could feel the drag of the barrel, and grave doubts assailed me. How would it be when we attempted to tack?

As we neared the shore-line at the head of the inlet, I saw two ways divided by a point of land; the one to the left led to a narrow outlet under a low railroad bridge. To pass this, we must take down the sail, and I was not sure of what lay beyond. We decided to go to the right of the point. A half hour later, we found ourselves near the beach of an enclosed cove. In silence, we turned about, and took up the oars, for we could not sail out against the wind, and there was no room to tack. A thick mass of sea grass rose close to the surface, and rendered our progress doubly hard. We tugged at the oars doggedly. They were constantly tangled in the grass. The barrel, at first a mere dead weight, seemed finally to possess a personality and purpose of its own, dragging us back with a sullen, tireless strength. We moved, however, inch by inch, and after two hours of grim straining, we reached the point of land, and rounding it, dropped our oars, and drifted before the wind toward the railroad bridge.

Passing under this, we made a clear, straight course for half a mile, reaching the end of Mason's Island. We were now compelled to turn southeastward. Another cove lay directly before us, opening on our left into the wide channel. If we could make this opening, and could tack with our barrel, we could reach Noank, and the island would be an easy port from there.

I brought the boat to the wind as much as I could, and just missed the opening. Another struggle with the oars cleared the point that enclosed us, and we started on our first tack. My arms were weary, and the barrel behind, drifting sideways, thwarted my efforts to steer. Tom, holding the sail, had lapsed into a disconsolate, exhausted indifference. To make any progress at all, it was now necessary to hold the sail close in, and to keep it full.

"Keep your eye on the sail," I panted. "She is flapping at the mast."

He looked wearily up, and in a moment was gazing again at the shore-line, as if taking his last look of land.

"Keep your eye on the sail!" I shouted. "Can't you see we are just drifting?"

He turned on me fiercely, and said:

"Do you think I am going to break my neck craning up at the sail?"

"Well, some one's got to. I can't handle this boat alone without a rudder."

"You are intolerable," he cried, throwing the rope from him. "I'll let the damned thing go."

"You are a crazy, incompetent fool," I retorted, out of my head with the long, exasperating strain.

There was a moment's ominous silence after this, in which we glared at each other, while the boat went its own way swiftly, blown sideways toward the land.

And then Tom said, with a husky, appealing voice, and a moistened eye:

"Come, now, let's not quarrel. My God, man, shall we let a worthless barrel break up our friendship?"

Something seemed to snap in my head, and a load of distress and anger fell from me.

Let's dump the old thing on shore," said I.

A light of relief shone from his face. He reached out his hand, and we gripped each other, as men do when they have escaped death together. We had drifted to a point on the Connecticut shore, as far as we could readily get from our destination, and here we beached the barrel and anchored it to some stones. Then we pushed away, and as the boat settled easily into a course for home, we laughed and hallooed till our rasped and haggard spirits were restored.

"Well," said Tom, "you can easily see how just such a miserable little mess like that might end in murder."

"Yes," I replied, and saw more clearly than before, that whether here or there, we are straws in the wind. We may move with the forces, keeping our eyes open and our souls in sympathy, or we may be tossed about by them in ignorant, blind and passionate discord. This is the difference between love and hatred, happiness and misery, good and evil. On sea or land, in town or country, in wealth or poverty, in big and little things, the same law holds.

CHAPTER IX

T HE week passed with us in much the same manner as the first two days. Tom worried over the work, and I continued to be irritated by his fretting. He was afraid of the water, and gave up attempting to sail, but he resolutely went with me in fair or stormy weather. He could not learn to understand a boat and the elements, nor adjust himself to the conditions about him, but, relieved of responsibility or the need for action, he could face danger, whether real or fancied, with at least an outward quiet.

Time and again Tom suggested that we buy sail cloth to enclose the porches.

"They will make two big, nice extra rooms," he said.

I had built the wide porches for shade, and I wanted them open. In fair weather they were certainly pleasanter so, and the house was large enough to shelter us all in a storm.

I admitted that cloth curtains hung on rollers, to be lowered or raised at will, would be well to have, but, as neither of us had any money to spare, it seemed foolish to harp on such an incidental need.

An oil stove came by express from New York. It was sent by Nancy. "Ruth would not enjoy cooking at a fireplace," she wrote, "and it will be a nice thing to have."

It was certainly a great convenience. I could not have bought one myself, and since I must do without, I had taken a delight in mastering the primitive method. But I turned from the embers to the blue flame burners with a grateful satisfaction. My kettles were no longer covered with soot; my hands and face were no longer burned; the smoke did not fill my eyes. I believe in conveniences, but I believe in cheerfully doing well without them, if you must.

At least ten times a day Tom would sigh for Ruth. "If she were here," he would say, "I could stay forever. I cannot do housework. I cannot look after my things. She has spoiled me, and I am lost without her."

Ruth is the best wife I know, and one of the sweetest and truest of women. For Tom's sake, and for my own, I wished for her. In my heart I longed for Nancy. Among women, she is my best companion. I had missed her presence before, but I long ago learned to busy myself with what I have, and to find my satisfaction in what each day brings. Since Tom's arrival, I had drifted from my course. I had been irritated. I was anything's man. Having admitted one malformed vagabond to my soul, the whole herd of tramps came after, and I began to count the hours, to run ahead of time, to fret and find fault, and long for Nancy.

Ruth came up by the Stonington boat, and we sailed to Noank early in the morning to meet her. As we neared the town dock, we saw her, sitting on her trunk, her back toward us. The girlish figure and glorious mass of red hair, the familiar hat and dress, were a welcome sight to us, and we hallooed noisily. She paid no heed. She was acting mad, because we had not met her at the train, and because she had been almost an hour on the dock, waiting. But when Tom pulled her from her trunk and beat her publicly, that all men might know he was the master of his house, she threw up both hands and capitulated. She kissed us both, for it has always been understood that, up to a certain point, Tom and I had share and share alike in her.

Ruth was afraid to venture over in our little boat, and said so frankly, with an affectionate appeal to our generosity in her bright blue eyes. She would not have chosen to live on an island, but had come to us because Tom wished it. She was not a philosopher, but just a complex combination of child and woman, a being of affectionate impulses and stubborn fidelity, devoted to the comfort of her husband, and managing, in some mysterious fashion, to reconcile her traditional beliefs with his unorthodox thoughts and ways.

I have sought to maintain toward her an attitude of passive affection. She is not for me to analyze nor fashion, for she is mine only as the wife of my friend. We three have been happy together, because I have carefully preserved this attitude and because she has accepted me, through him, and when necessary, he has pleaded with her for me.

"Tom," I said, "we can hire Mr. Main to take Ruth and the trunk over."

"Good!" he replied. "We'll do that."

Ruth sat serenely in the larger boat, and seemed to enjoy her voyage, smiling back at us as we followed, gazing placidly about her, over the rippling water, and feeling her way to Mr. Main's heart by the sympathetic converse she is able to adapt to any one.

As we approached the island, Ruth viewed it with delight, and when we stood upon its beach and walked up the path and looked about us, her wonder and admiration grew.

"It is so much higher than I thought," she said, "and more beautiful. It seems perfectly safe here to me. The water never could reach to the top, could it?"

"Nowhere near," I said confidently.

"It's beautiful. I am sure no one could want a lovelier spot."

"Well," said Tom resignedly, "I am glad you like it. But you had better come in and look at the beds. We can get a couple of cots, if you say so."

Ruth followed us inside, and thought the lower room was exceedingly bright and cozy.

"We were going to scrub the floor," I said, "but we did not have time this morning."

"It doesn't need scrubbing," said Ruth quietly. "It is perfectly clean."

We went to the garret, and here again she expressed delight. The airy, sunny quarters seemed sweet and pleasant to her. We showed her the ticks and spread them on the floor.

"They are good enough," she said. "It would be foolish to buy cots. They would only be in the way. I think this is all just lovely here."

Tom turned away in bewilderment, and went downstairs.

"He is not used to camping out," said Ruth pleasantly, "and I am. He'll be all right now. He needed me, I guess."

I found Tom outside, and I was glad to see a change in him. His eyes were brighter, his face more serene. His body was like that of a man relieved of a heavy load.

"I'm going to enjoy this place," said he, "now that Ruth is here. Let's go over and get a beefsteak for dinner."

"We will have Ruth for dinner," I replied, "and that is enough luxury for one day."

"But wouldn't you enjoy a steak?"

"Yes. But that is not the way to live on two dollars a week."

It is astonishing how much of her personality a woman can put into the food she cooks. Ruth served us a meal of fish, potatoes and onions, taken from the stock I had drawn from, prepared in the same frying-pan, and, so far as I could see, by the same method as my own, and yet how superior it was to any I had served. It seemed to possess something of the delicacy and sweetness of her own nature. We did, in truth, have her for dinner, and it was luxury enough.

"We would be all right here now," said Tom, "if we could enclose one of the porches for a kitchen and have the cooking done outside."

"That would be nice," said Ruth. "We could use canvas for that, and it would not cost very much."

"What do you say?" asked Tom.

Now, I could afford absolutely nothing more. The house and its simple furnishings had exhausted my resources, and what Nancy was able to spare. If I lived on two dollars a week, I could stay here quietly until October. If I spent any more than that, I must get out and hustle for it. I would rather have the stove inside and the porch open and stay here than to form a kitchen and leave it two weeks sooner.

"Fix it as you want it," I said, "and I will pay half."

Nancy would not arrive until the 8:43 train in the evening, and I very unwisely devoted the rest of the day to expecting her. I might better have dwelt upon the beauty of patience and serenity until these qualities again possessed me.

I do not know how the afternoon passed, for I was not busy with it. I sailed alone to Noank in the evening, and stood in the dark, on the station platform, waiting for the train, with all the foolish impatience of any haphazard man.

When Nancy stepped out and stood before me, the light of the car on her upturned, beaming face, her arms full of bundles, her eyes luminous with good spirits and affection, I looked at life more tranquilly. I lit my pipe, took her bundles, and walked slowly along the winding street, listening to her budget of news and enjoying the best smoke of two weeks. But our devils are not removed by the virtue of others, and the delight we receive, even from those who love us, is short-lived, unless it finds a companion within ourselves to welcome it.

"Is anything the matter?" asked Nancy suddenly, her happy countenance becoming a shade more grave.

"I have had a hard week of it with Tom," I said.

"You have?"

"I have. I am amazed by the way he takes things here."

Then all the devils I had harbored got up and talked, pouring forth the story of his faultfindings, his misgivings, his constant suggestions, involving expense and trouble. Our beautiful walk under the trees was lost to us. We reached the town dock, got into the boat and pushed off. There was no moon, but it was a clear, starry night, and a light breeze was blowing.

Nancy came to the stern seat beside me, laid her hand on my knee, and looked smilingly at me, her eyes expressing both amusement and affectionate sympathy.

"Never mind," she said, "he will be all right now that Ruth is here."

"As soon as she came, he suggested cots, a kitchen and a beefsteak. You laugh now, but you will see."

"I know," she answered softly, "but remember how much you wanted them to come and what good friends they are."

"That's what I ought to do, I know. It's a shame for me to be this way. But I expected so much from Tom."

During all the voyage to the island, Nancy listened to me sweetly and sought to divert my thoughts to Tom's virtues, to her own presence and to the beauty of the night.

It was very dark on the beach when we landed, but over the top of the brush above us, the light from the cabin windows shone with a soft, comfortable glow.

"I am so glad to get back," sighed Nancy. "It's home to me."

She called a joyful announcement of our arrival, while waiting for me to anchor the boat for the night. Ruth looked from the window and answered her. There was an interval of silence, and then, what I had been hoping for happened. From the darkness came a sound of purring, and Yannie rubbed against Nancy's ankle.

"A kitten!" she exclaimed. "Why—when did you get it?"

She stopped and took it to her breast. It crawled to her shoulder, rubbed against her neck, and jumping down, came to me as I waded ashore.

"I thought she would be here to welcome you," I answered. "Wherever you go around here, day or night, you are liable to find that Yannie is with you. She does not mind the rain or wind. She has stayed out with me in the storm, dripping wet, and minded it no more than I."

"What a beauty! Here, Yannie, come along."

As we walked up the path, we met Betty, a little late, as usual, but friendly and interested, in her own more deliberate way. I could see that Nancy's delight in the kittens was all that I had expected.

Tom was in the hammock, stretched across the room. Ruth was sewing by the table. Nancy entered with that exaggerated demonstration of a natural good-will and delight that must always be a source of trouble to those who indulge it. There are few simple beings in whom nature has herself properly adjusted the instruments by which we receive impressions and express what they mean to us. Most of us have that to do for ourselves, but how few there are who realize it. We go rattling about together, exclaiming at the jolts, complaining of the misunderstandings and discords, and doing little or nothing toward the establishment of harmony within ourselves.

Tom is one who seeks honestly to express at all times neither more nor less than what he feels. I believe in this, and, except for these few weeks on the island, when I was all at fault, if I am not pleased with his attitude, the pleasure I take in his truthful expression of it suffices. Ruth has been remarkably well served by nature in this respect. Her emotions and her manners, like twins, go hand-in-hand, the one giving a natural and simple expression to what the other is.

There are times when most people would call Nancy affected, a word, like many others we use, that relieves us of the task of penetration. Tom thinks her so, and often adopts toward her an attitude of watchfulness, not very sympathetic and somewhat cynical in its nature.

It was Tom who taught me to appreciate a being like Sam, but he is not so apt to estimate truly a woman like Nancy. Such an attitude, of course, makes a tranquil friendship impossible. We four had found an almost uninterrupted pleasure in each other before this, because while I had lived with Tom, Nancy had only met him occasionally. She took him as my friend, was permitted to serve him constantly, and found a pleasure in doing so. When they met, she took his half-playful, half-cynical jibes and railleries in a merry spirit, artfully concealing the wounds from him and from herself. It is this method of defense such natures often employ that makes them seem affected and renders a correct reading of them difficult.

Nancy, easily led away by her impulses of good-will and generosity, giving an exaggerated expression of them in her eagerness to have all about her as happy as herself, exceedingly sensitive, quick to resent, and holding to her resentment with a passionate and bitter tenacity, was an easy mark for Misery, and she was hard hit by it.

The first evening was a very pleasant one. Tom was in an agreeable, quiet humor. He greeted Nancy's exuberant entrance with a jovial, skeptical glance, and retired again to the absorption of a pleasant reverie, humming a plaintive tune. Ruth entered at once into her mood, took her bundles from her, eagerly helped her to undo them, and exclaimed over their contents.

"What gay colors!"

"Aren't they lovely?"

"I should say so."

"Only ten cents a yard at Loeser's. Won't they make pretty dresses? Short, you know—up to your knees. You'll wear one, won't you?"

"Of course, I will. It's just the thing for here."

"I wore my bathing suit before, but I thought these would be better. There is enough for us both. Now, how would you make them?"

Ruth has a fine knack for dressmaking, and in a twinkling she had conceived a design, marking the pattern on her person with a nimble forefinger as she rapidly explained.

"Great," said Nancy, following her movements eagerly. "How simple that is!"

I'll be a sight with my thin legs."

"No more than I, with my fat ones. We'll wear red stockings, blue dresses and green sunbonnets. It's color we want."

Nancy ran upstairs and returned in a bath-robe.

"I'm going for a swim," she said.

"Not to-night?" exclaimed Ruth.

"Yes, indeed, I'm used to it."

"Won't you take cold?"

"I never take cold."

I was standing near the door outside. As she passed me, she asked in a whisper:

"Why are the windows all closed upstairs?"

"To keep the dampness out," I replied solemnly.

She laughed softly and went to the beach. The sound of her splashing tempted me. I went to the ledge, undressed and plunged in. When I returned to the cabin, the girls were making a pattern for their dresses and talking in whispers. Tom was asleep.

At ten o'clock the girls went upstairs and threw down the ticks. Tom and I were to sleep below.

Even in July the nights were cold on the island, and if the wind was from the east, it frequently brought mist or fog or rain. Tom tumbled from the hammock and prepared for bed.

"We ought to have shut the doors and windows," he said. "It's getting damp in here. If we close up evenings until we get in bed, we can open the windows then and have fresh air and dry beds."

He shut everything but one window, and no wind came through that, and asked me if it would be enough.

"We can open more if you say so," he said hesitatingly.

"That will be all right," I answered, but Nancy, upstairs, was expressing my real sentiments as she talked to Ruth.

"I like to feel the wind blowing on me," she said.

"I can't stand too much of it," Ruth replied. "This damp air would give me rheumatism."

I don't know how the matter was settled up there, but I could see in the morning that Nancy had not slept well. We had punched the house full of windows that we might have it wide open, day and night, in all sorts of weather. This was its principal charm to us. The wind and weather is to Nancy what a good name is to most women. Talk about her as you will, but leave her windows open and she will sleep serenely, providing she has not gained her way by distressing you.

And so it was with Tom and Ruth; they feared the draught and dampness, but they could take no comfort in a shelter where others were distressed.

I left Tom to build the kitchen alone. I can truthfully say that had I been entirely free to do so, I would have helped him. But the cabin was not all paid for. I was in debt to Nancy; there were other imperative calls for money from outside, and I had not written a line for over a month. You may have your island if you will take it, but you will find that no sea is wide enough to separate you from the world. All that has been undone on land will find you out. So long as we live, we must remain in the meshes that hold mankind together. Whether we move with the jostling crowds or dwell in isolation, we will gain only the happiness we create and add to the world's store of happiness.

All this I realized. I knew that I could not possess this fair retreat in idleness. I must be making some use of its beauty if I would continue to delight in it. I used to think that we should not work for money, but for the furtherance of our ideals. This is a narrow view. It springs from the egotism of the idealist. He imagines that his conceptions are altogether his own, and that he is bestowing what he reveals as a free and personal gift upon a world that declines to accept it at its peril. He who is able to perceive what the whole world is earnestly seeking is the real idealist. His power of perception is a gift to him from the people of all ages past and present. He only finds what all are looking for. It is there for him to find, because it is the next step in the logical advance of his kind. The ideal is what the world is to attain, and there are few who are not eager to know what this may be. All the world labors, and all the labor of the world promotes its progress. Money is as truly a medium of exchange in morals as in commerce. We must meet upon a common ground in all things. The brick-layer who lays bricks to suit the idealist will be paid by him from the proceeds of his poem. The poet who can present his ideal to move the mason will be paid by him from the wages of his trowel.

To enjoy my island cabin, I must pay some tribute to the world that gives it me. The needs of the world have opened markets for both fish and philosophy, and it will give me a dollar for a dollar's worth of either.

I had not labored for a month. Necessity was beginning to sting me like a lash.

"Tom," I thought, "can spare a few days now. I will get to my trade and let him tinker at his wishes by himself."

He put up four shelves, fixed a large box to serve for a kitchen cupboard and table and measured the porch for the canvas. Ruth and Nancy were busy with their dresses. They were eager to see the effect of their designs, and they laughed and chatted amiably as their needles followed the seams and hems and button-holes. Nancy, however, could not sew constantly. She frequently put her work aside and went to the beach for driftwood, bringing up the dry pieces and piling them on the porch.

"I found a lot of your trash around here," Tom called to her, "and threw it in the sea. When Ruth is in a place two minutes, it begins to look like home."

Nancy opened her eyes very wide and laughed. It is her way of meeting unexpected pricks that do not quite wound her to resentment.

She took the bait pail and went for crabs. I heard her at the end of the island, talking to the cats. I went to the edge of the jungle and peeped over. She was wading in the water, Yannie on her shoulder, and Betty on a rock near by.

"We are just wild creatures," I heard her say, "you kit-cats and I. We are supposed to be domestic animals, you know, and to come in when it rains. We thought we could do as we pleased and be happy on this far-off island, with only the wind and the weather, the bugs and the birds for our neighbors. But it seems we are to be civilized. Never mind, my Yannie cat. Just try and not mind."

Nancy, with the kittens, pushed off in the boat, and sailed out to the pole buoy to fish. I took my pad to the rocks, where I could watch her as I wrote. But I could not write. All I could see in this vast scene of beauty was Nancy, in the little boat, striving in vain to reach the pole buoy. She pulled the sail in when it should be out. She came about the wrong way, and instead of taking the necessary long tack, tried to force the boat to a straight course. At last she abandoned the sail, and picking up the oars, rowed to her spot, threw over the anchor, and settled down to fish.

Tom came and sat by me. He had probably forgotten his lightly considered jibe at Nancy as soon as it was uttered. He was, at least, not thinking of her now, but of the serene and sunny day and of the conceptions their influence brought to him. We talked pleasantly together of impersonal things, until Nancy returned with her catch. I skinned the fish, Ruth cooked the dinner, and it was served on a wide, flat ledge by the water side.

In the afternoon, Nancy sailed Tom to Noank, that he might go to the sail loft for the canvas, while she did the marketing. They took five pails for water with them. I watched their voyage with a restless eye. They made a safe port, but it was by accident. A fair wind blew them over, in spite of the fact that Nancy paid little attention to sail or rudder. She followed a zigzag course, and betrayed the most complete ignorance of all I had taught her. I had remained behind to write, but my pad was a blank when they returned. My friends were here, and yet I felt a curious sense of desolation. Something was wrong with us. We all seemed to be enjoying ourselves, but I scented a thickening atmosphere of distress, and began to suffer in helpless apprehension.

In the evening, Tom and I sat upon the great rock, overlooking the island, and all its surroundings, while the girls were happily at work inside. Ruth had finished her dress and was helping Nancy with hers. We heard their low voices and their laughter, and were content with our silent reveries.

"The mist is falling," said Tom. "We had better go in."

The girls, arrayed in their gay new costumes, received us after the fashion of light opera maids at a mountain inn. We looked them over and admired them. I built a fire, for a glowing, crackling fireplace is a thing to have when it is possible, and here, even in July, we were not uncomfortable with one. Nancy brewed us a milk punch, Tom sang a fine old German ballad, and we passed, by degrees, into a quiet, sentimental mood. And then came Memory, that strolling wight, half-minstrel, half-peddler, undoing his fiddle and his pack. We looked with tender eyes at the familiar wares he held before us, and listened to the strains of his bow until we were undone. The fire burned low, and some one spoke of bed.

"Look here," I said, "let Tom and Ruth have the attic and Nancy this room below. I will sleep on the porch. We can all have the air to suit us then."

"You can't sleep on the porch in this mist," said Ruth.

"Indeed, I can. I really want to. I'm not putting myself out. I have just found the courage at last to do as I long to do"

And it was so arranged. Nancy helped me make my bed on the porch.

"You have the best room of all," she said, holding her cheek to the wind and mist. "I see the stars dimly, as through a veil."

"Why is it that people shrink so from the rain?"

"To save their clothes."

"That was how the habit began, no doubt, but now a man in rags will run to shelter. We have so separated ourselves from nature that we don't like to get wet. I love the rain. A drenching gives me the finest sensation I can feel. My whole body is thirsty for this good mist."

A little later I slipped under my covers with a sigh of content. I listened to the murmur of the wind in the jungle, to the wash of the tide, and with my face cool and wet, passed into a tranquil sleep.

CHAPTER X

W build castles in the air, and fancy that could we dwell in them, with a few chosen friends, our occasional joys alone would interrupt our serenity. But these castles of the air are thin as air, and could we be transported to them, we would find them without form or substance. If we become citizens of the clouds, we must still build our habitations from the materials we carry with us. Let those who think they are unhappy, because of an unfriendly world, retire to a wilderness, and they will discover the source of all their sorrows is in themselves.

In all the world, there is no lovelier retreat than this island, where Nancy, Ruth, Tom and I were together for a month. And yet, we became more and more unhappy as the days passed.

Fogs were frequent in July. If Tom ventured to Noank, all the world was filled with apprehension until his return. The distant bank of mist, approaching slowly from the sea, was hailed with alarm. Or the day might be clear with us, while the horn at Race Rock, nine miles away, told of a fog down the Sound. In the ears of Tom and Ruth, its distant voice was ominous, and they listened, hour after hour, speaking of it now and then, watching the horizon, unwilling to venture from the island and viewing the indifference of Nancy and my own delight, as recklessness and folly.

If it rained, it was a dismal day.

Tom grew tired of fish, and made frequent purchases of meat and cake. If we did have fish, he wanted it boiled, for a change. Nancy would not consent to this, for her mood had grown bitter now, and the fish was always fried.

We now used five pails of fresh water where we had used one before. Ruth would not go to Dodge's Island to wash the clothes. She emptied the pails serenely, and we kept them full. But our serenity was gone. When we had used but a pailful or two a day, it had been easy to keep a supply on hand. This necessity had, in fact, been one of our sources of delight. During May and June, I would sometimes fill the five pails, and they would last us for almost a week, if we wished them to. But I managed to keep a pailful fresh without any special effort.

If I went for a sail, when the wish to sail moved me, I could put a bucket in the boat and fill it, if the wind and my fancy took me in the region of a well. If not, there was no distress. And now and then I could make the water an excuse for an idle hour or so, sailing to Noank or to Dodge's Island or to Mystic Island, as the wind might blow. On such voyages as these, I had been free to take my time, to study the tides and its courses, to lean over the edge of the boat and acquaint myself with the nature of the under world around me. In this way, I had learned where to sail, to keep with a vagrant current, when the tide of the channel was against me, for the water does not flow as a mass in one direction. And the grasses and rocks I had come to know became my guides if the fog overtook me.

But there was no idling now. There were times when the water was exhausted in the morning, and dinner must wait for a fresh supply. Wherever we went, the pails were with us. Tom heard that the water of the town pump was brackish, and it would no longer do. We must hunt through Noank for a friendly well, and carry our five pails to a distance.

The climax of our miseries came with Susan. We only needed this one addition to our household to disrupt it. Susan was Ruth's maid. She was anxious to come to the island and help with the work, if we would pay her expenses up and back. Under the circumstances, it seemed well to do this. Nancy could not trot in harness with Ruth as with Elizabeth.

The housework had somehow become work again. All the romance was gone from it. Tom liked Ruth's cooking best, and as he is exceedingly particular and difficult to please, in this and in all affairs of the household, she was tacitly conceded the mistress of the cabin. Nancy would gladly have washed the dishes if she could have done so on the beach with sea water and sand, but neither Tom nor Ruth could have endured this. She busied herself gathering driftwood, going to market, fishing and keeping the bait-pail full. She took her clothes and mine to Dodge's Island and washed them. She was roaming the island or voyaging to neighboring shores, the cats for her constant companions, but she was not happy. For two weeks I did not hear her piping voice, nor see a cheerful look from her. When Nancy is bitter or distressed her face grows thin and unlovely. It is both pathetic and repellent. She becomes twenty years older in a moment. Her eyes, at other times clear, luminous, alluring, grow hard and treacherous. She sees then nothing but meanness in the world.

Susan, when she came, was constantly troubled with a stomach ache before meal time, and always recovered when it was served. Ruth seemed to have as much to do as ever. She worked, while Susan fished and complained.

Every day Nancy went to Noank for the mail and groceries, taking a pail or two for water, if she went alone, and all five, if Tom or I went with her. One morning, the sight of the pails all empty irritated her. She took them to the boat and suggested to Ruth that Tom go with her to carry them from the well.

"I don't think he can go over to-day," she replied, "he is painting."

"Then Susan had better come and help me with it."

Ruth looked across the water, in all directions.

"I heard the Race Rock horn a while ago. I am almost afraid to let her."

"Well, I can't carry all the water alone."

"I'd like to go," said Susan. "I've not been to Noank yet. I'd like to go."

Ruth consented pleasantly. There was not wind enough to sail, and Nancy rowed over. They were not gone long before the distant growl of the Race Rock horn came up the Sound.

"I wish I had kept Susan here," said Ruth.

Tom looked up from his easel, near the door, and scanned the southern horizon.

"The fog is coming on this time, sure enough."

Ruth watched the advancing cloud of mist. North Dumpling and Fishers Island were swallowed up. Long Point grew dim, and disappeared. A thin vapor floated before the town of Noank, and presently obscured it. An impenetrable fog was about us. We could not see the edge of our island. Even the bushes close to us were ghostly.

"They probably will wait until it clears," said Tom.

"Yes, I guess Susan has sense enough to stay. I don't believe Nancy could get her to start back in a fog."

"Well," said I, "you may be sure they will arrive here safely if they start."

"People just go round and round in a fog," said Ruth.

"There are people in Noank that have been lost for hours right off here," said Tom.

"Nancy has come through safely before. I will go to the beach now and then and call. The light-ship bell and my voice will guide her."

"Sounds are misleading in a fog. The fog might easily take them away. And if they don't keep clear of the channel, a passing boat might run them down."

"I don't believe Susan will start until it clears. She has good sense," said Ruth, in an effort to remain tranquil.

I went to the beach and shouted. From far away, through the dense white vapor, came a faint call in answer. It was Nancy's voice. Listening intently, I could now hear another voice raised in constant screams. I shouted again, and heard Nancy's answering call. Then the voices were silent. I shouted at intervals, and presently I heard the sound of oarlocks. The fog lifted for a moment, and revealed the boat headed straight for the island, not five hundred feet away. Nancy was rowing steadily. The fog enclosed them. The sound of the oarlocks was lost in the panting of a naphtha launch that loomed suddenly near the beach, and, circling about, disappeared again. It returned in a few moments with our boat in tow. Mr. Rathbun, hearing the screams of Susan, had put out from Noank to the rescue.

"It was good of you to come," said Nancy.

"I see you were making port all right," he replied, "but we thought over in Noank something was wrong with you."

"I don't wonder. All that screaming was pure insanity,—nothing else. But it was good of you to come, just the same."

The ghost of Mr. Rathbun waved its hand and vanished. The girls came ashore. Susan went to the house with Ruth, loud in her complaints against Nancy, and proud of her violent clamor. She seemed to think she had just escaped death by virtue of her shrieks. Nothing was said of Nancy's good rowing and her true homing instinct. Susan was the hero of the occasion, and Nancy was the culprit.

"She was as mean as she could be to me," said Susan.

"I told her," replied Nancy, "that if she screamed again, I would not row another stroke. We were as safe out there as we are here. I knew I could keep a straight course, and I did so."

"Susan had good sense to scream," snapped Ruth. "I don't wonder at it. And she was over-persuaded to go, in the first place."

Then Ruth burst into tears, distressed beyond control by her own anger and anxiety. She looked appealingly at Tom, and hurried upstairs, saying:

"I am sorry it happened, Tom, but I am responsible for that child."

Nancy turned to leave the house, but I called her back, and drew her to a seat beside me. Tom was exceedingly troubled. He looked at us with the best expression in his eyes I have ever seen when they are turned toward Nancy, and said sincerely:

"It's too bad. I will go away, if that will do any good."

"That's not the way," I answered earnestly.

Tom followed Ruth upstairs, and Nancy and I went to the beach.

"I am angry—angry," said she. "Can you blame me?"

"It is never a question of where the blame lies," I said. "Let's not be angry, if we can help it. It is not lovely. It disfigures us as much, whether we or others are in fault."

"I know. I am doing my best. If it were not for you, I would have left here a week ago, or asked them to. I know I am hard to endure just now, but I can't help it. I have longed so for this island, and worked so hard to get here. They don't seem to enjoy it much, and they are spoiling it for me."

"It's all my fault," I exclaimed. "When you came up this time, I met you with complainings. I began at once to force unpleasant things upon you, and I have not since helped you as I should, to meet them properly."

Tom came to us and asked us to come back. "Ruth is all right now," he said gently.

We followed him to the porch, and found Ruth, smiling and tearful. Nancy tried to greet her cordially, but her heart was sore and her effort painfully apparent. The quarrel was over, but its taint remained.

After this, we all tried bravely to be happy. When we came together, we talked politely. We were solicitous as to each other's wants, trying to resign ourselves to them. Then came a second outburst, as unexpected as the first. But as this one served to reveal my own shortcomings, I can relate it with a better zest. No one can know with what misgivings, what shame and groanings I have been tattling of my friends. I cannot do them justice. I can only ask indulgence in this use I make of them. As I look back upon my lines, they seem to form but an abusive tirade against the three persons in the world whose virtues I admire most.

Of the four, I was, in reality, the most disagreeable. You can surely see me stalking through this narrative, the overbearing, self-satisfied man

I was. The truth we proclaim, the beauty we depict, is by no means lost, because we fail to live by it. What I perceive is valuable to me in just so far as it becomes my life, but if I fail to profit by what I see, another may give it a being in himself, and so make it good. As for me, if I have been saved from becoming the unbearable champion of ideals I do not follow, it is because old Captain Louis, after sixty years of the sea, is now in his haven, sitting under a huge cherry tree that shades his dooryard, working at his weedless garden, tinkering in his woodshed, or dozing in the evening in his corner of the kitchen, behind the stove. There is an old-fashioned well under his cherry tree, with a bucket and windlass. It is the best water in Noank, and we went there frequently for a drink or a pailful. Close to the well was a perch where an ancient parrot stood with ruffled feathers, rolling a wicked eye at me, and muttering to himself.

I first saw the Captain in a little woodshed near the well. It was dark in there, and his form was vaguely outlined. He had just finished a washing, and was wringing the clothes through a wringer. He was very short and thick-set. His broad back was humped, and his head was very large. He looked like a gnome at work. Another day I entered the yard through a gate in the back fence, and as I walked up the path, I heard the sound of a hammer in a little outhouse close to me. I stopped at the open window and looked in. The Captain was putting up a shelf. I spoke to him, and he turned toward me. This was the first time I had seen his face, and it was a surprise to me. It was broad, coarsely formed, misshapen with age and wrinkles, and dyed with the indelible stains of weather, but I had never seen a sweeter human countenance. The broad mouth smiling up at me, the dim, gentle eyes, the soft, full voice with which he answered my greeting, warmed my heart, and caused me to linger near him, though I had nothing to say. I saw him again in his garden, bending over a row of corn. He leaned on his hoe when I approached, and gave me a smiling welcome.

"I hear you were once a sea captain," I said.

"Aye," he answered slowly, "I sailed the sea for sixty years, and two and forty on 'em in a ship of my own. I was master of three good ships. One went to pieces on the rocks off Gibraltar; one was burned by pirates off the coast of Africa, and one was sunk by a Confederate gunboat."

As he said this, he looked so out of place, leaning on his hoe, that I asked him if he was contented here.

"I can't complain," he said. "I've had my life. I'm living on borrowed time, an' I can't complain." With a glance whimsical and pathetic, he added: "I do sometimes wish I could be young again, for I miss the sea."

His voice was so mellow, his smile so sweet and simple, that my eyes filled, and I walked away.

Now, during these days I was having a hard time with Nancy, teaching her to sail. Wherever we went, she would take her pastille box, her bottles, her purse, her pad and her handkerchief, holding them in her lap. She could not make a move in the boat without first dropping and picking these things up. We were constantly upon the water, for we had much to talk about alone. Our relations with Tom and Ruth formed a restless theme. When Nancy has turned from a friend, she becomes as unjust to him as she was generous before. The bitterness of her attitude now toward Tom and Susan appalled me. But the thing that moved me most was her own distress in her bitterness. It was now my one concern to banish her resentment. I could see that Tom was beginning to realize his own misconduct and was seeking to amend it. If Nancy would but become her generous and open-hearted self again, we might all be happy here.

I blamed myself for all my complaints against him. I spoke to her of his fine sympathetic qualities, of his friendly acts for me. She tried again and again to yield to my pleadings, but the blood in her veins still smacks of her ancestors, who dwelt in the hills of Ireland, and held to a feud for a thousand years. But I believe that she would have prevailed against even this inheritance if I had not interrupted my plea with abuse. We sailed as we talked, and my recommendations of patience, sincerity and gentleness were frequently cut short, that I might scold her for her carelessness.

We sailed to Dodge's Island one evening for water. A furious storm had been raging all day, and prevented our going before. At sunset the wind abated some, but it was still a gale. I had learned to push my boat from shore, its nose toward the wind, and to see that Nancy's lap was rid of its trinkets, and her rudder ready to slip in place, before a move was made. We got off successfully, and sped past the rocks at the end of the island, and out to the channel with a speed that made our blood tingle. I think there are few sailors who would have risked a twelve-foot sharpie in such a wind and sea. But men are truly saved by faith, and in such matters Nancy and I had the faith of saints, and we felt secure. There was one long gash of crimson in the sky above Noank. Except for this, it was black and lowering above and around us. Huge masses of clouds were scudding overhead. The rush of wind, the wash and roll of waters, the dashing of the boat upon the waves, filled our ears. Tom and Ruth were sitting on the observatory rock, watching the storm. They disappeared, and the island itself became but an obscure shape in the darkness.

"Oh!" cried Nancy, as she gripped the straining rope and laughed at the water dashing over her, "what a joy this is! I have not been so happy for a week."

"Nancy," I shouted, for the wind whirled my words away, "take this spirit back to the cabin with you, and all will be well. To-day Ruth asked Tom and me how to cook the fish. I did not care myself, but I did not know what to say. I was afraid if Tom told her to boil it, you would be angry, and I was afraid he would complain if I said to fry it—"

I don't like boiled fish, and I love it fried," interrupted Nancy. "Tom says he don't care for it either way, but I notice that he eats his share."

"I would rather eat it raw and be pleasant about it," I replied, irritation and the wind now raising my voice to a yell. "But I started to tell you this to show that Tom has changed. While I hesitated, he looked up and said pleasantly, 'For my part, I would like it fried.' Now, Nancy, please be good again. Be gentle and warm-hearted for your own sake and mine, if for nothing else." The sail caught my eye. Nancy had pulled it in too close, at the same time changing our course to one straight before the wind. "Let the sail out!" I bellowed. She gave it a startled jerk and the wind, catching it behind, threw it violently over the boat. The rope was torn from her hand. We dashed sidewise over a hissing billow, and the crest of a second one broke over us. We would have been capsized, if Nancy could have held to the rope. As it was, we kept our keel, but the sail was now free and was hanging straight before the boat over the water. I clambered to the prow and, hugging the mast, tried to pull the sail around. I could not move it against the wind with my short purchase. I slipped the end of the pole, that held it stretched, from its noose at the mast, and, shaking it free at the other end, put it in the boat. The loose sail cracked and flapped violently. Reaching out on each side of the mast, I managed to pull it in by degrees, and to fasten it. There was now no danger of capsizing, and I could row to shore. But that was unnecessary. The gale rushing in our direction blew us before it, and landed us safely on the beach of Dodge's Island. We filled our pails in silence. I put the sail in shape again, and we started back. It was now a voyage against a head wind, and we must tack far out beyond Ahoy, through the tossing tide race of the channel. Nancy took the seat in the centre.

"You sail," she said.

"No," I replied. "You will either sail this boat correctly, or you will never go alone again."

She bit her lips and changed places with me, gathering up her trinkets and almost lurching headlong overboard in her effort to hold them. I caught her arm, got her to her seat and snatching the pastille box, the bottles and the pad, threw them in the sea. I brushed the purse and handkerchief to the bottom of the boat and kicked them forward.

"Now," I roared, "you sail us home. I will not help you out of any trouble that comes from carelessness, if we drown for it."

For nearly two hours, we were tossed about in the storm and darkness. I was frequently obliged to bail. Nancy, her face white and drawn and miserable, handled the boat as if inspired. Not a word was spoken.

We came to our beach with a rush and took the pails out, half-full. In spite of the wildness of the night, Yannie was close to the surf, watching for us. Nancy picked her up and, holding her to her throat, stumbled up the path to the cabin. I made the boat secure and carried the pails to the kitchen. Tom and Ruth were still on the rock, but came in presently and went upstairs. Nancy made her bed inside and I took mine to the porch. We smiled an apologetic good-night, but our hearts were heavy and sore.

The next morning, after a subdued breakfast meeting, I sailed Tom to Noank. He was going into the country for the day, with his easel to paint a farmer who had agreed to pose for him in the field with his ox-team and plow. I returned to the Island, and, going to the shelter of the rocks, sat down dejectedly. In a few moments, Yannie jumped to my knee. As I stroked her head and listened to her gentle purr, I could have wept. Nancy joined me, her face hard set with a purpose.

"I have something to say," she said.

"What is it?"

"Do you know what is troubling me most? You are doing nothing. For two months you have not written."

I knew what was in her heart. She was afraid that in helping me she would destroy me, that I would become idle and ineffective; but her words stung me none the less.

"When I write," I exclaimed, "I wish to tell of the beauty about us and our delight in it. How can I do that in this present wretched atmosphere?"

"You could do nothing before, because you were too happy. Now you are too miserable. It makes me wretched to say this to you. I care nothing at all for the money you owe, but it is because I know you think of it and because you will be dissatisfied with yourself, that I cannot see you idle. I am miserable!"

For the second time in my life, I now saw Nancy break into sobs. She checked them presently, and said:

"You have become cold and tyrannical. You think I am unjust, and

I think you are. Since we feel that way, we had better separate. I have decided to leave. I cannot stay here!"

"You shall not," I said. "I will go myself. I will go at once. You can come with me now to Noank, and bring the boat back. You can telegraph for Elizabeth and Jim. I will go at once."

I got up and strode to the cabin. Nancy followed and wished to help me pack my bundle, but I would not let her.

"Go downstairs," I said, "and wait for me."

"You have bullied me until I can't stand it," cried Nancy, stamping her foot. "Even Tom and Ruth have noticed how cross you are to me."

"So you have been talking me over between you!" I exclaimed.

"We are your friends."

"They are no friends of mine if they speak of me to you like that."

"You know they are. We all love you dearly. Don't go."

I waved her aside, tied up my bundle, and walked down to the ledge, where Ruth and Susan were fishing. Nancy had preceded me and told Ruth I was going, and why.

"Good-bye," I said, holding my hand toward her. She kissed me and begged me not to go. "Wait until Tom comes back," she pleaded. "Don't go."

I went to the beach, followed by the girls.

"Tom and I had a quarrel once," whispered Ruth. "I was peevish, and he left me and said he wasn't coming back any more. But he did come back that night, and I was the happiest woman in the world. Don't go."

Nancy and I got into the boat and pushed off. Before we had reached the bush buoy, Nancy looked at me with the light in her eyes that is irresistible, and said softly:

"Please come back with me."

"All right," I said. "I will."

"And don't be cross with me."

"I will maul you unmercifully until you learn to sail," I replied. "You must expect nothing else than that. Do you know why all sea captains are such gruff old fellows? Those who sail a boat safely, must move quickly, and a skipper must have instant obedience. To get this from his crew, he must hold a hard hand over them. As a passenger, I could be good to you, but you wish to sail, and I must hammer your feminine habits out of you, and force you to move quickly and keep your whole mind on the wind and sail."

As I spoke, the gentle face of Captain Louis rose before me, and I heard his mellow voice repeating "I miss the sea." I tried to imagine his roar of wrath, his face glowering fiercely upon his surly crew, but the kindly eyes and broad, smiling lips would not obey me; they were kind and smiling still.

This made me thoughtful. We sailed within hailing distance of the Island, and shouted to Ruth that we would both return. Then we made for Noank. Nancy looked young again and quite happy, but we were both very quiet. While Nancy was shopping, I strolled round to Captain Louis's. I wished to see him, to talk with him, and yet I hardly knew why. He was in his rocking-chair, behind the stove, the old parrot on a perch beside him. This bird was forty-one years old. She was a malicious creature. She permitted the Captain to maul her as he pleased, but no one else could touch her. The Captain had bought her fresh from the shell in South America, and brought her home. There were years at a time when the parrot was with Mrs. Louis and the children alone. They could feed her, but if they came too near, she bit them. However long the voyage, she talked of the Captain during his absence, and greeted him joyously on his return. She called him Father. Now they were seldom apart. Their plates were side by side at the table. The parrot ate with a spoon and helped herself to her food.

The Captain was born in France. Mrs. Louis comes from the best and purest of New England stock. She is a very intelligent, very positive old lady, with white hair, fine, bright eyes, strong, sweet face and a voice as clear and good as a woman's at forty. She can only move with great difficulty by the aid of a cane, because of rheumatism.

The captain helps her therefore with the housework. I have usually found her in her chair by the window, sewing.

This morning, she was standing by the table, making a pie.

"I declare," she said, as I entered. "This is the wrong fruit. You will have to get me another can—currants."

The Captain started from a doze, got up slowly, and, seeing me at the door, invited me to a chair. As he got up, the parrot opened her eyes. She, too, had been dozing. She moved restlessly on her perch, watching the old man closely. The Captain went outside to go down cellar, and the parrot called anxiously, "Father! Father!" She craned her neck and cried softly to herself until the Captain returned. Then she nodded on her perch again.

"I was just taking a little nap," said the Captain. "I don't know why it is, but I seem to sleep a good deal."

He beamed upon me with the most ingenuous friendliness. He reached out, and absently tousselled the parrot's head.

"Captain," I said, "you were sixty years at sea, were you?"

"Aye—for sixty years I sailed the sea, and two and forty on 'em in my own ships. One was lost on the rocks off Gibraltar and one the rebels sunk and one was burned by the pirates off the coast of Africa."

"You must have had all sorts of crews in those forty-two years."

"Pretty much every kind," he said, with a smile and nod.

"Ever have any trouble with them?"

"Never a cross word or look."

"How did you manage them?"

"Just told 'em what to do—gave 'em good rum, good food, good tobacco and good pay. Never spoke a cross word to one on 'em."

"That's rather remarkable, isn't it?"

"I don't know," he said slowly. "I never thought much about it. Your asking me now just made me think how it was."

"He's a great one to have things kind of pleasant and agreeable," said his wife. "I tell him sometimes," she added, with an amiable shake of the head, "he's most too much that way."

"Yes," he admitted with an apologetic smile and glance, "I *do* like things agreeable. I'd a been a poor Captain, I guess, if it hadn't been for the good feeling we always had all round."

I left him with a full heart. This unknown man, scarcely noticed by any one but his wife and parrot, who could say so little and who had done so much—how sublime he was! I stood at his gate and looked back. I blessed him for his revelation. I joined Nancy at the corner, and walked with her to the boat.

"Will you sail, Nancy?"

We smiled upon each other, and as we moved from the dock, glanced across the water toward the island with returning contentment.

"Surely," I thought, "if he could encompass the seas with every kind of crew for forty-two years, and not speak a cross word or give a harsh command, I can teach one willing woman how to sail without abusing her."

All the way over we talked of the wind and its ways with a boat. We experimented and laughed at mistakes, and tried again, until we corrected them.

Ruth met us on the beach, and we made merry over our follies. The afternoon was clear, and I took my pad to the shade of the great rock and wrote. The wind died away, and a soothing quiet was about us. I heard Nancy singing. As the evening approached, I went to the beach to watch the brilliant afterglow of the sunset. The water between the island and Noank was very still. All the world seemed hushed and waiting. A sudden impulse possessed me, and putting my hands around my mouth like a trumpet, I called, "Hello!

Tom!" There was a full minute of profound silence, and then from the darkness under the hill of Noank, came a familiar voice, faint and clear:

"Hello!—Come over."

"All—right," I hallooed.

The girls came hurriedly down the path, and marveled. I pushed off in the boat, and rowed away for Tom, singing as I rowed.

CHAPTER XI

AUGUST and September were two wonderful months for me. Tom and Ruth returned to the city the last of July, and no amount of persuasion could tempt them up again. Every Friday night brought Nancy and Elizabeth, who remained over Sunday. My five days of solitude each week were days of delight. The apparently aimless hours of reverie were over, for I was now at work with my pad and pencil, and I began to find a purpose in what I saw and felt. But I will show you a letter presently, which, written at the time, gives a truer picture of these days than I can now create.

It is necessary first to tell how a new member of our family came to us. The pleasure we had found in Yannie and Betty caused us to wish for more creatures like them.

"I would like the island filled with cats," said Nancy.

"If I only had a good dog!" I kept repeating. "I would not part with our cats, but I long for a dog."

Royal is the real keeper of Mystic Island. He is a huge brute of a beast, of many tribes. He owes his color to some bygone Irish setter; his build to a Newfoundland. I think there is some mastiff blood in him, as well. Gibbie's anger is the one thing in the world of which he is afraid, but this is because he loves his master. Except in this, he knows no fear. He would leap into the belching cannon's mouth. He permits Gibbie to say who shall come on the island and who shall not, remaining quiet and watchful, ready to receive a friend, or rush a designing intruder. He is not permitted to go to Noank, for at the sight of another dog, he becomes unmanageable. He seems to have no sentiment in this respect, and will kill a spaniel or a bulldog with equal relish. He has never found his match in a brawl. There are from ten to fifteen cats on the island. Royal has been there seven years, and has killed more than thirty of them in that time. He has not tasted cat flesh for two years, however, for the present inhabitants are descended from those grown wise in avoiding him. They dwell under the house. There they come into the world, and are securely guarded until old enough to leap for their life. There is a little hole under a step at an unused kitchen door, opening, at the back of the house, onto a wide grass plot. The cats slip through this hole and lie in the sunlight. But they do not sleep. They are ready to disappear at an instant's notice.

"I will have a kitten or two for you soon," said Mrs. Wilcox one day. "I can hear the litter under the house, but the old cat has not brought them out yet."

"Can we have them all?" asked Nancy.

"If you don't take them, they will be drowned. We have all we can keep."

The litter, however, was composed of one.

Nancy and Elizabeth were obliged to leave Sunday night without seeing it. On Wednesday, Sam brought it over to me. It was about three weeks old, a little black and white ball of fat and fur. Sam unpinned his coat pocket, pulled it forth and placed it on the porch. I caught one glance from its eyes, but before I could move, it had dashed under the house. This kitten had brought its terror with it. It did not see my friendly look, it could not hear any comfort in my voice. During the day, I called to it in vain. It remained hidden. The next morning after breakfast, I heard its anxious cry. Yannie and Betty pricked up their ears, and, trotting from the room, looked under the house, craning their necks, sniffing and listening. The cry was repeated, and Yannie crawled under to investigate. A little later, she returned, bringing the stranger. When I appeared, she dashed from sight again. I was tempted to leave a dish of milk near by and go away, for I knew the kitten must be hungry. But that would not do. She must learn, first of all, that she was safe here and she must be brought boldly to her food with the others. It required the rest of the week and the most systematic patience to accomplish this. By Friday, she was beginning to make herself at home. Her round, staring eyes had lost their senseless alarm. She came and went with her companions, playing with them, eating with them and joining in the hunt for bugs and grasshoppers. As her terror left her, she became possessed of a greedy, selfish spirit. Whether in man or beast, it is true that the soul which flies in a panic when pressed, will as readily impose upon kindness. Fear is but one manifestation of a narrow, self-centered selfishness, and greed may easily replace it. I first named this kitten Dumpling, but we shortened it to Dump, a word expressive of her spirit.

The girls listened to my account of her behavior, and seemed to find a curious pleasure in her. They laughed at her increasing boldness, for she became now as forward as she had been wild before. She was the first at the food dish, and ate more than both the others. If she wished for a nap, she would never find a place under the bushes alone, but would seek first the plump shoulders of Elizabeth, or if this was denied her, she would curl about Nancy's throat, a resting-place quite as soft, but not quite so spacious. If neither of the girls could take her, she would hunt up Betty and lie down across her body.

In September, the mackerel came in great numbers, and I was able to get my food, take my pleasure and compose my chapters, all at the same time. Mackerel fishing is, for one of my stamp, the most attractive kind. The only bait required is a little piece of white rag, which lasts all day, and does not once require replacing. At this time of the year, there is always a good breeze. Every morning, when the breakfast was over, I spent an hour or two gathering wood, bringing up the chips and small pieces, and using the saw and axe on the logs and barrels. I now required a fire whenever I was in the cabin, and during the evenings, the louder it roared and crackled, the better it was, for, with the falling of the sun, the watery world around me grew cold and drear.

But the days were warm with sunshine, and when the wood was gathered, I called the cats to the boat and pushing off, set sail through the run and off toward the channel of the Sound or the ocean. I tied the sail to an oar-lock, threw a small mackerel hook overboard and let it trail on the surface of the water, about fifty feet behind, tying the line to my finger. So long as we kept moving, it did not matter where we went, for the mackerel might be here or there, and so, with my pad on my knee, I sailed and fished and wrote, hour after hour. Yannie preferred to sit on the narrow prow before the mast and watch the water. Betty slept on the seat beside me. Dump would lie across her or crawl to my shoulder, if I did not move about too much. When we struck a school, and I began to pull the mackerel in, the cats woke up, and all three gathered eagerly to watch the sport. Yannie and Betty never attempted to molest the catch, but I was obliged to watch Dump closely.

During these days, I had much to think about. I was not only meditating on the summer that was gone, in the hope of making some use of it, but our misunderstandings still grieved and puzzled me. I knew, also, that Tom and Ruth were not to me as they once had been, and that Nancy was still suffering from the wounds she had received and what remained of her own bitterness. The last Sunday in September and the first one in October she was not able to come up.

"But I have been able to do something that I know will console you," she wrote. "I have found you a dog—a pure-blooded Scotch collie—a son of Mr. Morgan's Ruffled Ornament. He is just three months old. We got him through Jim, who makes a great mystery of the way he came by him. I shall see that he is shipped to you tonight, so that he will be with you Sunday, that you may not miss Elizabeth and me. I wish that I could see the arrival, and witness the first lessons in his bringing up. You will have a busy, happy time with him, and Bess and I will try to imagine what is happening up there.

"And now I want you to know that I am succeeding better with my own self. I have not had a harsh nor an unkind thought since I came from the Island this time. Our talks have surely done me good, and I shall succeed, if only for your sake."

I read this letter with a full heart. My answer to it seems to me now but a poor expression of all that I felt, and yet to Nancy it was a true expression of it. I offer it here as the best explanation I can give of the nature of the relations between us. In this complex life of ours, wherein each must find his way through a maze of half-formed perceptions, beset by conflicting desires, laws, opinions and personalities, it seems impossible for any man to shape his course in accord with all his fellows. As for me, I wish to be most with those who, defective as I am, can use me most in their progress toward a happier and sweeter life. What joy or comfort comes to me in the process, I take with gratitude, but my own comfort or the love of others must serve the ideal as I see it, or I will let them slip from me, if I must. I know that, were I a wiser and a broader man, I could pursue such a course without prejudice to anyone, and so bring nothing but good to myself and others.

In this letter to Nancy, you may find all that there is to know of the bonds between us.

I HAVE not been very lonesome this time. It does seem best for me to stay here, and I am glad that I can do it. From Tuesday until Friday I wrote constantly from morning until late at night. Then your letter came, saying you would not be up. My chapter was finished, and I was tempted to go down. I knew if I felt a sense of desolation here, I could not write, and I thought it might be wise to go to you and the city for a few days, while I was getting the next thing in shape. I did not sleep any Friday night. I could not get an idea Saturday, and I decided to take the evening train. Then I thought once more of the six dollars it would cost, of you, cheerfully and courageously working where you don't want to be, and I knew I must stay.

Yannie was at my feet looking up at me with questioning eyes.

"Yannie!" I said, "I shall stay. And since that is decided, how shall I be—desolate, restless, homesick, heavy-eyed and lonely, or patient and serene? We can be what we wish to be, Yannie cat, if we think more about that than of the things that would disturb us. I will be patient and serene."

So I put the sail in the boat, and went over to Noank in my old clothes and got the mail.

Your letter warmed me through.

Of all the countless things you have done for me, this is the most beautiful. I don't mean about the dog—that is one of the countless things—but I mean your loving attitude and my insistent requirements concerning you. A nature as generous and sensitive as yours, cannot afford to recognize resentment for an instant. If you do, you will have it as a frequent guest, for, of course, the fact that you possess these virtues makes you liable to the encroachments of those who have them in a less degree. The only way a sensitive person can remain generous and sweet is for him to love these qualities for their own sake. If we are more anxious to retain them than to lose them, we may do so by constantly increasing them and adding, for their protection, other virtues. If another injures us, or is unkind, or unlovely, resentment in us is neither kind nor lovely. It is as great a defacement of ourselves, without and within, as is the thing in our neighbor that calls it forth.

Many sensitive people, generous and sweet to begin with, become embittered, because, while possessing these qualities by nature they do not love them for their own beauty, and lose them in resentment. There are thousands who think it wise to become less generous as they find the world unkind. But this is not wisdom. We should not lose our virtues because many we meet do not possess them.

You are quick to see the beautiful and the ugly traits and habits in others. You love the beautiful and despise the ugly. This is the approved, orthodox attitude. Your view, however, is not orthodox. You perceive informally and true. But neither the orthodox view nor the orthodox attitude is good. We should not despise the ugliness of others. Loathing, disgust, and all kindred feelings, even ridicule, are as ugly as anything that can inspire them. To see the faults in others that we may help them, and correct our own, is to use our keener intellect to a purpose worthy of it. Otherwise we cut ourselves with our own sharp tools.

Wisdom is all in all. If we are wise we will be happy, beautiful and strong. You and I have forty years together. We must live them in this world as it is. We can do very little toward shaping others to our ways, but we can do everything with ourselves. Let us lose none of the delight we might have in each other. Every moment that we are unlovely is so much lost to both of us.

You tell me there have been many times when you have tried to conform to my ideal of you, for my sake. You say in your letter you are doing so these days. This is the greatest thing you can do for me. But I know it is not alone for my sake. If it were, you would not succeed. You are doing this most of all because you see truly what is lovely in character and because you love these qualities, and because you possess a sunny, warm and generous nature. I only serve as a prompter. You will, some day, become your own, entirely. Then peace will be with us.

I began this letter to tell you of the dog.

They told me at the depot that there would be no express Sunday. I waited for the six o'clock train, and he did not come. The agent and Bill assured me several times that it would be impossible for him to get here until Monday morning, since he did not come then. So I returned to the Island to coax my lazy thoughts. All Sunday morning I sat by the door, gazing seaward, my mind alert, and willing, but chasing hither and yon, like a good dog that has lost the scent. It was a perfect September day. Since Tuesday, we had experienced breathless, sultry weather, the most oppressive of the season. For the first time, the mosquitoes came in numbers, and made themselves at home. Saturday night a strong north wind blew down and drove them off. Sunday morning it was still a gale, cold and fresh. As the day passed, the wind moderated to a good breeze. The water was all one shade of blue, dark and rich, the first fall coloring just laid on. Its surface was broken by brisk, short waves, with dancing peaks. They were not quite large enough to crest and break. A long line of schooners and smacks were bearing steadily up and down the Sound, and all kinds of smaller craft were criss-crossing over it. Their sails gleamed very white in contrast with the unusually blue water.

In my next chapter, I am to tell of—I have held my pencil poised for an hour trying to decide what—I don't know. Please send me a set of those I have written, that I can go over it all and see what it needs.

It seems to me I have failed to give any sense of our delight so far. In what I have written, I seem to be talking all the time, whereas, in reality, I was not. I said and thought all that I have written, and it is true that our enjoyment of a scene comes largely from the thoughts and emotions it awakens, and our ability to express them.

Emotions unexpressed produce melancholy, as I have found when here alone. This is the cause of much of the world's sadness. It is well to make this clear, for most of us long for beautiful surroundings that we may receive delight without much effort. But those who long for an island like ours, should know that its beauty would be lost to them when they cease to find a meaning in it to delight in, and if they failed to give any expression to what they perceived and felt. But I fear I have allotted too much of my space to this phase. It is only one of many. We found much of our delight in our activity, and in the long, silent hours, when we drifted, sailed, or lay upon the rocks and dreamed. But how can this be shown? Every day, we gathered driftwood, searched for bait, discovered new forms of life, and new habits. We fished, got the meals, scrubbed the cabin, added some adornment here and convenience there. Every day, these and countless other things, large and small, were repeated, and brought us each time a fresh enjoyment. How important it would be to show this in the smallest detail! It is hard to convey the delight you may feel in catching a floating stick from the water as you sail past it, in gathering up what has floated to your beach, in bringing a boatload from some foreign shore you have explored.

It is still more difficult to shape the delight we felt in our housework, the drudgeries of life, and even in our inconveniences, so that another may see and feel it. If I fail, it will be in this.

All day Sunday I sat by the door, recalling, smiling to myself, making sudden sallies at my subject, sighing because it eluded me. Memory at her easel is prone to subdue her colors, so that even the joys of former times, portrayed by her, appear in too soft and tender hues. Time and again I held her hand, delaying and delaying, because of this. I want those days to have the true color. I must present them now, as they were to us then.

About five o'clock, a boy came around the corner of the cabin, carrying a box.

"Hello," I exclaimed, for he took me by surprise, "what's that?"

"A dog."

He put the box at my feet, and a little pointed nose came up between the slats. There was a low, mournful cry. I carefully brought the box inside and placed it on the floor in the middle of the room. I put the cats out, so that neither they nor the dog would be frightened. I got a soup plate of condensed milk, diluted, and put it near the box. Then I removed the slats so carefully that the little fellow was licking my hands as I worked.

"That's right, Bobbie," I said in a quiet, conversational tone. "You're all right now."

It was a critical moment as I lifted him from the box. It is easier to spoil a full-blooded Scotch collie than a sensitized plate. A blow, a fright, or even a hard scolding, will often ruin a pup of this breed in a moment, and once the damage is done, it can never be corrected.

Of course, the moment I lifted him out, petting and talking to him, he fawned at my feet, but the moment I removed my hands, he stood up and looked into my face, his nose in the air. This was a good sign, but it was his eyes and tail that must tell the story. The eyes were open, round, exceedingly bright, and without a shade of fear. But how susceptible! A soul, gentle and affectionate beyond our human conception, was in them. The eyes of most pups are gentle. There is something grave and heavy in those of a St. Bernard. A Newfoundland's are more inquisitive and playful. A bull's are more bold and watchful. Those of an Irish setter are a little stupid in comparison. But the eyes of an unspoiled Scotch collie are more gentle than a fawn's, more alert than a young fox's.

Bob's were limpid bright.

I clapped my hands and reached for him quickly. He jumped back in a flash, pricked his ears, held his head up, and looked squarely at me. His eyes were sparkling like stars. His left ear lopped a little. His tail was straight out. This was the last good sign.

I showed him the plate of milk.

"Here you are, Bob," said I, "good dog."

He came to it eagerly, and lapped it up. I watched his tail. He dropped it while eating, but did not draw it under his legs. I filled the plate three times before he was satisfied.

I gave the boy thirty-five cents for rowing over. It was not too much, for there was a good wind blowing and a rough sea. I waited until he was some distance from the shore and then I opened the door and walked out. Bob was close at my heels. He tumbled over the sill on his nose, but was up in a moment and after me. I stepped up on the porch. He tried to follow, but could not. He put his fore paws on the edge, looked up at me anxiously, crying and barking sharply. I went to the corner, and leaning around the rainbarrel, called to him. He came scurrying around and followed the path after me down to the beach. The wind almost toppled him over, and he seemed surprised at it. The waves washing the shore caught his eye. He leaped into them, barked, caught at them playfully and ran out again to me, jumping up to my knees. He kept close to my feet, and I had to move carefully not to step on him. I saw that I must not play with him much. He is too nervous and excitable now. He must learn to look at things quietly, to form calm and correct opinions, before he is frightened by them. The traits that render him so readily spoiled are those that may make him the best of dogs. He never forgets. He is more generous and sensitive than even you. He will be guided eventually by the emotion that becomes dominant. If it be fear or grief, he will be a pitiful creature. If it be affection, and if the one he loves treats him wisely and quietly, subduing his flighty impulses, guarding him from injury and alarm until his judgment has matured, he will be a wise dog and a very brave one for affection's sake.

While we were on the beach, I kept a close watch on the path. At last I saw Yannie, attracted by the strange sounds, come slowly around the turn in the bushes. I was glad that it was Yannie. She would be the most sensible and help me afterwards with the others. She saw the dog jumping about me and stopped, opening her clear gray eyes very wide, thrusting her head forward and crouching a little. The hair of her back rose slightly in a narrow ridge. I called Bob to me, and, sitting on a stone, took him to my lap.

"Come on, Yannie," I called; "come along." She looked into my face, stood up, rubbed against a bush and moved slowly toward me, stopping now and then to stare at the dog.

"Come on, Yannie. Come along."

I spoke in a coaxing, natural way, and snapped my fingers. When she heard my voice, she looked at me, and the quiet, sympathetic expression of her eyes returned. She stopped, however, to rub against every stone and to take a peep at Bob, while doing so. She jumped up behind me, purring. I reached around, and stroked her, bringing her by degrees to my lap. Bob, under my caresses, was lying blissfully in my lap. Yannie poked her head under my arm and her nose came in contact with Bob's. She sniffed at it, growled and drew back. Bob lifted his head and looked at her curiously.

"Good Bob," I said. "Good Yannie," still stroking them. Bob licked my chin, wagged his tail and looked at the cat again, cocking his ears. By degrees, I got Yannie, purring and growling alternately, into my lap and induced her to lie beside him quietly. Then I put them both down, and clapping my hands, ran along the beach, Bob bounding and stumbling and barking in front, Yannie trotting behind.

As we came back, I saw Betty sitting in the path, just where it leaves the bushes. She was craning her head, watching us, in great excitement. As she caught my eye, she recovered her composure. But there were unmistakable signs of profound emotion. She was exceedingly beautiful. Her body seemed very big, her fur fluffy and alive. Her eyes assumed their darkest shades of blue and green. They were sombre and wide, deep-set and watchful. She sat still upon her haunches, her tail, like a fox's brush, curled around her legs.

I called to her, but she would not come. She looked at me for a moment and fixed her gaze again upon the dog. Three times we ran up and down the beach, clambering over the rocks at the southeast point, Bob leaping at them, falling between them, panting and barking in his eagerness to go where I went, Yannie springing nimbly from rock to rock and keeping as close to me now as he. As we returned the last time, I ran ahead and up the path first, stopping to pet Betty. She humped her back into my hand and purred once; then she squatted on her haunches, watching the dog. Bob came clumsily after me, panting and stumbling. He passed Betty with an awkward bound, brushing against her. She did not get up, but drew her body and head away, laid her ears back, lifted one fore-paw and held it toward him, but the claws were sheathed and she did not touch him.

I was very proud of the cats, and gave them some fish for supper, keeping Bob inside. Dump was asleep in a basket in the kitchen, and coming forth when the meal was ready, ate two thirds of it, as usual. Then she returned to the basket. She had been spared so far because for the first few days, I thought she missed you and I don't like to kill anything just because I don't like it. To slay a cat, for this reason, is as much of a murder as if I slew a man.

A few moments later I returned to the kitchen, and Bob ran ahead of me, before I knew it. As he passed the basket, in a bound, Dump ducked. I was surprised at her calmness. She rose slowly and looked over the edge at him. He came running back towards me and this time there was an explosion. A flash of wild terror shot from Dump's eyes, popping them out like balls. She flew up in the air, all four legs stiff as rods, the claws exposed, her back and tail a-bristle. The violence of her start threw her back under the bench, spitting and scratching at the air. Bob wheeled about, flopped down on his haunches and looked at her, the picture of perplexed astonishment. I held him where he was, with one hand, and with the other, I reached for Dump, stroking her until she was quiet. I finally induced her to come out, and brought her close to Bob. She made a vicious reach for his face and backed off, spitting. The terror had left her eyes. They took again their natural expression—round, protruding, glossy, soulless. I walked by her, Bob following me. She watched us, but as we did not come too close, held her peace. When we went inside, she jumped to the window-sill and sat there, her face close to the glass, all the evening, watching him. Yannie came in once or twice to have a look at him and finally went out for good, seemingly satisfied and unconcerned. Soon after I was seated, with the lamp lit, Betty appeared in the doorway and looked at me and the dog at my feet. She walked across the room like one with a purpose, and jumped on my lap. She sat with her head over my knee, looking solemnly, sometimes sullenly at the dog. If he moved, she uttered an ominous growl. Then I would speak to her reproachfully, pat her head and say: "Good Bobbie. Be good to him, Betty, for he is just a foolish, tender-hearted pup." In a little while she ceased to growl, and once, when I had him stand up beside her, she permitted it without a protest. Before closing up, I put her on the floor and induced Bob to a frolic. I wanted her to understand that his wild, uncouth antics were harmless. She watched him a little contemptuously, I thought, and when he made a playful plunge at her, she gave him two swift but gentle raps upon the nose, with the mitten of her foot. Then she walked out sedately.

I blew out the light and went upstairs. Bob came hurrying and stumbling after me. So far, all was going well with my household. Bob had met with surprises, but no serious alarms, and the worst was over, so far as Yannie and Betty were concerned. I had my doubts about Dump, but I would do my best with her in the morning.

I forgot to tell you I gave Bob a bath with soap and soft water and dried him in the sun. He seemed to enjoy this, and was sweet and clean afterwards. When we went upstairs, I took my blue wrapper, and folding it, placed it near my tick, in the corner.

"There is your bed, Bob. Go lie down."

He cast a curious, crestfallen glance at me and turned toward the stairs. This was the first bad sign. There is something unpleasant in his mind associated with a bed. I coaxed him to it, however, and he lay there quietly through the night.

When I awoke in the morning, I saw him, lying with his head between his paws, watching me intently. The moment I opened my eyes, he lifted his head and pricked up his ears. His eyes snapped with inquiry. "Shall we get up?" they said.

"You bet!" I called. In an instant, he was at me and we raced downstairs together. I caught a towel and hurried to my bath. He followed me to the edge of the ledge. I dove in, and coming up, saw him looking toward me in still anxiety. There was a great relief in his eyes when he saw me swimming back. Collies do not take naturally to the water, and I don't know just what is the best way to teach them to like it. I must feel my way in this. He is not afraid of it, but if I threw him in, he might learn to hate it, and it would be all up with that. You can't drive a collie. If you attempt to, he will either die of a broken heart or become mean and stubborn and treacherous. Bob is the sort to die. This is no exaggeration. You could kill him with a little unkindness or the use of stern measures.

As I left the water, Yannie and Betty came running down. I could hardly dry myself because of them. Yannie caught at the towel and jumped on my bare shoulders, biting at my ears and chin. Betty rubbed against my legs, keeping between me and the dog. It looked very much as if they had talked it over during the night, under the house, and were now carrying out their plan.

We all went into the kitchen. Dump was on the bench. She bristled up at our approach, but became quiet again. When I stood by the box, Yannie and Betty stood by me; when I stooped to light the burners, they laid down close behind me, facing the dog. Wherever I moved, they were close to my feet. I mixed a wash-basinful of milk and placed it on the floor. They ran to it; Bob and Dump followed. All four were drinking together, without concern, their noses close together. I smiled in satisfaction, for fast friends are often made at a feast, and I thought my concerns were over. Bob's lusty lapping disturbed Dump. She jumped back and spit at him loudly. Yannie and Betty growled approvingly and Bob withdrew. I tried to talk to Dump, but there was no reasoning with her. She pulled away from me and went to the dish, looking up now and then to growl. When the cats were through, Bob finished the milk.

After breakfast, I went out by the door, put a board across the arms of my chair, after Tom's example, and began this letter to you. Yannie went off about her business. Betty jumped up on the board, and lying down by my pad, dozed and purred alternately. Bob lay at my feet, looking wistfully up at me for a long time; then he got up and looked about him.

"That's right," I said; "run around. You must entertain yourself, old man."

He trotted off, and presently Betty got down. She stretched herself lazily and followed him. I saw Dump peering at me from the kitchen porch. She saw Betty disappear around the corner, and vanished. There was mischief in her fishy eye.

"My girl," I said, "I am afraid your end is near."

I wrote for a while, and laying my board and pad upon the ground, went around the house toward the beach. As I came to the head of the path, I saw Bob at the foot of it, looking wistfully up. Directly in front of him, barring the way, sat Dump, meeting every move of his with a menacing dab and a spiteful spit. Back of her were Yannie and Betty, very quiet, indeed, but wavering, I could see, between their natural decency and the barbaric impulses Dump's conduct stirred to life. I hurried toward them, hoping to reach Dump that I might reason with her before any injury was done. But when Bob saw me, he lifted his head high and dashed up the path. Dump made a wild reach for him, just missing his eye. Yannie and Betty made tentative dabs at him, but he escaped untouched. He followed me to my chair and stood up beside me, his paws on my knees, his head between them. When I picked up my board and began to write, he lay down at my feet quietly. He had learned to leave me alone when I took my pad and pencil. I had given him no instruction in this. His observation, feelings and affection had taught him.

In a few moments, Betty jumped into my lap and crept to her place on the board. For a time there was peace.

It was a glorious autumn day. A cool, strong wind was blowing from the south-west and it was pleasant to sit in the lee of the house, on the north side, upon the grass, in the warm sunshine. Back of me, there was a constant sighing and swishing among the tall bushes and vines of the jungle. The little patch of sod that forms the dooryard, is enclosed now by a fringe of goldenrod, in full bloom, wild rose-bushes, with here and there a belated blossom, young sumacs, about two feet high, and a tall grass, shaded green and silver and gold, with a heavy head like barley.

Bees and butterflies were hovering around the goldenrod. It was a fragrant, delicately tinted border. Its graceful foliage stirred pleasantly in the spent breeze. Over it, I could see the white, clean ridge of rocks and the far stretch of water, shaded blue and amber. It rippled gently in the lee of the island. Farther out, there were white-caps. When I had looked a while before, it was wind-swept, dark blue and foam-crested between the island and Noank. I could now hear the surf washing the beach.

For some time I mused tranquilly in the sheltered, murmuring dooryard, now and then writing a line or two. As my pencil moved, Betty followed it lazily with her paw. Bob dropped his head on my foot and slept. Suddenly I heard a low growl. Dump was perched on the door-sill, her back ruffled, her yellow, pop eyes fixed on Bob. An impulse of rage possessed me. "You little devil," I thought. "Nothing interests you but food, a soft spot and trouble. You are not content with your own safety and comfort, but must disturb that of others. Why can't you leave him alone?"

My inclination was to put a stone to her neck and throw her in the sea. While I was weighing the matter, she crept under the chair. If Bob moved in his sleep, she growled and spit at him. Betty grew restless, and craning over the board, looked down at him, the shades of her ancestors darkening her eyes. I waited until my mood was gracious, and my spirit more sympathetic. Then I reached under for Dump and brought her to my lap.

"My girl," I said, "be reasonable. He is a kind-hearted boy, foolish and awkward now, but too gentle to harm you. Just look at this beautiful home of ours. There is nothing here to disturb its loveliness for us but ourselves. If you are a good girl, that is, if you will just not *hunt* for trouble, you may feed your fill here day after day and sleep your long sleeps. If you continue to be spiteful, you will corrupt our good conduct, make spitting creatures of us all, and work a trail of malice and fear through our Eden. Unless you mend your ways, you will be cast out. I will give you to the lobsters. Behold, I am your God—and I have spoken."

Bob, hearing my voice, lifted his head, and through all the discourse, Dump growled and spit at him, sticking her claws in my knee. Bob got up and walked away. He was evidently weary of this nagging. He vanished around the house, and Dump, jumping down, crept stealthily after him. Betty soon followed. I was very much perplexed. It was so easy to kill Dump. Was there no other way? I could not dispose of her elsewhere, for there is small demand for girl cats. It was so easy to kill her! It would be no credit to me. This act must lie at the end of my wisdom, and I disliked to feel it was limited by that.

All day I followed them about, coaxing, watching and instructing. I carried my pad and pencil, now writing on the windy beach, now on the sheltered ledge. Betty never left me when the dog was near. She would keep between him and me as we walked, rubbing against my legs. If I sat down to write, she was on my lap or my shoulder. Dump followed us persistently, preferring to stand near us, a little back of Bob, growling and fretful. Yannie roamed at large, pouncing upon grasshoppers and devouring them. She would disappear into the jungle for long periods. As I sat by the great rock, writing, I heard a sudden commotion in the bushes to my left. There was a shrill squeaking, and presently, Yannie ran out, her head up, her ears pricked, her eyes bright, a good-sized rat dangling from her mouth. She trotted past me and carried her prey to the dooryard. I followed quietly to watch. This was her first rat. At least, we have never seen any on the island. I knew that this would be important news for you. In fancy, I see your look of alarm as you read this, but I know your pride and confidence in Yannie will comfort you.

It was certainly brave of Yannie, and although showing some surprise and excitement, she handled the affair like an old hand. For some time, she played with her victim, allowing him to run under the house, to the edge of the tall grass, or behind the rocker of my chair. Then she pounced upon him, and brought him back to the centre of the open ground. She carried him lightly, uninjured, and dropped him on the grass. He grew accustomed to the handling. I was surprised to see him lift himself suddenly on his haunches and sniff at her face. Again he lifted his paws and felt of it. Once they rubbed noses, and finally the rat, no longer seeking to escape, scampered back and forth, seeming to enjoy the sport. I began to think another member had joined our household when, without warning, Yannie closed her teeth, first in his back, and then in his neck, and killed him. She ate the body under a little sumac bush, and I threw the remains in the sea. I was at first distressed by her conduct. It seemed unnecessarily cruel to win his affection, to bring a new delight into his benighted, outcast life, only to devour him.

ARTHUR HENRY

But I could not blame her long, for I knew that even we, with our wider knowledge, our holy ideals, our heritage of religion, philosophy and song, still eat the sheep that have clothed us, caress and feed the confiding creatures we would fatten for our stomachs, and for the sake of an Easter hat, drive our pets to the slaughter pen.

In the evening, I devoted myself entirely to Dump and the dog. I was this cat's judge and jury, her prosecution and defense. I labored to preserve her and to save myself from the hangman's task. Had I been more of a saviour and less of a judge, I might have succeeded. As it was, I failed. After three hours of exhortation, caresses and example, I kicked her from the room into the night, and closed the door.

She was the first at breakfast in the morning, standing, as usual, in the plate and menacing Bob when he came to eat. When she was through, I carried her to the beach, waded out to the fish box, opened it, threw her in, and shutting the cover, pressed it quickly under water with my foot. There was a great gurgling as the water rushed through the holes. I felt two sharp bumps against the cover. Through a crack in the top, I could see the black and white spots of Dump's body. They flashed across it at short intervals, as she swam swiftly in a circle. It seemed that she would never stop. I watched and listened with a growing sickness. I would have felt no horror if I could have justified the deed. Poor Dump was dying because my love was not perfect nor my wisdom whole. These are the forces that will some day abolish courts and penalties, but they were not strong enough in me.

I lifted the box and opened it. Dump was lying in a corner, limp and dead. I took her out, and carrying her in the boat, rowed some distance into the channel. I would not risk her drifting to my shore. I would not bury her on it. I wanted none of her in my soil. I felt a passing fear that she would return, in spite of the tide race; that I would not get rid of her; that I would find her returning body, day after day, in my tours on the coast, until it rotted.

Near the bush buoy, I got up, and reaching from the boat, dropped her overboard. She fell with a splash and sank slowly, head down, all four legs extended, her tail straight up. When I saw her last, she looked like a hide hung up to dry.

I solemnly rowed back and found Yannie and Betty watching me from the beach. Yannie jumped upon my shoulder, purring loudly. Betty looked quietly up. I put the memory of Dump from me. The whole island seemed to feel a relief, and I returned to my chair in the dooryard, a little quiet, perhaps, but serene.

> *"'Tis the law, 'tis the law,*
> *And the duty of the old turnkee."*

CHAPTER XII

As the fall advanced, the forces of nature became steadily more active and insistent. All through September, the wind blew constantly. There were no gales, but there were no quiet days. The tides were higher and lower than before, rolling far in upon my beach, and changing its shape with its great washing eddies. Day and night, the sound of the water was in my ears. The wind-swept island was stripped of its leaves. The once green and fragrant jungle became a mass of bare sticks, and the cabin, no longer sheltered, felt every strong gust. The water was always blue and white-capped. The nights were lowering and intensely cold. In the sunlight it was still possible to find a warm corner in the shelter of the rocks, but on gray days the frosty air bit persistently and the wind penetrated to the bones. This little island, surrounded by such a reach of sea, is the last place to choose for the winter. I would prefer a cave in the woods, a steam-heated hall bedroom, apartments in the Waldorf, or an easy chair by the fireplace in Brooklyn, with Nancy, her mother and Elizabeth. It was not the cold nor the high weather that troubled me, but it was the lack of room and the right kind of labor, the continuous exposure. A mountain forest must be the place for winter. I would rather climb through the woods after partridges, and swing my axe, and find my night's shelter in a warm hut under the trees, than to sit in an open boat, fishing, with the bitter wind benumbing me, the ice-cold water dashing over me, and my only refuge a cabin set on a bleak hummock of the sea.

The first week in October Nancy and Elizabeth came up to help me close the cabin for the season. I expected them on the eight-forty-three train Friday night. For two days the wind had blown steadily from the west, increasing in strength with every change of the tide. The water, grown cold and heavy, rolled in ponderous breakers between the island and Noank. Friday afternoon the wind moderated and shifted east. The sky, clear before, became slowly overcast and dull. A frosty vapor came in gusts from the ocean. I kept a fire going all day, and if a piece of drift-wood came to my shore, I brought it in to dry. The outgoing tide was al-ways freighted with timber from the shipyards. Most of it remained in the channel, and passed around me to the north, but with this west wind, a barrel and chips would occasionally be blown from their course, and come ashore. I watched the water closely, and if I saw a fine oak beam, a barrel or a long plank drifting past, I ran to the beach and put after it with the boat. I wanted wood enough to last over Sunday. In all this labor, Bob and Yannie and Betty were as busy as I. If I ran to the beach, they were scampering before me, or close at my heels. They jumped in the boat as I launched it, Yannie crouching on the prow, Betty climbing to my shoulders, and clinging there through all my exertions. I could work without considering her, for though I pushed hard with an oar to get the boat off, and rowed with vigor, and struggled to seize the timber and make it fast to the boat, she remained comfortably on her perch, purring in my ear, regulating her position as my arm and shoul-ders strained and heaved. Bob, as soon as he was aboard, jumped to the stern seat, where, upon his haunches, with head erect and ears pricked, he watched all my motions with shining eyes. He knew what I was after, and if a small stick came near him, he would reach over the stern and pick it from the water with his mouth.

At sunset there was half an hour of calm, but the brilliant colors were suddenly swept from sky and sea. A long bank of clouds rose in the east and, filling the heavens, hid the moon and stars, and plunged my world into black night, premature and threatening. At seven o'clock I put two damp logs on the fire, placed the lamp in the window, that it might guide us on our return, and went to the beach. Bob and the cats were with me. By some means, still unknown to me, they had learned what this trip to Noank, Friday night, meant to us. Ordinarily, if I did not want them in the boat, a word was sufficient. But on these occasions, they became frantic. I had learned that commands were useless. It was so dark on this night that I could not see six feet before me. I got into the boat, and reaching under the seats, found Yannie and Betty. Bob was crouched in the prow. I threw them high upon the beach, and seizing an oar, attempted to get away with one strong push. My oar slipped on a flat stone, and I stumbled to my knees. I heard them coming with a rush, and before I could move, they were in the boat again. They did not try to hide this time, but crowded close about me. Bob was crying like a child, his whole body trembling. The cats yowled piteously. It is a terrible thing to be so closely related to creatures with whom you cannot speak. I could not tell them that they must stay behind, because the terrors and strangeness of Noank would confuse them; that we might become separated, and lost to each other. I could only suffer in sympathy with them and relentlessly ignore their appeal. I got the boat a few feet from shore, and threw them to the beach. Then I bent my whole strength upon the oars, until I was out of the lee of the island, and the wind could fill my sail. Half-way to Noank, I heard the voice of Bob raised in long-drawn, plaintive howls. The island was lost in the night. The light of the window, distinguishable from the planets only by its position and greater size, alone marked its location. But, in fancy, I could see Bob distinctly, sitting on the beach, his long nose pointed to the heavens, his sorrowful eyes rolled upward as he poured forth that complaint, more melancholy, more desolate than all earthly sounds.

Before I reached the dock, a rush of wind brought a storm of rain and sleet. The waves lifted me and plunged me forward. I swept past the moored boats, around the corner of the wharf, between the huge fish cars anchored here, seeing nothing, but following the oft-traveled way instinctively. I wore only a painter's suit of thin cotton cloth, an old slouch hat and rubber boots. I was wet through with rain and sea water. Fine sleet was clinging to me, but I was tingling with enjoyment, and I was warm. Perhaps, if I had seen the train rush in and stop, and move on again, bringing no one to me; if I had turned from the depot, and walked through the wet streets alone, and beat back across the mile of water against the wind and sleet alone, with another week of cold and dreary solitude before me, I would have shivered some. As it was, Nancy, Elizabeth and I walked merrily through Noank, stopping to make purchases and to greet our neighbors.

"You are not going over to-night?" asked the grocer.

"We can make it safely."

"I wouldn't try it. You'll be drowned—you will. Yes, you will."

On the street, we met Mr. Ashbey. He stopped and peered into our faces.

"Well," said he slowly, "I'm not surprised to see you. It's your kind of a night. You remind me of a piece I used to speak, 'The Black Horse and Its Rider.' I was always a great hand to declaim, and I tell you, that poem seemed to fill me with fire. I would forget where I was. My whole soul was up and away where the battle was fiercest, alongside of the black horse and his rider."

As he had said this, his voice, strong and rich, rang in my ears. His eyes, usually mild as with dreams, flashed. For an instant, a magnetic influence, emanating from him, shook me to my feet. His eyes became mild and dim again, and he moved on with a friendly nod and smile. Here was surely a stray spark of that genius that, burning as a flame in some, illumes a way and inspires a world to follow it.

Captain Green joined us at the foot of the hill, and walked to the dock.

"I won't urge you not to venture over," said he, "for it would do no good."

"Don't you think it is possible to get there?" asked Nancy.

"Everything is possible. It is probably safe enough for you people."

"You would not be afraid to do it," I said.

"I would go if there was any need. Of course, I'd go, but I would not choose to in your little boat."

"Well, Captain, I look at it this way. That island is ours, and our place is there. I should lose my comfort in it, and my delight in the wind and water if they kept me from my own. I don't believe they will. I feel safe in making this voyage, and I wish to feel so. I never care to risk danger for the risk's sake, but when I begin to dodge, and hide and hang back, and look upon life anxiously, I hope to die."

The wind shrieked over our heads, the rain whipped us, the roll and break of water sounded far into the darkness, we heard the boat pounding against the dock.

"None but those who brave its dangers, comprehend its mystery," murmured the Captain, in his beard. "They say," he added thoughtfully, "that our destiny is not in our own keeping. If that is so, why should we concern ourselves with it?"

Nancy and Elizabeth walked away until they were concealed by the darkness. When they returned, their rubber coats bulged with bundles under them. The Captain held the boat until we were seated, and gave it a strong push off, that rid us safely of the dock, and brought the nose of the boat around toward the wind; the sail filled, and, wrenching at my hand, hauled us swiftly from the land. I slipped off my boots and the girls removed their shoes. The bundles were composed of their skirts. If we capsized, they could slip from their rubber coats and swim.

The girls were saved from the anxiety they might have felt, by the darkness. They could not see the size of the billows. There is something appalling in a tempestuous sea when viewed from a little boat. The waves, rising on every hand higher than your craft, the great ridges of water rushing toward you with an appearance of power irresistible and relentless, towering over you as they advance, are terrible to behold if you are one to apprehend death, and to fear it. We had never been in so rough a sea, but the darkness hid its threats, and Elizabeth whose tranquillity would have been most disturbed, sat quietly where I had placed her, enjoying the adventure with us, for the rain and wind did not trouble her.

The girls, both on the windward side of the boat, acted as ballast. I sat upon the edge in the stern, and leaned far over the water, holding fast to the sail rope and the rudder. We shot through the water with great speed, for there is no better sailing craft than a long, narrow, flat-bottom sharpie, with a centreboard, if you keep it right side up. We would have made the voyage in ten minutes if we could have sailed straight for port. But the wind blew direct from our island, and we were obliged to make a long tack toward the north.

"Where is the island?" asked Nancy. "Did you leave the lamp burning? Can you see it?"

"Ours is the second light off the starboard bow."

"What is the first one?"

"I have been wondering. I can't make it out. It don't belong here. I thought at first it was on a large boat coming in, but it remains stationary."

We kept our eyes on this light, for we were making close to it. A huge shape loomed through the rain and darkness.

"It is a ship," said Nancy.

"At anchor!" I exclaimed. "It could not land at the dock on account of the storm, or, if outward bound, is afraid of it, and has anchored here."

"It has two masts," said Elizabeth.

"We are doing very well with our mutton-leg," said Nancy proudly, and I must confess that the sight of this towering vessel, held safe from the storm we were breasting, sent a thrill of elation through me. I am not proud of this feeling, however. I wish to be fearless, to unhesitatingly face all things, attempt all things, but I wish to find my joy in the pursuit itself, and in the thing I win, not in another's failure. It has been said that we should comfort ourselves in our distresses by remembering that thousands are more unfortunate than we. It would be better if we dispensed with distresses altogether, for if in those things that cause us distress we looked for wisdom, we would find them brimming with it.

Our boat was half-filled, and hard to manage when we left the violent strip of tide race, and came into quieter water in the lee of our island. We had been almost an hour on the way, for the wash of the waves, the adverse tide, the strong head wind, had been almost too much for us. As we passed the bush buoy, and neared the island, Nancy, as was her custom, lifted her voice in a long, penetrating call to the family at home. There was an explosive answer from the invisible beach ahead. Bob barked so frantically that his voice broke and his efforts ended in a series of discordant yelps. We almost ran him down, for he had leaped into the surf to meet us. We now heard the fainter voices of the cats. Yannie, leaping for the prow of the boat, as we dashed in, missed her footing and splashing into the water, was rolled upon the beach.

I fastened the boat, threw the sail, the oars and rudder far beyond high water mark, and hurried after the others to the cabin. Elizabeth had piled the fireplace full of dry wood, and as I entered, its roar and crackle greeted me as shouts of laughter, sparks from the pine sticks flew beyond the hearth in harmless showers, the room gleamed and twinkled with its light, and I could almost discern the forms of the fairies as they danced—their shadows on ceiling, walls and floor were plain enough.

The voices of the wind, the rain and water filled the night, and the cabin creaked and trembled constantly. There were gusts that we thought would surely lift us up and hurl us into the sea.

Clothed in warm wrappers, we sat by the fire and kept it howling up the chimney at the storm. At midnight, Elizabeth prepared a feast. We had a market basket full of fine fat oysters I had gathered at the last low tide, a stew of potatoes, onions, canned tomatoes and fresh mackerel, wood toast, tea, and jelly made two weeks before from wild grapes we had gathered two miles down the coast.

We sipped milk punches afterward, lolled before the fire, listened to the storm, grew warm and dry and drowsy.

"I hope it storms for a week," said Nancy.

"So do I," murmured Elizabeth, with a sleepy smile.

"We must have two days of bright sunshine. Everything must be thoroughly aired and dried before we put them away."

"Even if it does not storm," I said, "we may have no sun to speak of, for a week."

"I hope not. Oh, if Satan would but attend to me. If all manner of disaster would only befall me—if my business were ruined, my home disrupted, my reputation gone—if all my friends and relations disowned me, I might, perhaps, be permitted to be happy then. For my part, I would gladly endure all the triumphs of Napoleon, if I knew that in the end I should be overthrown and banished here."

"Let's go to bed," said Elizabeth.

I could no longer keep my pipe lit, and, vigorous as her sentiment had been, Nancy spoke with frequent yawns.

Ten minutes later, I might have been blown to New London, and not have known it, for I was asleep on a bed made comfortable by the hands of Elizabeth.

Saturday afternoon the rain ceased. Sunday was a cold, gray day, with an east wind. We spent it with Captain Green aboard the *Eric Lief,* cruising along the coast of Fishers Island, slipping out into the ocean and back, trolling for mackerel, and coaxing him to make us a boat like his own.

"If I should promise you," he kept repeating, "I should have to do it. It took me several years to build this one. I might not be able to find just the timber to suit." This was the substance of his reply, and he neither refused nor promised.

"I think he will do it," said Nancy in the evening.

I could not agree with her, but she was confident and happy.

"We could sail around the world in such a boat."

"I would rather have it than the finest yacht afloat, but that is too much to expect of him."

"I believe he will do it."

Monday a northwest wind was blowing. There was not a cloud. The sun blazed down upon us clear and strong. This was the end. There was no longer an excuse for delay. We covered the island with beds and bedding, and our clothing. We emptied the cabin, scrubbed it and left it open to the wind and sunlight. By evening, it was thoroughly dry. We put the chairs and table in the centre of the room, and spread the ticks and bedding on them. Our clothing we left hanging in the attic. In the afternoon Mr. Ashbey sailed over to measure the windows for wooden shutters. He would make them and fasten them in when we were gone. Captain Green made two trips in his little skiff, once to see if we were leaving, and once to bring us a basket of fruit and two bouquets of asters from his garden.

We put the cats in a covered basket, turned the key in the cabin door, and loading the boat with baskets and boxes, told Bob to jump in, and set sail for the dock of Mystic Island.

Gibbie had told me to leave our boat there for the winter, and he would paint it in the spring. And Bob was to be left there, too. I had taken him over there one day, and, to the surprise of every one, Royal had received his bold and boisterous advances in a friendly but dignified spirit. This was probably because Bob had come with me, and he understood that we were neighbors. He took him off to hunt rats along the beach, and taught him to dig holes in the ground.

A dinner had been prepared for us by Mrs. Wilcox. It was eaten in silence. There are few people in this world that Nancy and I love as we do Gibbie and his wife, Nora. I have said very little concerning them, for I could not say enough. It seemed to us that, in leaving our island and these neighbors, we were children venturing for the first time from home. As Nora was taking the coffee-pot from the stove, I saw her surreptitiously lift the corner of her apron to her eyes. They were brimming over when we said good-bye.

"It will be a lonely winter," she said, looking away from us quickly, beyond Latimer's Reef to the dull horizon of sky and water.

The twilight was falling as we left the island with Gibbie, in his sail-boat. Bob watched us move swiftly from the dock, and seeming to realize that he was deserted, lifted his nose and howled. Royal pushed against him, wagging his tail, and tried to induce him to a run, but Bob would not heed him. It grew dark rapidly, and by the time we landed at Ash-bey's dock, we could see only the rough form of things. Gibbie handed our bundles up to us, and we said good-bye, and watched him push away. A voice came from a lobster boat moored near by.

"Are you going?"

"Yes, we have closed up for the season."

"I am sorry. I shall miss the light in your window."

We could not see the speaker, and did not recognize the voice.

"Good-bye, neighbor," came another voice from a dock close to us.

"Good-bye," we called, "and good luck to you."

"You will be back in the spring?"

"We hope so."

"Well, good luck to you."

We carried the cats to the Ashbey house, where they found a harbor-age for the winter, and then, as we had an hour before train time, walked silently through the shipyard to Captain Green's. He was just coming from his workshop, a lantern in his hand.

"I just looked across," he said, "and there was no light on the island. I have got used to seeing it there."

"You may be sure," said Nancy, "that it was always a friendly light for you."

"I felt that," he said hastily, "and I have laid my course by it oftener than you think. Come inside," he added, opening the shop door.

We entered, and the Captain, holding up the lantern, revealed a long oak beam resting on blocks, and a shorter piece, curving like a duck's breast, fastened to one end. It was the keel and prow of a boat.

"O Captain," cried Nancy, "you have begun it."

"I won't promise," said he.

Then he showed us how thoroughly sound and seasoned the wood was, how the keel was not straight, as in most boats, but curved upward from the centre to both ends, and how the piece for the prow had not been cut to its peculiar shape, but had grown that way, as if nature herself from the beginning had intended it for this particular boat.

"I may never finish it," he said, "but here are two good timbers for it, anyway."

AS I write these lines, we are sitting in a row on the depot steps, our bundles and bags about us, waiting for the New York train. I am dressed in my city clothes, for the first time in four months and a half. My face is red and my hands are scarred and rough. I feel exceedingly strange,—an adventurer returning to the almost forgotten land of his youth, and I am bringing treasures with me. Although invisible, they are as real as any yet hauled from the sea, or dug from the earth, or found in an oyster's shell. I am bringing with me pictures, experiences, sounds and revelations that have become my indestructible possessions. Where shall I go now; what shall I do? Shall I choose the inland fields, the mountain forest, or the city? In any of these places, I may meet the requirements of winter with little more than my bare hands. I may be warmed and fed. More than shelter, clothing and food, the world cannot give me, unless I possess the spirit to receive, and if this spirit is mine, it does not matter where I am, or what I do, how great or little is my wealth, how conspicuous or obscure my position; all that can delight or profit a man will come to me until my heart and mind are full.

"It is wonderful," said Nancy just now, "that in all these months, we have received nothing from any one around here but the most unstinted kindness—not one unfriendly word or look; even the reserved glance, the hesitating speech, the cold or questioning glint has not once been offered us."

"That is true, and it is an exceedingly important fact to think over."

"Why don't you close with that statement, then?"

"I guess I will."

And still, I am not satisfied, for I can not give to these written words the grace with which she spoke them; the tender cadence, the moistened eyes, the memories that lived in them.

THE END

Wash day on Dodge's Island. The skiff has its sail lowered a bit to ease its repose. Enders Island before the monastery was built is to the right, Noank hovers faintly on the western horizon. Ahoy and Quirk seem to be one island from this angle and the "narrow run" between Quirk and Ram is obscured by the woman's body. Over the low spot on Ram looms the drumlin North Dumpling a good five nautical miles to the southwest. The woman's attire would seem to be more the everyday gear that the Quirk Island women would adopt. (Photo from Second Edition)

Short Stories by Theodore Dreiser

A Doer Of The Word

The Village Feudists

A Cripple Whose Energy Gives Inspiration
(The Noank Boy)

A DOER OF THE WORD

By Theodore Dreiser

NOANK is a little played-out fishing town on the southeastern coast of Connecticut, lying half-way between New London and Stonington. Once it was a profitable port for mackerel and cod fishing. Today its wharves are deserted of all save a few lobster smacks. There is a shipyard, employing three hundred and fifty men, a yacht-building establishment, with two or three hired hands; a sail-loft, and some dozen or so shops or sheds, where the odds and ends of fishing life are made and sold. Everything is peaceful. The sound of the shipyard axes and hammers can be heard for miles over the quiet waters of the bay. In the sunny lane which follows the line of the shore, and along which a few shops struggle in happy-go-lucky disorder, may be heard the voices and noises of the workers at their work. Water gurgling about the stanchions of the docks, the whistle of some fisherman as he dawdles over his nets, or puts his fish ashore, the whirr of the single high-power sewing machine in the sail-loft, often mingle in a pleasant harmony, and invite the mind to repose and speculation.

I was in a most examining and critical mood that summer, looking into the nature and significance of many things, and was sitting one day in the shed of the maker of sailboats, where a half-dozen characters of the village were gathered, when some turn in the conversation brought up the nature of man. He is queer, he is restless; life is not so very much when you come to look upon many phases of it.

"Did any of you ever know a contented man?" I inquired idly, merely for the sake of something to say.

There was silence for a moment, and one after another met my roving glance with a thoughtful, self-involved and retrospective eye.

Old Mr. Main was the first to answer.

"Yes, I did. One."

"So did I," put in the sailboat maker, as he stopped in his work to think about it.

"Yes, and I did," said a dark, squat, sunny, little old fisherman, who sold cunners for bait in a little hut next door.

"Maybe you and me are thinking of the same one, Jacob," said old Mr. Main, looking inquisitively at the boat-builder.

"I think we've all got the same man in mind, likely," returned the builder.

"Who is he?" I asked.

"Charlie Potter," said the builder.

"That's the man!" exclaimed Mr. Main.

"Yes, I reckon Charlie Potter is contented, if anybody be," said an old fisherman who had hitherto been silent.

Such unanimity of opinion struck me forcibly. Charlie Potter—what a humble name; not very remarkable, to say the least. And to hear him so spoken of in this restless, religious, quibbling community made it all the more interesting.

"So you really think he is contented, do you?" I asked.

"Yes, sir! Charlie Potter is a contented man," replied Mr. Main, with convincing emphasis.

"Well," I returned, "that's rather interesting. What sort of a man is he?"

"Oh, he's just an ordinary man, not much of anybody. Fishes and builds boats occasionally," put in the boat-builder.

"Is that all? Nothing else?"

"He preaches now and then—not regularly," said Mr. Main.

A-ha! I thought. A religionist!

"A preacher is expected to set a good example," I said.

"He ain't a regular preacher," said Mr. Main, rather quickly. "He's just kind of around in religious work."

"What do you mean?" I asked curiously, not quite catching the import of this "around."

"Well," answered the boat builder, "he don't take any money for what he does. He ain't got anything."

"What does he live on then?" I persisted, still wondering at the significance of "around in religious work."

"I don't know. He used to fish for a living. Fishes yet once in a while, I believe."

"He makes models of yachts," put in one of the bystanders. "He sold the New Haven Road one for two hundred dollars here not long ago."

A vision of a happy-go-lucky Jack-of-all-trades arose before me. A visionary—a theorist.

"What else?" I asked, hoping to draw them out. "What makes you all think he is contented? What does he do that makes him so contented?"

"Well," said Mr. Main, after a considerable pause and with much of sympathetic emphasis in his voice, "Charlie Potter is just a good man, that's all. That's why he's contented. He does as near as he can what he thinks he ought to by other people—poor people."

"You won't find anybody with a kinder heart than Charlie Potter," put in the boat-builder. "That's the trouble with him, really. He's too good. He don't look after himself right, I say. A fellow has to look out for himself some in this world. If he don't, no one else will."

"Right you are, Henry," echoed a truculent sea voice from somewhere.

I was becoming both amused and interested, intensely so.

"If he wasn't that way, he'd be a darned sight better off than he is," said a thirty-year-old helper, from a far corner of the room.

"What makes you say that?" I queried. "Isn't it better to be kind-hearted and generous than not?"

"It's all right to be kind-hearted and generous, but that ain't sayin' that you've got to give your last cent away and let your family go hungry."

"Is that what Charlie Potter does?"

"Well, no, maybe he don't, but he comes mighty near to it at times. He and his wife and his adopted children have been pretty close to it at times."

You see, this was the center, nearly, for all village gossip and philosophic speculation, and many of the most important local problems, morally and intellectually speaking, were here thrashed out.

"There's no doubt but that's where Charlie is wrong," put in old Mr. Main a little later. "He don't always stop to think of his family."

"What did he ever do that struck you as being over-generous?" I asked of the young man who had spoken from the corner.

"That's all right," he replied in a rather irritated and peevish tone; "I ain't going to go into details now, but there's people around here that hang on him, and that he's give to, that he hadn't arter."

"I believe in lookin' out for Number One, that's what I believe in," interrupted the boat-maker, laying down his rule and line. "This givin' up everything and goin' without yourself may be all right, but I don't believe it. A man's first duty is to his wife and children, that's what I say."

"That's the way it looks to me," put in Mr. Main.

"Well, does Potter give up everything and go without things?" I asked the boat-maker.

"Purty blamed near it at times," he returned definitely, then addressing the company in general he added, "Look at the time he worked over there on Fishers Island, at the Ellersbie farm—the time they were packing the ice there. You remember that, Henry, don't you?"

Mr. Main nodded.

"What about it?"

"What about it! Why, he give his rubber boots away, like a darned fool, to old drunken Jimmy Harper, and him loafin' around half the year drunk, and worked around on the ice without any shoes himself. He might 'a' took cold and died."

"Why did he do it?" I queried, very much interested by now.

"Oh, Charlie's naturally big-hearted," put in the little old man who sold cunners. "He believes in the Lord and the Bible. Stands right square on it, only he don't belong to no church like. He's got the biggest heart I ever saw in a livin' being."

"Course the other fellow didn't have any shoes for to wear," put in the boat-maker explanatorily, "but he never would work, anyhow."

They lapsed into silence while the latter returned to his measuring, and then out of the drift of thought came this from the helper in the corner:

"Yes, and look at the way Bailey used to sponge on him. Get his money Saturday night and drink it all up, and then Sunday morning, when his wife and children were hungry, go cryin' around Potter. Dinged if I'd'a' helped him. But Potter'd take the food right off his breakfast table and give it to him. I saw him do it! I don't think that's right. Not when he's got four or five orphans of his own to care for."

"His own children?" I interrupted, trying to get the thing straight.

"No, sir; just children he picked up around, here and there."

Here is a curious character, sure enough, I thought—one well worth looking into.

Another lull, and then as I was leaving the room to give the matter a little quiet attention, I remarked to the boatmaker:

"Outside of his foolish giving, you haven't anything against Charlie Potter, have you?"

"Not a thing," he replied, in apparent astonishment. "Charlie Potter's one of the best men that ever lived. He's a good man."

I smiled at the inconsistency and went my way.

A day or two later the loft of the sail-maker, instead of the shed of the boat-builder, happened to be my lounging place, and thinking of this theme, now uppermost in my mind, I said to him:

"Do you know a man around here by the name of Charlie Potter?"

"Well, I might say that I do. He lived here for over fifteen years."

"What sort of a man is he?"

He stopped in his stitching a moment to look at me, and then said: "How d'ye mean? By trade, so to speak, or religious-like?"

"What is it he has done," I said, "that makes him so popular with all you people? Everybody says he's a good man. Just what do you mean by that?"

"Well," he said, ceasing his work as though the subject were one of extreme importance to him, "he's a peculiar man, Charlie is. He believes in giving nearly everything he has away, if any one else needs it. He'd give the coat off his back if you asked him for it. Some folks condemn him for this, and for not giving everything to his wife and them orphans he has, but I always thought the man was nearer right than most of us. I've got a family myself—but, then, so's he, now, for that matter. It's pretty hard to live up to your light always."

He looked away as if he expected some objection to be made to this, but hearing none, he went on. "I always liked him personally very much. He ain't around here now any more—lives up in Norwich, I think. He's a man of his word, though, as truthful as kin be. He ain't never done nothin' for me, I not bein' a takin' kind, but that's neither here nor there."

He paused, in doubt apparently, as to what else to say.

"You say he's so good," I said. "Tell me one thing that he ever did that struck you as being preeminently good."

"Well, now, I can't say as I kin, exactly, offhand," he replied, " there bein' so many of them from time to time. He was always doin' things one way and another. He give to everybody around here that asked him, and to a good many that didn't. I remember once"—and a smile gave evidence of a genial memory— "he give away a lot of pork that he'd put up for the winter to some colored people back here — two or three barrels, maybe. His wife didn't object, exactly, but my, how his mother-in-law did go on about it. She was livin' with him then. She went and railed against him all around."

"She didn't like to give it to them, eh?"

"Well, I should say not. She didn't set with his views, exactly—never did. He took the pork, though—it was right in the coldest weather we had that winter—and hauled it back about seven miles here to where they lived, and handed it all out himself. Course they were awful hard up, but then they might 'a' got along without it. They do now, sometimes. Charlie's too good that way. It's his one fault, if you might so speak of it."

I smiled as the evidence accumulated. Houseless wayfarers, stopping to find food and shelter under his roof, an orphan child carried seven miles on foot from the bedside of a dead mother and cared for all winter, three children, besides two of his own, being raised out of a sense of affection and care for the fatherless.

One day in the local postoffice I was idling a half hour with the postmaster, when I again inquired:

"Do you know Charlie Potter?"

"I should think I did. Charlie Potter and I sailed together for something over eleven years."

"How do you mean sailed together?"

"We were on the same schooner. This used to be a great port for mackerel and cod. We were wrecked once together."

"How was that?"

"Oh, we went on rocks."

"Any lives lost?"

"No, but there came mighty near being. We helped each other in the boat. I remember Charlie was the last one in that time. Wouldn't get in until all the rest were safe."

A sudden resolution came to me.

"Do you know where he is now?"

"Yes, he's up in Norwich, preaching or doing missionary work. He's kind of busy all the time among the poor people, and so on. Never makes much of anything out of it for himself, but just likes to do it, I guess."

"Do you know how he manages to live?"

"No, I don't, exactly. He believes in trusting to Providence for what he needs. He works though, too, at one job and another. He's a carpenter for one thing. Got an idea the Lord will send 'im whatever he needs."

"Well, and does He?"

"Well, he lives." A little later he added:

"Oh, yes. There's nothing lazy about Charlie. He's a good worker. When he was in the fishing line here there wasn't a man worked harder than he did. They can't anybody lay anything like that against him."

"Is he very difficult to talk to?" I asked, meditating on seeking him out. I had so little to do at the time, the very idlest of summers, and the reports of this man's deeds were haunting me. I wanted to discover for myself whether he was real or not—whether the reports were true. The Samaritan in people is so easily exaggerated at times.

"Oh, no. He's one of the finest men that way I ever knew. You could see him, well enough, if you went up to Norwich, providing he's up there. He usually is, though, I think. He lives there with his wife and mother, you know."

I caught an afternoon boat for New London and Norwich at one-thirty, and arrived in Norwich at five. The narrow streets of the thriving little mill city were alive with people. I had no address, could not obtain one, but through the open door of a news-stall near the boat landing I called to the proprietor:

"Do you know any one in Norwich by the name of Charlie Potter?"

"The man who works around among the poor people here?"

"That's the man."

"Yes, I know him. He lives out on Summer Street, Number Twelve, I think. You'll find it in the city directory."

The ready reply was rather astonishing. Norwich has something like thirty thousand people.

I walked out in search of Summer Street and finally found a beautiful lane of that name climbing upward over gentle slopes, arched completely with elms. Some of the pretty porches of the cottages extended nearly to the sidewalk. Hammocks, rocking-chairs on verandas, benches under the trees—all attested the love of idleness and shade in summer. Only the glimpse of mills and factories in the valley below evidenced the grimmer life which gave rise mayhap to the need of a man to work among the poor.

"Is this Summer Street?" I inquired of an old darky who was strolling cityward in the cool of the evening. An umbrella was under his arm and an evening paper under his spectacled nose.

"Bress de Lordl" he said, looking vaguely around. "Ah couldn't say. Ah knows dat street—been on it fifty times—but Ah never did know de name. Ha, ha, ha!"

The hills about echoed his hearty laugh.

"You don't happen to know Charlie Potter?"

"Oh, yas, sah. Ah knows Charlie Potter. Dat's his house right ovah dar."

The house in which Charlie Potter lived was a two-story frame, overhanging a sharp slope, which descended directly to the waters of the pretty river below. For a mile or more, the valley of the river could be seen, its slopes dotted with houses, the valley itself lined with mills. Two little girls were upon the sloping lawn to the right of the house. A stout, comfortable-looking man was sitting by a window on the left side of the house, gazing out over the valley.

"Is this where Charlie Potter lives?" I inquired of one of the children.

"Yes, sir."

"Did he live in Noank?"

"Yes, sir."

Just then a pleasant-faced woman of forty-five or fifty issued from a vine-covered door.

"Mr. Potter?" she replied to my inquiry. "He'll be right out."

She went about some little work at the side of the house, and in a moment Charlie Potter appeared. He was short, thickset, and weighed no less than two hundred pounds. His face and hands were sunburned and brown like those of every fisherman of Noank. An old wrinkled coat and a baggy pair of gray trousers clothed his form loosely. Two inches of a spotted, soft-brimmed hat were pulled carelessly over his eyes. His face was round and full, but slightly seamed. His hands were large, his walk uneven, and rather inclined to a side swing, or the sailor's roll. He seemed an odd, pudgy person for so large a fame.

"Is this Mr. Potter?"

"I'm the man."

"I live on a little hummock at the east of Mystic Island, off Noank."

"You do?"

"I came up to have a talk with you."

"Will you come inside, or shall we sit out here?"

"Let's sit on the step."

"All right, let's sit on the step."

He waddled out of the gate and sank comfortably on the little low doorstep, with his feet on the cool bricks below. I dropped into the space beside him, and was greeted by as sweet and kind a look as I have ever seen in a man's eyes. It was one of perfect courtesy and good nature — void of all suspicion.

"We were sitting down in the sailboat maker's place at Noank the other day, and I asked a half dozen of the old fellows whether they had ever known a contented man. They all thought a while, and then they said they had. Old Mr. Main and the rest of them agreed that Charlie Potter was a contented man. What I want to know is, are you?"

I looked quizzically into his eyes to see what effect this would have, and if there was no evidence of a mist of pleasure and affection being vigorously restrained I was very much mistaken. Something seemed to hold the man in helpless silence as he gazed vacantly at nothing. He breathed heavily, then drew himself together and lifted one of his big hands, as if to touch me, but refrained.

"Yes, brother," he said after a time, "I am."

"Well, that's good," I replied, taking a slight mental exception to the use of the word brother. "What makes you contented?"

"I don't know, unless it is that I've found out what I ought to do. You see, I need so very little for myself that I couldn't be very unhappy."

"What ought you to do?"

"I ought to love my fellowmen."

"And do you?"

"Say, brother, but I do," he insisted quite simply and with no evidence of chicane or make-believe—a simple, natural enthusiasm. "I love everybody. There isn't anybody so low or so mean but I love him. I love you, yes, I do. I love you."

He reached out and touched me with his hand, and while I was inclined to take exception to this very moral enthusiasm, I thrilled just the same as I have not over the touch of any man in years. There was something effective and electric about him, so very warm and foolishly human. The glance which accompanied it spoke, it seemed, as truthfully as his words. He probably did love me—or thought he did. What difference?

We lapsed into silence. The scene below was so charming that I could easily gaze at it in silence. This little house was very simple, not poor, by no means prosperous, but well-ordered—such a home as such a man might have. After a while I said:

"It is very evident that you think the condition of some of your fellowmen isn't what it ought to be. Tell me what you are trying to do. What method have you for improving their condition?"

"The way I reason is this-a-way," he began. "All that some people have is their feelings, nothing else. Take a tramp, for instance, as I often have. When you begin to sum up to see where to begin, you find that all he has in the world, besides his pipe and a little tobacco, is his feelings. It's all most people have, rich or poor, though a good many think they have more than that. I try not to injure anybody's feelings."

He looked at me as though he had expressed the solution of the difficulties of the world, and the wonderful, kindly eyes beamed in rich romance upon the scene.

"Very good," I said, "but what do you do? How do you go about it to aid your fellowmen?"

"Well," he answered, unconsciously overlooking his own personal actions in the matter, "I try to bring them the salvation which the Bible teaches. You know I stand on the Bible, from cover to cover."

"Yes, I know you stand on the Bible, but what do you do? You don't merely preach the Bible to them. What do you do?"

"No, sir, I don't preach the Bible at all. I stand on it myself. I try as near as I can to do what it says. I go wherever I can be useful. If anybody is sick or in trouble, I'm ready to go. I'll be a nurse. I'll work and earn them food. I'll give them anything I can—that's what I do."

"How can you give when you haven't anything? They told me in Noank that you never worked for money."

"Not for myself alone. I never take any money for myself alone. That would be self-seeking. Anything I earn or take is for the Lord, not me. I never keep it. The Lord doesn't allow a man to be self-seeking."

"Well, then, when you get money what do you do with it? You can't do and live without money."

He had been looking away across the river and the bridge to the city below, but now he brought his eyes back and fixed them on me.

"I've been working now for twenty years or more, and, although I've never had more money than would last me a few days at a time, I've never wanted for anything and I've been able to help others. I've run pretty close sometimes. Time and time again I've been compelled to say, 'Lord, I'm all out of coal,' or 'Lord, I'm going to have to ask you to get me my fare to New Haven tomorrow,' but in the moment of my need He has never forgotten me. Why, I've gone down to the depot time and time again, when it was necessary for me to go, without five cents in my pocket, and He's been there to meet me. Why, He wouldn't keep you waiting when you're about His work. He wouldn't forget you—not for a minute."

I looked at the man in open-eyed amazement.

"Do you mean to say that you would go down to a depot without money and wait for money to come to you?"

"Oh, brother," he said, with the softest light in his eyes, "if you only knew what it is to have faith!"

He laid his hand softly on mine.

"What is car-fare to New Haven or to anywhere, to Him?"

"But," I replied materially, "you haven't any car-fare when you go there—how do you actually get it? Who gives it to you? Give me one instance."

"Why, it was only last week, brother, that a woman wrote me from Malden, Massachusetts, wanting me to come and see her. She's very sick with consumption, and she thought she was going to die. I used to know her in Noank, and she thought if she could get to see me she would feel better.

"I didn't have any money at the time, but that didn't make any difference.

"'Lord,' I said, 'here's a woman sick in Malden, and she wants me to come to her. I haven't got any money, but I'll go right down to the depot, in time to catch a certain train,' and I went. And while I was standing there a man came up to me and said, 'Brother, I'm told to give you this,' and he handed me ten dollars."

"Did you know the man?" I exclaimed.

"Never saw him before in my life," he replied, smiling genially.

"And didn't he say anything more than that?"

"No."

I stared at him, and he added, as if to take the edge off my astonishment:

"Why, bless your heart, I knew he was from the Lord, just the moment I saw him coming."

"You mean to say you were standing there without a cent, expecting the Lord to help you, and He did?"

"'He shall call upon me, and I shall answer him,'" he answered simply, quoting the Ninety-first Psalm.

This incident was still the subject of my inquiry when a little colored girl came out of the yard and paused a moment before us.

"May I go down across the bridge, papa?" she asked.

"Yes," he answered, and then as she tripped away, said:

"She's one of my adopted children." He gazed between his knees at the sidewalk.

"Have you many others?"

"Three."

"Raising them, are you?"

"Yes."

"They seem to think, down in Noank, that living as you do and giving everything away is satisfactory to you but rather hard on your wife and children."

"Well, it is true that she did feel a little uncertain in the beginning, but she's never wanted for anything. She'll tell you herself that she's never been without a thing that she really needed, and she's been happy."

He paused to meditate, I presume, over the opinion of his former fellow townsmen, and then added:

"It's true, there have been times when we have been right where we had to have certain things pretty badly, before they came, but they never failed to come."

While he was still talking, Mrs. Potter came around the corner of the house and out upon the sidewalk. She was going to the Saturday evening market in the city below.

"Here she is," he said. "Now you can ask her."

"What is it?" she inquired, turning a serene and smiling face to me.

"They still think, down in Noank, that you're not very happy with me," he said. "They're afraid you want for something once in a while."

She took this piece of neighborly interference in better fashion than most would, I fancy.

[198]

"I have never wanted for anything since I have been married to my husband," she said. "I am thoroughly contented."

She looked at him and he at her, and there passed between them an affectionate glance.

"Yes," he said, when she had passed after a pleasing little conversation, "my wife has been a great help to me. She has never complained."

"People are inclined to talk a little," I said.

"Well, you see, she never complained, but she did feel a little bit worried in the beginning."

"Have you a mission or a church here in Norwich?"

"No, I don't believe in churches."

"Not in churches?"

"No. The sight of a minister preaching the word of God for so much a year is all a mockery to me."

"What do you believe in?"

"Personal service. Churches and charitable institutions and societies are all valueless. You can't reach your fellowman that way. They build up buildings and pay salaries—but there's a better way." (I was thinking of St. Francis and his original dream, before they threw him out and established monasteries and a costume or uniform—the thing he so much objected to.) "This giving of a few old clothes that the moths will get anyhow, that won't do. You've got to give something of yourself, and that's affection. Love is the only thing you can really give in all this world. When you give love, you give everything. Everything comes with it in some way or other."

"How do you say?" I queried. "Money certainly comes handy sometimes."

"Yes, when you give it with your own hand and heart—in no other way. It comes to nothing just contributed to some thing. Ah!" he added, with sudden animation, "the tangles men can get themselves into, the snarls, the wretchedness! Troubles with women, with men whom they owe, with evil things they say and think, until they can't walk down the street any more without peeping about to see if they are followed. They can't look you in the face; can't walk a straight course, but have got to sneak around corners. Poor, miserable, unhappy—they're worrying and crying and dodging one another!"

He paused, lost in contemplation of the picture he had conjured up.

"Yes," I went on catechistically, determined, if I could, to rout out this matter of giving, this actual example of the modus operandi of Christian charity. "What do you do? How do you get along without giving them money?"

"I don't get along without giving them some money. There are cases, lots of them, where a little money is necessary. But, brother, it is so little necessary at times. It isn't always money they want. You can't reach them with old clothes and charity societies," he insisted. "You've got to love them, brother. You've got to go to them and love them, just as they are, scarred and miserable and bad-hearted."

"Yes," I replied doubtfully, deciding to follow this up later. "But just what is it you do in a needy case? One instance?"

"Why, one night I was passing a little house in this town," he went on, "and I heard a woman crying. I went right to the door and opened it, and when I got inside she just stopped and looked at me.

"'Madam,' I said, 'I have come to help you, if I can. Now you tell me what you're crying for.'

"Well, sir, you know she sat there and told me how her husband drank and how she didn't have anything in the house to eat, and so I just gave her all I had and told her I would see her husband for her, and the next day I went and hunted him up and said to him, 'Oh, brother, I wish you would open your eyes and see what you are doing. I wish you wouldn't do that any more. It's only misery you are creating.' And, you know, I got to telling about how badly his wife felt about it, and how I intended to work and try and help her, and bless me if he didn't up and promise me before I got through that he wouldn't do that any more. And he didn't. He's working today, and it's been two years since I went to him, nearly."

His eyes were alight with his appreciation of personal service.

"Yes, that's one instance," I said.

"Oh, there are plenty of them," he replied. "It's the only way. Down here in New London a couple of winters ago we had a terrible time of it. That was the winter of the panic, you know. Cold—my, but that was a cold winter, and thousands of people out of work—just thousands. It was awful. I tried to do what I could here and there all along, but finally things got so bad there that I went to the mayor. I saw they were raising some kind of a fund to help the poor, so I told him that if he'd give me a little of the money they were talking of spending that I'd feed the hungry for a cent-and- a-half a meal."

"A cent-and-a-half a meal!"

"Yes, sir. They all thought it was rather curious, not possible at first, but they gave me the money and I fed 'em."

"Good meals?"

"Yes, as good as I ever eat myself," he replied.

"How did you do it?" I asked.

"Oh, I can cook. I just went around to the markets, and told the market-men what I wanted—heads of mackerel, and the part of the halibut that's left after the rich man cuts off his steak—it's the poorest part that he pays for, you know. And I went fishing myself two or three times —borrowed a big boat and got men to help me—oh, I'm a good fisherman, you know. And then I got the loan of an old covered brick-yard that no one was using any more, a great big thing that I could close up and build fires in, and I put my kettle in there and rigged up tables out of borrowed boards, and got people to loan me plates and spoons and knives and forks and cups. I made fish chowder, and fish dinners, and really I set a very fine table, I did, that winter."

"For a cent-and-a-half a meal!"

"Yes, sir, a cent-and-a-half a meal. Ask any one in New London. That's all it cost me. The mayor said he was surprised at the way I did it."

"Well, but there wasn't any particular personal service in the money they gave you?" I asked, catching him up on that point. "They didn't personally serve—those who gave you the money?"

"No, sir, they didn't," he replied dreamily, with unconscious simplicity. "But they gave through me, you see. That's the way it was. I gave the personal service. Don't you see? That's the way."

"Yes, that's the way," I smiled, avoiding as far as possible a further discussion of this contradiction, so unconscious on his part, and in the drag of his thought he took up another idea.

"I clothed 'em that winter, too—went around and got barrels and boxes of old clothing. Some of them felt a little ashamed to put on the things, but I got over that, all right. I was wearing them myself, and I just told them, 'Don't feel badly, brother. I'm wearing them out of the same barrel with you—I'm wearing them out of the same barrel.' Got my clothes entirely free for that winter."

"Can you always get all the aid you need for such enterprises?"

"Usually, and then I can earn a good deal of money when I work steadily. I can get a hundred and fifty dollars for a little yacht, you know, every time I find time to make one; and I can make a good deal of money out of fishing. I went out fishing here on the Fourth of July and caught two hundred blackfish—four and five pounds, almost, every one of them."

"That ought to be profitable," I said.

"Well, it was," he replied.

"How much did you get for them?"

"Oh, I didn't sell them," he said. "I never take money for my work that way. I gave them all away."

"What did you do?" I asked, laughing— "advertise for people to come for them?"

"No. My wife took some, and my daughters, and I took the rest and we carried them around to people that we thought would like to have them."

"Well, that wasn't so profitable, was it?" I commented amusedly.

"Yes, they were fine fish," he replied, not seeming to have heard me.

We dropped the subject of personal service at this point, and I expressed the opinion that his service was only a temporary expedient. Times changed, and with them, people. They forgot. Perhaps those he aided were none the better

"I know what you mean," he said. "But that don't make any difference. You just have to keep on giving, that's all, see? Not all of 'em turn back. It helps a lot. Money is the only dangerous thing to give—but I never give money—not very often. I give myself, rather, as much as possible. I give food and clothing, too, but I try to show 'em a new way— that's not money, you know. So many people need a new way. They're looking for it often, only they don't seem to know how. But God, dear brother, however poor or mean they are—He knows. You've got to reach the heart, you know, and I let Him help me. You've got to make a man over in his soul, if you want to help him, and money won't help you to do that, you know. No, it won't."

He looked up at me in clear-eyed faith. It was remarkable.

"Make them over?" I queried, still curious, for it was all like a romance, and rather fantastic to me. "What do you mean? How do you make them over?"

"Oh, in their attitude, that's how. You've got to change a man and bring him out of self-seeking if you really want to make him good. Most men are so tangled up in their own errors and bad ways, and so worried over their seekings, that unless you can set them to giving it's no use. They're always seeking, and they don't know what they want half the time. Money isn't the thing. Why, half of them wouldn't understand how to use it if they had it. Their minds are not bright enough. Their perceptions are not clear enough. All you can do is to make them content with themselves. And that, giving to others will do. I never saw the man or the woman yet who couldn't be happy if you could make them feel the need of living for others, of doing something for somebody besides themselves. It's a fact. Selfish people are never happy."

He rubbed his hands as if he saw the solution of the world's difficulties very clearly, and I said to him:

"Well, now, you've got a man out of the mire, and 'saved,' as you call it, and then what? What comes next?"

"Well, then he's saved," he replied. "Happiness comes next—content."

"I know. But must he go to church, or conform to certain rules?"

"No, no, no!" he replied sweetly. "Nothing to do except to be good to others." "True religion and undefiled before our God and Father is this," he quoted, "to visit the widow and the orphan in their affliction and to keep unspotted from the world. Charity is kind," you know. 'Charity vaunteth not itself, is not puffed up, seeketh not its own.'"

"Well," I said, rather aimlessly, I will admit, for this high faith staggered me. (How high! How high!) "And then what?"

"Well, then the world would come about. It would be so much better. All the misery is in the lack of sympathy one with another. When we get that straightened out we can work in peace. There are lots of things to do, you know."

Yes, I thought, looking down on the mills and the driving force of self-interest—on greed, lust, love of pleasure, all their fantastic and yet moving dreams.

"I'm an ignorant man myself, and I don't know all," he went on, "and I'd like to study. My, but I'd like to look into all things, but I can't do it now. We can't stop until this thing is straightened out. Some time, maybe," and he looked peacefully away.

"By the way," I said, "whatever became of the man to whom you gave your rubber boots over on Fishers Island?"

His face lit up as if it were the most natural thing that I should know about it.

"Say," he exclaimed, in the most pleased and confidential way, as if we were talking about a mutual friend, "I saw him not long ago. And, do you know, he's a good man now—really, he is. Sober and hard-working.

And, say, would you believe it, he told me that I was the cause of it—just that miserable old pair of rubber boots—what do you think of that?"

I shook his hand at parting, and as we stood looking at each other in the shadow of the evening I asked him:

"Are you afraid to die?"

"Say, brother, but I'm not," he returned. "It hasn't any terror for me at all. I'm just as willing. My, but I'm willing."

He smiled and gripped me heartily again, and, as I was starting to go, said:

"If I die tonight, it'll be all right. He'll use me just as long as He needs me. That I know. Good-by."

"Good-by," I called back.

He hung by his fence, looking down upon the city. As I turned the next corner I saw him awakening from his reflection and waddling stolidly back into the house.

THE VILLAGE FEUDISTS

By Theodore Dreiser

IN a certain Connecticut fishing-town sometime since, where, besides lobstering, a shipyard and some sail-boat-building there existed the several shops and stores which catered to the wants of those who labored in those lines, there dwelt a groceryman by the name of Elihu Burridge, whose life and methods strongly point the moral and social successes and failures of the rural man.

Sixty years of age, with the vanities and desires of the average man's life behind rather than before him, he was at the time not unlike the conventional drawings of Parson Thirdly, which graced the humorous papers of that day. Two moon-shaped eyes, a long upper lip, a mouth like the sickle moon turned downward, prominent ears, a rather long face and a mutton-chop-shaped whisker on either cheek, served to give him that clerical appearance which the humorous artists so religiously seek to depict. Add to this that he was middle-sized, clerically spare in form, reserved and quiet in demeanor, and one can see how he might very readily give the impression of being a minister. His clothes, however, were old, his trousers torn but neatly mended, his little blue gingham jumper which he wore about the store greasy and aged. Everything about him and his store was so still and dark that one might have been inclined on first sight to consider him crusty and morose.

Even more remarkable than himself, however, was his store. I have seen many in my time that were striking because of their neatness; I never saw one before that struck me as more remarkable for its disorder. In the first place it was filled neck-deep with barrels and boxes in the utmost confusion. Dark, greasy, provision-lined alleys led off into dingy sections which the eye could not penetrate. Old signs hung about, advertising things which had long since ceased to sell and were forgotten by the public. There were pictures in once gilt but now time-blackened frames, wherein queerly depicted children and pompous-looking grocers offered one commodity and another, all now almost obliterated by fly-specks. Shelves were marked on the walls by signs now nearly illegible. Cobwebs hung thickly from corners and pillars. There were oil, lard, and a dust-laden scum of some sort on three of the numerous scales with which he occasionally weighed things and on many exteriors of once salable articles. Pork, lard, molasses, and nails were packed in different corners of the place in barrels. Lying about were household utensils, ship-rigging, furniture and a hundred other things which had nothing to do with the grocery business.

As I entered the store the first afternoon I noticed a Bible open at Judges and a number of slips of paper on which questions had been written. On my second visit for oil and vinegar, two strangers from off a vagrant yacht which had entered the little harbor nudged one another and demanded to know whether either had ever seen anything like it. On the third, my companion protested that it was not clean, and seeing that there were other stores we decided to buy our things elsewhere. This was not so easily accomplished.

"Where can I get a flatiron?" I inquired at the Post Office when I first entered the village.

"Most likely at Burridge's," was the reply.

"Do you know where I can get a pair of row-locks?" I asked of a boy who was lounging about the town dock.

"At Burridge's," he replied.

When we wanted oars, pickles of a certain variety, golden syrup, and a dozen other things which were essential at times, we were compelled to go to Burridge's, so that at last he obtained a very fair portion of our trade despite the condition of his store.

During all these earlier dealings there cropped up something curt and dry in his conversation. One day we lost a fruit jar which he had loaned, and I took one very much like it back in its place. When I began to apologize he interrupted me with, "A jar's a jar, isn't it?"

Another time, when I remarked in a conciliatory tone that he owed me eight cents for a can of potted ham which had proved stale, he exclaimed, "Well, I won't owe you long," and forthwith pulled the money out of the loose jacket of his jumper and paid me.

I inquired one day if a certain thing were good. "If it isn't," he replied, with a peculiar elevation of the eyebrows, "your money is. You can have that back."

"That's the way you do business, is it?"

"Yes, sir," he replied, and his long upper lip thinned out along the line of the lower one like a vise.

I was in search of a rocking-chair one day and was directed to Burridge's as the only place likely to have any!

"Do you keep furniture?" I inquired.

"Some," he said.

"Have you a rocking-chair?"

"No, sir."

A day or two later I was in search of a table and on going to Burridge's found that he had gone to a neighboring city.

"Have you got a table?" I inquired of the clerk.

"I don't know," he replied. "There's some furniture in the back room, but I don't know as I dare to sell any of it while he's away."

"Why?"

"Well, he don't like me to sell any of it. He's kind of queer that way I dunno what he intends to do with it. Gar!" he added in a strangely electric way, "he's a queer man! He's got a lot of things back there—chairs and tables and everything. He's got a lot more in a loft up the street here. He never seems to want to sell any of 'em. Heard him tell people he didn't have any."

I shook my head in puzzled desperation.

"Come on, let's go back and look anyway. There's no harm in seeing if he has one."

We went back and there amid pork and molasses barrels, old papers, boxes and signs, was furniture in considerable quantity—tables, rocking-chairs, washstands, bureaus—all cornered and tumbled about.

"Why, here are rocking-chairs, lots of them," I exclaimed. "Just the kind I want! He said he didn't have any."

"Gar! I dunno," replied the clerk. "Here's a table, but I wouldn't dare sell it to you."

"Why should he say he didn't have a rocking-chair?"

"Gar! I dunno. He's goin' out of the furniture business. He don't want to sell any. I don't know what he intends to do with it."

"Well," I said in despair, "what about the table? You can sell that, can't you?"

"I couldn't—not till he comes back. I don't know what he'd want to do about it."

"What's the price of it?"

"I dunno. He could tell you."

I went out of the thick-aired stuffy backroom with its unwashed windows, and when I got opposite the Bible near the door I said:

"What's the matter with him anyhow? Why doesn't he straighten things out here?"

Again the clerk awoke. "Huh!" he exclaimed. "Straighten it out! Gar! I'd like to see anybody try it."

"It could be," I said encouragingly.

"Gar!" he chuckled. "One man did try to straighten it out once when Mr. Burridge was away. Got about a third of it cleaned up when he come back. Gar! You oughta seen him! Gar!"

"What did he do?"

"What did he do! What didn't he do! Gar! Just took things an' threw them about again. Said he couldn't find anything."

"You don't say!"

"Gar! I should say so! Man come in an' asked for a hammer. Said he couldn't find any hammer, things was so mixed up. Did it with screws, water-buckets an' everything just the same. Took 'em right off the shelves, where they was all in groups, an' scattered 'em all over the room. Gar! 'Now I guess I can find something when I want it,' he said." The clerk paused to squint and add, "There ain't anybody tried any straightenin' out around here since then, you bet. Gar!"

"How long ago has that been?"

"About fourteen years now."

Surprised by this sharp variation from the ordinary standards of trade, I began thinking of possible conditions which had produced it, when one evening I happened in on the local barber. He was a lean, inquisitive individual with a shock of sandy hair and a conspicuous desire to appear a well-rounded social factor.

"What sort of person is this Burridge over here? He keeps such a peculiar store."

"Elihu is a bit peculiar," he replied, his smile betraying a desire to appear conservative. "The fault with Elihu, if he has one, is that he's terribly strong on religion. Can't seem to agree with anybody around here."

"What's the trouble?" I asked.

"It's more'n I could ever make out, what is the matter with him. They're all a little bit cracked on the subject around here. Nothing but revivals and meetin's, year in and year out. They're stronger on it winters than they are in summer."

"How do you mean?"

"Well, they'll be more against yachtin' and Sunday pleasures when they can't go than when they can."

"What about Elihu?" I asked.

"Well, he can't seem to get along, somehow. He used to belong to the Baptist Church, but he got out o' that. Then he went to a church up in Graylock, but he had a fallin' out up there. Then he went to Northfield and Eustis. He's been all around, even over on Long Island. He goes to church up at Amherst now, I believe."

"What seems to be the trouble?"

"Oh, he's just strong-headed, I guess." He paused, and ideas lagged until finally I observed:

"It's a very interesting store he keeps."

"It's just as Billy Drumgold told him once: 'Burridge,' he says, 'you've got everything in this store that belongs to a full-rigged ship 'cept one thing.' 'What's that?' Burridge asks. 'A second-hand pulpit.' 'Got that too,' he answered, and takes him upstairs, and there he had one sure enough."

"Well," I said, "what was he doing with it?"

"Danged if I know. He had it all right. Has it yet, so they say."

Days passed and as the summer waned the evidences of a peculiar life accumulated. Noank, apparently, was at outs with Burridge on the subject of religion, and he with it. There were instances of genuine hard feeling against him.

Writing a letter in the Post Office one day I ventured to take up this matter with the postmaster.

"You know Mr. Burridge, don't you—the grocer?"

"Well, I should guess I did," he replied with a flare.

"Anything wrong with him?"

"Oh, about everything that's just plain cussed—the most wrangling man alive. I never saw such a man. He don't get his mail here no more because he's mad at me, I guess. Took it away because I had Mr. Palmer's help in my fight, I suppose. Wrote me that I should send all his mail up to Mystic, and he goes there three or four miles out of his way every day, just to spite me. It's against the law. I hadn't ought to be doing it, re-ad-dressing his envelopes three or four times a day, but I do do it. He's a strong-headed man, that's the trouble with Elihu."

I had no time to follow this up then, but a little later, sitting in the shop of the principal sailboat maker, which was situated in the quiet little lane which follows the line of the village, I was one day surprised by the sudden warm feeling which the name of Elihu generated. Something had brought up the subject of religion, and I said that Burridge seemed rather religious.

"Yes," said the sailboat maker quickly, "he's religious, all right, only he reads the Bible for others, not for himself."

"What do you mean by that?"

"Why, he wants to run things, that's what. As long as you agree with Elihu, why, everything's all right. When you don't, the Bible's against you. That's the way he is."

"Did he ever disagree with you?" I asked, suspecting some personal animus in the matter.

"Me and Elihu was always good friends as long as I agreed with him," he went on bitterly. "We've been raised together, man and boy, for pretty near sixty years. We never had a word of any kind but what was friendly, as long as I agreed with him, but just as soon as I didn't he took a set against me, and we ain't never spoke a word since."

"What was the trouble?" I inquired sweetly, anxious to come at the kernel of this queer situation.

"Well," he said, dropping his work and looking up to impress me, "I'm a man that'll sometimes say what I don't believe; that is, I'll agree with what I hadn't ought to, just to be friendly like. I did that way a lot o' times with Elihu till one day he came to me with something about particular salvation. I'm a little more liberal myself. I believe in universal redemption by faith alone. Well, Elihu came to me and began telling me what he believed. Finally he asked me something about particular salvation and wanted to know whether I didn't agree with him. I didn't, and told him so. From that day on he took a set against me, and he ain't never spoke a word to me since."

I was unaware that there was anything besides a religious disagreement in this local situation until one day I happened to come into a second friendly contact with the postmaster. We were speaking of the characteristics of certain individuals, and I mentioned Burridge.

"He's all right when you take him the way he wants to be taken. When you don't you'll find him quite a different man."

"He seems to be straightforward and honest," I said.

"There ain't anything you can tell me about Elihu Burridge that I don't know," he replied feelingly. "Not a thing. I've lived with him, as you might say, all my life. Been raised right here in town with him, and we went to school together. Man and boy, there ain't ever been a thing that Elihu has agreed with, without he could have the running of it. You can't tell me anything about him that I don't know."

I could not help smiling at the warmth of feeling, although something about the man's manner bespoke a touch of heartache, as if he were privately grieving.

"What was the trouble between you two?" I asked.

"It's more'n I could ever find out," he replied in a voice that was really mournful, so difficult and non-understandable was the subject to him. "Before I started to work for this office there wasn't a day that I didn't meet and speak friendly with Elihu. He used to have a good many deeds and papers to sign, and he never failed to call me in when I was passing. When I started to work for this office I noticed he took on a cold manner toward me, and I tried to think of something I might have done, but I couldn't. Finally I wrote and asked him if there was anything between us if he wouldn't set a time and place so's we might talk it over and come to an understanding." He paused and then added, "I wish you could see the letter he wrote me. Comin' from a Christian man—from him to me—I wish you could see it."

"Why don't you show it to me?" I asked inquisitively.

He went back into the office and returned with an ancient-looking document, four years old it proved to be, which he had been treasuring. He handed me the thumbed and already yellowed page, and I read:

"MATTHEW HOLCOMB, ESQUIRE,

"DEAR SIR:—In reply to your letter asking me to set a time and place in which we might talk over the trouble between us, would say that the time be Eternity and the place where God shall call us to judgment.

"Very truly,

"ELIHU BURRIDGE."

His eyes rested on me while I read, and the moment I finished he began with:

"I never said one word against that man, not one word. I never did a thing he could take offense at, not one thing. I don't know how a man can justify himself writing like that."

"Perhaps it's political" I said. "You don't belong to the same party, do you?"

"Yes, we do," he said. "Sometimes I've thought that maybe it was because I had the support of the shipyard when I first tried to get this office, but then that wasn't anything between him and me," and he looked away as if the mystery were inexplicable.

This shipyard was conducted by a most forceful man but one as narrow and religionistic as this region in which it had had its rise. Old Mr. Palmer, the aged founder of it, had long been a notable figure in the streets and private chambers of the village. The principal grocery store, coal-yard, sail-loft, hotel and other institutions were conducted in its interests. His opinion was always foremost in the decision of the local authorities. He was still, reticent, unobtrusive. Once I saw him most considerately helping a cripple up the lane to the local Baptist Church.

"What's the trouble between Burridge and Palmer?" I asked of the sail-maker finally, coming to think that here, if anywhere, lay the solution of the difficulty.

"Two big fish in too small a basket," he responded laconically.

"Can't agree, eh?"

"They both want to lead, or did," he said. "Elihu's a beaten man, though, now." He paused and then added, "I'm sorry for Elihu. He's a good man at heart, one of the kindest men you ever saw, when you let him follow his natural way. He's good to the poor, and he's carried more slow-pay people than any man in this country, I do believe. He won't collect an old debt by law. Don't believe in it. No, sir. Just a kind-hearted man, but he loves to rule."

"How about Palmer?" I inquired.

"Just the same way exactly. He loves to rule, too. Got a good heart, too, but he's got a lot more money than Elihu and so people pay more attention to him, that's all. When Elihu was getting the attention he was just the finest man you ever saw, kind, generous, good-natured. People love to be petted, at least some people do—you know they do. When you don't pet 'em they get kind o' sour and crabbed like. Now that's all that's the matter with Elihu, every bit of it. He's sour, now, and a little lonely, I expect. He's drove away every one from him, or nearly all, 'cept his wife and some of his kin. Anybody can do a good grocery business here, with the strangers off the boats" —the harbor was a lively one— "all you have to do is carry a good stock. That's why he gets along so well. But he's drove nearly all the local folks away from him."

I listened to this comfortable sail-loft sage, and going back to the grocery store one afternoon took another look at the long, grim-faced silent figure. He was sitting in the shadow of one of his moldy corners, and if there had ever been any light of merriment in his face it was not there now. He looked as fixed and solemn as an ancient puritan, and yet there was something so melancholy in the man's eye, so sad and disappointed, that it seemed anything but hard. Two or three little children were playing about the door and when he came forward to wait on me one of them sidled forward and put her chubby hand in his.

"Your children?" I asked, by way of reaching some friendly understanding.

"No," he replied, looking fondly down, "she belongs to a French lady up the street here. She often comes down to see me, don't you?"

and he reached over and took the fat little cheek between his thumb and forefinger.

The little one rubbed her face against his worn baggy trousers' leg and put her arm about his knee. Quietly he stood there in a simple way until she loosened her hold upon him, when he went about his labor.

I was sitting one day in the loft of the comfortable sail- maker, who, by the way, was brother-in-law to Burridge, when I said to him:

"I wish you'd tell me the details about Elihu. How did he come to be what he is? You ought to know; you've lived here all your life. "

"So I do know," he replied genially. "What do you want me to tell you?"

"The whole story of the trouble between him and Palmer; how he comes to be at outs with all these people."

"Well," he began, and here followed with many interruptions and side elucidations, which for want of space have been eliminated, the following details:

Twenty-five years before Elihu had been the leading citizen of Noank. From operating a small grocery at the close of the Civil War he branched out until he sold everything from ship- rigging to hardware. Noank was then in the height of its career as a fishing town and as a port from which expeditions of all sorts were wont to sail. Whaling was still in force, and vessels for whaling expeditions were equipped here. Wealthy sea-captains frequently loaded fine three-masted schooners here for various trading expeditions to all parts of the world; the fishers for mackerel, cod and herring were making three hundred and fifty dollars a day in season, and thousands of dollars' worth of supplies were annually purchased here.

Burridge was then the only tradesman of any importance and, being of a liberal, strong-minded and yet religious turn, attracted the majority of this business to him. He had houses and lands, was a deacon in the local Baptist Church and a counselor in matters political, social and religious, whose advice was seldom rejected. Every Fourth of July during these years it was his custom to collect all the children of the town in front of his store and treat them to ice-cream. Every Christmas Eve he traveled about the streets in a wagon, which carried half a dozen barrels of candy and nuts, which he would ladle out to the merry shouting throng of pursuing youngsters, until all were satisfied. For the skating season he prepared a pond, spending several thousand dollars damming up a small stream, in order that the children might have a place to skate. He created a library where all might obtain suitable reading, particularly the young.

On New Year's morning it was his custom to visit all the poor and bereaved and lonely in Noank, taking a great dray full of presents and leaving a little something with his greetings and a pleasant handshake at every door. The lonely rich as well as the lonely poor were included, for he was certain, as he frequently declared, that the rich could be lonely too.

He once told his brother-in-law that one New Year's Day a voice called to him in church: "Elihu Burridge, how about the lonely rich and poor of Noank?" "Up I got," he concluded, " and from that day to this I have never neglected them."

When any one died who had a little estate to be looked after for the benefit of widows or orphans, Burridge was the one to take charge of it. People on their deathbeds sent for him, and he always responded, taking energetic charge of everything and refusing to take a penny for his services. After a number of years the old judge to whom he always repaired with these matters of probate, knowing his generosity in this respect, also refused to accept any fee. When he saw him coming he would exclaim:

"Well, Elihu, what is it this time? Another widow or orphan that we've got to look after?"

After Elihu had explained what it was, he would add:

"Well, Elihu, I do hope that some day some rich man will call you to straighten out his affairs. I'd like to see *you* get a little something, so that

I might get a little something. Eh, Elihu?" Then he would jocularly poke his companion in charity in the ribs.

These general benefactions were continuous and coeval with his local prosperity and dominance, and their modification as well as the man's general decline the result of the rise of this other individual— Robert Palmer,— "operating" to take the color of power and preeminence from him.

Palmer was the owner of a small shipyard here at the time, a thing which was not much at first but which grew swiftly. He was born in Noank also, a few years before Burridge, and as a builder of vessels had been slowly forging his way to a moderate competence when Elihu was already successful. He was a keen, fine-featured, energetic individual, with excellent commercial and strong religious instincts, and by dint of hard labor and a saving disposition he obtained, soon after the Civil War, a powerful foothold. Many vessels were ordered here from other cities. Eventually he began to build barges in large numbers for a great railroad company.

Early becoming a larger employer of labor than any one else in the vicinity he soon began to branch out, possessed himself of the allied industries of ship-rigging, chandlering, and finally established a grocery store for his employees, and opened a hotel. Now the local citizens began to look upon him as their leading citizen. They were always talking of his rise, frequently in the presence of Burridge. He said nothing at first, pretending to believe that his quondam leadership was unimpaired. Again, there were those who, having followed the various branches of labor which Palmer eventually consolidated, viewed this growth with sullen and angry eyes. They still sided with Burridge, or pretended still to believe that he was the more important citizen of the two. In the course of time, however—a period of thirty years or more—some of them failed; others died; still others were driven away for want of a livelihood. Only Burridge's position and business remained, but in a sadly weakened state. He was no longer a man of any great importance.

Not unnaturally, this question of local supremacy was first tested in the one place in which local supremacy is usually tested—the church where they both worshiped. Although only one of five trustees, Burridge had been the will of the body. Always, whatever he thought, the others had almost immediately agreed to it. But now that Palmer had become a power, many of those ardent in the church and beholden to him for profit became his humble followers. They elected him trustee and did what he wished, or what they thought he wished. To Burridge this made them sycophants, slaves.

Now followed the kind of trivialities by which most human feuds are furthered. The first test of strength came when a vagrant evangelist from Alabama arrived and desired to use the church for a series of evening lectures. The question had to be decided at once. Palmer was absent at the time.

"Here is a request for the use of the church," said one of the trustees, explaining its nature.

"Well," said Burridge, "you'd better let him have it."

"Do you think we ought to do anything about it," the trustee replied, "until Mr. Palmer returns?"

Although Burridge saw no reason for waiting, the other trustees did, and upon that the board rested. Burridge was furious. By one fell stroke he was put in second place, a man who had to await the return of Palmer —and that in his own church, so to speak.

"Why," he told some one, "the rest of us are nothing. This man is a king."

From that time on differences of opinion within the church and elsewhere were common. Although no personal animosity was ever admitted, local issues almost invariably found these two men opposed to each other. There was the question of whether the village should be made into a borough—a most trivial matter; another, that of creating public works for the manufacture of gas and distribution of water; a third, that of naming a State representative. Naturally, while these things might be to the advantage of Palmer or not, they were of no great import to Burridge, but yet he managed to see in them an attempt or attempts to saddle a large public debt upon widows and orphans, those who could not afford or did not need these things, and he proceeded to so express himself at various public meetings. Slowly the breach widened. Burridge became little more than a malcontent in many people's eyes. He was a "knocker," a man who wanted to hold the community back.

Although defeated in many instances he won in others, and this did not help matters any. At this point, among other things the decay of the fishing industry helped to fix definitely the position of the two men as that of victor and vanquished. Whaling died out, then mackerel and cod were caught only at farther and farther distances from the town, and finally three- and even two-masted schooners ceased entirely to buy their outfits here, and Burridge was left dependent upon local patronage or smaller harbor trade for his support. Coextensively, he had the dissatisfaction of seeing Palmer's industries grow until eventually three hundred and fifty men were upon his payrolls and even his foremen and superintendents were considered influential townspeople. Palmer's son and two daughters grew up and married, branched out and became owners of industries which had formerly belonged to men who had traded with Burridge. He saw his grocery trade dwindle and sink, while with age his religiosity grew, and he began to be little more than a petty disputant, one constantly arguing as to whether the interpretation of the Bible as handed down from the pulpit of what he now considered *his* recalcitrant church was sound or not. When those who years before had followed him obediently now pricked him with theological pins and ventured to disagree with him, he was quick and sometimes foolish in his replies. Thus, once a former friend and fellow-church-member who had gone over to the opposition came into his store one morning and said:

"Elihu, for a man that's as strong on religion as you are, I see you do one thing that can't quite be justified by the Book."

"What's that?" inquired Burridge, looking up.

"I see you sell tobacco."

"I see you chew it," returned the host grimly.

"I know I do," returned his visitor, "but I'll tell you what I'll do, Elihu. If you'll quit selling, I'll quit chewing it," and he looked as if he had set a fancy trap for his straw-balancing brother, as he held him to be.

"It's a bargain," said Burridge on the instant. "It's a bargain!"

And from that day on tobacco was not offered for sale in that store, although there was a large local demand for it.

Again, in the pride of his original leadership, he had accepted the conduct of the local cemetery, a thing which was more a burden than a source of profit. With his customary liberality in all things reflecting credit upon himself he had spent his own money in improving it, much more than ever the wardens of the church would have thought of returning to him. In one instance, when a new receiving vault was desired, he had added seven hundred dollars of his own to three hundred gathered by the church trustees for the purpose, and the vault was immediately constructed. Frequently also, in his pride of place, he had been given to asserting he was tired of conducting the cemetery and wished he could resign.

In these later evil days, therefore, the trustees, following the star of the newer power, saw fit to intimate that perhaps some one else would be glad to look after it if he was tired of it. Instantly the fact that he could no longer boast as formerly came home to him. He was not essential any longer in anything. The church did not want him to have a hand in any of its affairs! The thought of this so weighed on him that eventually he resigned from this particular task, but thereafter also every man who had concurred in accepting his resignation was his bitter enemy. He spoke acidly of the seven hundred he had spent, and jibed at the decisions of the trustees in other matters. Soon he became a disturbing element in the church, taking a solemn vow never to enter the graveyard again, and not long after resigned all his other official duties—passing the plate, et cetera—although he still attended services there.

Decoration Day rolled around, the G.A.R. Post of which he was an ardent member prepared for the annual memorial services over the graves of its dead comrades. Early on the morning of the thirtieth of May they gathered before their lodge hall, Burridge among them, and after arranging the details marched conspicuously to the cemetery where the placing of the wreaths and the firing of the salute were to take place. No one thought of Burridge until the gate was reached, when, gun over shoulder and uniform in perfect trim, he fell conspicuously out of line and marched away home alone. It was the cemetery he had vowed not to enter, his old pet and protégé.

Men now looked askance at him. He was becoming queer, no doubt of it, not really sensible—or was he? Up in Northfield, a nearby town, dwelt a colonel of the Civil War who had led the very regiment of which Burridge was a member but who during the war had come into serious difficulty through a tangle of orders, and had been dishonorably discharged. Although wounded in one of the engagements in which the regiment had distinguished itself, he had been allowed to languish almost forgotten for years and finally, failing to get a pension, had died in poverty. On his deathbed he had sent for Burridge, and reminding him of the battle in which he had led him asked that after he was gone, for the sake of his family, he would take up the matter of a pension and if possible have his record purged of the stigma and the pension awarded.

Burridge agreed most enthusiastically. Going to the local congressman, he at once began a campaign, but because of the feeling against him two years passed without anything being done. Later he took up the matter in his own G.A.R. Post, but there also failing to find the measure of his own enthusiasm, he went finally direct to one of the senators of the State and laying the matter before him had the records examined by Congress and the dead colonel honorably discharged.

One day thereafter in the local G.A.R. he commented unfavorably upon the indifference which he deemed had been shown.

"There wouldn't have been half so much delay if the man hadn't been a deserter," said one of his enemies—one who was a foreman in Palmer's shipyard.

Instantly Burridge was upon his feet, his eyes aflame with feeling. Always an orator, with a strangely declamatory style he launched into a detailed account of the late colonel's life and services, his wounds, his long sufferings and final death in poverty, winding up with a vivid word picture of a battle (Antietam), in which the colonel had gallantly captured a rebel flag and come by his injury.

When he was through there was great excitement in the Post and much feeling in his favor, but he rather weakened the effect by at once demanding that the traitorous words be withdrawn, and failing to compel this, preferred charges against the man who had uttered them and attempted to have him court-martialed.

So great was the bitterness engendered by this that the Post was now practically divided, and being unable to compel what he considered justice he finally resigned. Subsequently he took issue with his former fellow-soldiers in various ways, commenting satirically on their church regularity and professed Christianity, as opposed to their indifference to the late colonel, and denouncing in various public conversations the double-mindedness and sharp dealings of the "little gods," as he termed those who ran the G.A.R. Post, the church, and the shipyards.

Not long after his religious affairs reached a climax when the minister, once a good friend of his, following the lead of the dominant star, Mr. Palmer, publicly denounced him from the pulpit one Sunday as an enemy of the church and of true Christianity!

"There is a man in this congregation," he exclaimed in a burst of impassioned oratory, "who poses as a Christian and a Baptist, who is in his heart's depth the church's worst enemy. Hell and all its devils could have no worse feelings of evil against the faith than he, and he doesn't sell tobacco, either !"

The last reference at once fixed the identity of the person, and caused Burridge to get up and leave the church. He pondered over this for a time, severed his connections with the body, and having visited Graylock one Sunday drove there every Sabbath thereafter, each time going to a different church. After enduring this for six months he generated a longing for a more convenient meeting-place, and finally allied himself with the Baptist Church of Eustis. Here his anchor might possibly have remained fast had it not been that subtle broodings over his wrongs, a calm faith in the righteousness of his own attitude, and disgust with those whom he saw calmly expatiating upon the doctrines and dogmas of religion in his own town finally caused him to suspect a universal misreading of the Bible. This doubt, together with his own desire for justification according to the Word, finally put the idea in his mind to make a study of the Bible himself. He would read it, he said. He would study Hebrew and Greek, and refer all questionable readings of words and passages back to the original tongue in which it had been written.

With this end in view he began a study of these languages, the importance of the subject so growing upon him that he neglected his business. Day after day he labored, putting a Bible and a Concordance upon a pile of soap-boxes near the door of his store and poring over them between customers, the store meantime taking care of itself. He finally mastered Greek and Hebrew after a fashion, and finding the word "repent" frequently used, and that God had made man in the image of Himself, with a full knowledge of right and wrong, he gravitated toward the belief that therefore his traducers in Noank knew what they were doing, and that before he needed to forgive them—though his love might cover all—they must repent.

He read the Bible from beginning to end with this one feeling subconsciously dominant, and all its loving commands about loving one another, forgiving your brother seventy times seven, loving those that hate you, returning good for evil, selling all that you have and giving it to the poor, were made to wait upon the duty of others to repent. He began to give this interpretation at Eustis, where he was allowed to have a Sunday-school, until the minister came and told him once, "to his face," as the local report ran: "We don't want you here."

Meekly he went forth and, joining a church across the Sound on Long Island, sailed over every Sunday and there advanced the same views until he was personally snubbed by the minister and attacked by the local papers. Leaving there he went to Amherst, always announcing now that he held distinctive views about some things in the Bible and asking the privilege of explaining. In this congregation he was still comfortably at rest when I knew him.

"All sensitiveness," the sail-maker had concluded after his long account. "There ain't anything the matter with Elihu, except that he's piqued and grieved. He wanted to be the big man, and he wasn't."

I was thinking of this and of his tender relationship with children as I had noticed it, and of his service to the late colonel when one day being in the store, I said:

"Do you stand on the Bible completely, Mr. Burridge?"

"Yes, sir," he replied, "I do."

"Believe every word of it to be true?"

"Yes, sir."

"If your brother has offended you, how many times must you forgive him?"

"Seventy times seven."

"Do you forgive your brothers?"

"Yes, sir—if they repent."

"If they repent?"

"Yes, sir, if they repent. That's the interpretation. In Matthew you will find, 'If he repent, forgive him.' "

"But if you don't forgive them, even before they repent," I said, "aren't you harboring enmity?"

"No, sir, I'm not treasuring up enmity. I only refuse to forgive them."

I looked at the man, a little astonished, but he looked so sincere and earnest that I could not help smiling.

THEODORE DREISER

"How do you reconcile that with the command, 'Love one another?' You surely can't love and refuse to forgive them at the same time?"

"I don't refuse to forgive them," he repeated. "If John there," indicating an old man in a sun-tanned coat who happened to be passing through the store at the time, "should do me a wrong—don't care what it was, how great or how vile—if he should come to me and say, 'Burridge, I'm sorry,'" he executed a flashing oratorical move in emphasis, and throwing back his head, exclaimed: "It's gone! It's gone! There ain't any more of it! All gone!"

I stood there quite dumbfounded by his virility, as the air vibrated with his force and feeling. So manifestly was his reading of the Bible colored by the grief of his own heart that it was almost painful to tangle him with it. Goodness and mercy colored all his ideas, except in relation to his one-time followers, those who had formerly been his friends and now left him to himself.

"Do you still visit the poor and the afflicted, as you once did?" I asked him once.

"I'd rather not say anything about that," he replied sternly.

"But do you?"

"Yes, sir."

"Still make your annual New Year round?"

"Yes, sir."

"Well, you'll get your reward for that, whatever you believe."

"I've had my reward," he said slowly.

"Had it?"

"Yes, sir, had it. Every hand that's been lifted to receive the little I had to offer has been my reward."

He smiled, and then said in seemingly the most untimely way:

"I remember once going to a lonely woman here on New Year's Day and taking her a little something—basket of grapes or fruit of some kind it was. I was stopping a minute—never stay long, you know; just run in and say 'Happy New Year!' leave what I have and get out—and so said,

'Good morning, Aunt Mary!'

"'Good morning, Elihu,' says she.

"'Can't stay long, Aunt Mary,' I said. 'Just want to leave you these. Happy New Year!'

"Well, sir, you know I was just turning around and starting when she caught hold of my sleeve and says:

"'Elihu Burridge,' she says, 'give me that hand!' and do you know, before I knew what she was about she took it up to her lips and kissed it! Yes, she did—kissed my hand!

"Now," he said, drawing himself up, with eyes bright with intense feeling, "you know whether I've had my reward or not, don't you?"

A CRIPPLE WHOSE ENERGY GIVES INSPIRATION
(THE NOANK BOY)

By Theodore Dreiser

"There is no excellence without great labor"

Noank is a small, grass-grown fishing town on the southeastern coast of Connecticut,—a little collection of pretty white cottages with green vines and ample shade trees. Years ago it was more important than it is to-day, for then vessels were fitted out there for long cruises into the Arctic Ocean, after whales, and for more certain if less profitable labor off Fishers Island, where mackerel and cod were to be found in abundance. Thousands of dollars were in those days made annually by men who ventured to sea in ships. But the whaling business died out. Mackerel and cod were caught in decreasing quantities. Finally, Noank became rather slow and unimportant, in its fishing ventures, and was compelled to confine itself to the trapping of lobsters. On this industry, and the rising importance of its one ship-building yard, it has existed for years, the drag of great cumulative enterprises in other places in no way disturbing it.

Docks and wharves are now silent. The weatherbeaten buildings which front the water's edge harbor a few old sailors and fishermen, engaged upon drowsy and only slightly profitable labors. Further up the hillside, two grocery stores, a barber shop, a dry goods store and a meat market stand near the public school and the post office. Back of these are lanes lined with white cottages,—lovely, flower-scented pathways where families seem to dwell in perfect quiet.

A friend of mine and myself were sitting on the lawn surrounding the local Baptist church, one morning, discussing the possibilities of life and development in so small and silent a place, when a trivial incident turned the argument to the necessity of doing something to promote the organization and intelligence of the world. A woman appeared upon the side porch of one of the nearby houses and began to knock the nails out of a box, which she was trying to break up for kindling. While she was doing this, she called two or three times and soon a boy, of twelve years came out and took from her the labor of breaking up the kindling. Then she went away and a sixteen-year-old girl came out of the house and sat down. Presently, the older woman returned, leaned against a post, and began criticising the work of the boy. The local meat-market clerk came up and rested a while. Finally a man, the husband, possibly, came around from the rear of the house, and then there were four people idling about the spot where one boy was indifferently laboring.

"There is a good illustration," said my companion. "Five people are trifling away a half-hour of a fine morning, and the whole world is waiting for deliverance from a thousand difficulties."

"Yes, indeed, there is endless labor to be done. Yet, if you should go to these people and ask them why they don't do something, they would tell you that there isn't anything to do in Noank."

"'Tell you,'—they have told me. The boy in the meat market told me, only yesterday, that there is no chance for anyone in Noank."

"I saw a lot of signs which tell much the same story; one in front of the post office, another in front of the public school, and one in the local fire house, reading, 'No loafing here.'"

"Yes," replied my companion, "there seems to be a great complaint on the part of the few merchants against those who think there is nothing to do. At least they try to warn them off their premises by signs."

While we were still pursuing this thought, a thickset, undersized cripple, of perhaps eighteen or nineteen years of age, came briskly down the lane which bordered the outer edge of the churchyard, and hurried up to the back entrance of the fire house next door. At first glance, he was rather commonplace-looking in his worn, baggy trousers; but a quick, sharp glance thrown our way, and a short return to his own thoughts, whatever they were, served to hold conjecture in abeyance. He went briskly to the door, unlocked it, entered, and threw open the windows. Soon he began moving the chairs about, and a few minutes later he was seen carefully sweeping the office of the fire house.

"There's the caretaker of that institution," said my companion.

"Yes, you'll usually find one boy, in a village of this sort, who works."

"It's curious that there shouldn't be more than one."

"It is curious that there aren't more great financiers than there are. There are hundreds of millions of people, but very few of them are doing anything in particular."

We talked on, paying no more attention to the young cripple, who finally came out, closed the door of the building, and hurried down the quiet street.

A day or two later, I was going up the main street from the railroad station, when I met the boy, hobbling energetically along, trundling a wheelbarrow in front of him. The barrow was full of mail sacks, and he was wheeling the load—which was considerable in the hot July sun,—as if it were nothing in particular. I nodded to him and he smiled. I turned, and, going after him, reached the station in time to see him meet a train. There were a half-dozen mail sacks to be taken off and put on, which he did so expeditiously that his crippled hip and foot seemed hardly an impediment. When the train had gone and his wheelbarrow was loaded and being pushed up the hill, toward the post office, I noticed that he was perspiring profusely.

In passing the local schoolhouse, one afternoon, I saw the doors and windows open, and, on espying the young cripple through one of the side windows, I went back and called to him.

"Do you take care of the school building, too?" I inquired.

"Yes, sir," he replied. smiling, "I'm the janitor in winter. I just open it once in a while to let in the fresh air and see that things are in order."

"You carry the mail in Noank, too, don't you?"

"Yes, sir."

"I saw you in the fire house the other morning."

"Yes, I take care of that."

"Anything else?"

"No, nothing in particular. I deliver papers, mornings and evenings."

"What time do you get up?"

"Oh, about six o'clock."

I did not ask about his income, though it occurred to me to do so at the time. But one day, happening to visit the neighboring city, I saw the same boy hobbling rapidly toward the principal wharf, his body fairly weighted with parcels of all sorts. He went down to the dock just in time to catch the local boat for Noank, and seemed in very high spirits. The captain and the crew of the little steamer seemed to know him well; and, after he had deposited his packages in the forward cabin, he came out and began an animated conversation with the former.

"How's marketing to-day?" asked the captain.

"Fair."

"Get all you went for?"

"Pretty nearly."

He talked seriously with his friend about some local matter; and, when he was through and alone, I ventured to say to him:—

"This is one of your occupations you didn't tell me about."

"No," he replied, greeting me pleasantly; "I forgot this. I run errands for people there occasionally."

"Private families?"

"Oh, everybody. They all know me. I get anything for anybody that can't come."

"Have you many other things to do?"

"No others,—that is,—nothing regular. I do odd jobs whenever I can get them."

"I should like to know how much you make out of all your labors," I said.

"Oh, I don't make so very much,—not in the summer time, anyhow. It's better in winter."

"How's that?"

"Well, I am janitor of the school in winter, and that doesn't pay anything during the summer months."

"I saw you working there, though."

"Oh, I take care of it just the same," he replied.

"How much do you get a month for your janitor work?"

"Forty dollars."

"How much does your post office work pay you?"

"Fourteen."

"A week?"

"A month."

"Then you have the fire house to take care of."

"Yes, I get ten dollars a month for that."

"What do you get for your errand-running?"

"Oh, I do that largely as a favor. Sometimes people pay me something, sometimes they don't."

"But you expend railroad fare on it."

"Oh, they pay me enough to bring me a little out of it,—five dollars a month, sometimes."

"What do you earn by selling newspapers?"

"Well, I make about as much out of that, possibly."

He looked at me and smiled, as I began to figure up his income.

"Seventy-five dollars a month!" I exclaimed. "That's pretty good for Noank."

"Yes, but you see I don't make that in summer. I only make about thirty a month until school opens," he said.

"I know," I said; "but, even so, that makes a yearly average of sixty dollars or thereabouts."

"Yes, about that," he said, shrewdly.

"That ought to put you in the way of making a fair income some day," I said.

"I have not seen my way to anything yet," he replied.

I thought of this energy and its curious ramification in a village seemingly so unpromising as Noank.

One afternoon, a company of boys, lounging in the shade of a sail-maker's loft, arrested my attention. They were of about the same age as the crippled mail carrier. All of them were sound in wind and limb. On meeting one and another of these idlers from time to time thereafter, I made it a point to get into conversation with them, and to find out, if possible, what their attitude to their life and surroundings was. One of them, a lounger in the shop of a local sailboat-maker, looked exceedingly disgusted when I asked him what sort of a village Noank is.

"'Tain't much of anything, that anybody could ever find out," he said.

"What do the boys do here when they grow up and want to earn a little money now and then?"

"They don't do anything, unless they get away from this place," he replied.

"That young fellow who carries the mail seems to be making a pretty good living out of it."

"He may," was the reply. "There ain't anybody else that does." Suddenly he brightened and added, "People favor him."

"Why?"

"Well, he's got a game leg."

I smiled at the thought of this being looked upon as an advantage instead of a disadvantage.

"Most people would look upon that as being something against him," I replied.

"Well, they don't around here," he answered.

"How do you expect to get a start?" I asked.

THEODORE DREISER

"Oh, I'll get out of here one of these days," he replied.

"Where do you think you'll go,—to New London."

"I don't know," he said. "I'll go somewhere, though, pretty soon."

Another boy rowed me over to Mystic Island, after I had induced him to by finding a boat free of charge and paying him a quarter.

"Well," I said, "what sort of a town is Noank for a boy to get along in?"

"There ain't anything to do here," he replied.

"Isn't there a chance to get something to do in the shipyards?"

"No," he said, "they don't hire anything but Canucks from up in Canada, who, when they get a dollar and a quarter a day, imagine they're in heaven."

"How much do you think they ought to get?" I asked.

"They ought'n't to get anything,—them fellows. If they didn't come down here, wages would be a lot higher than they are. It's them that's keeping the people around here, that would work, out of jobs."

"Couldn't you go in with them and earn more, if you should deserve it?"

"I wouldn't want to work among them fellows," he replied.

While we were talking, a lobster-trapping vessel went by, and that put me in mind of the endless quantity of free fishing there is in the sea. Anyone can go out into the waters of the bay about there and set a trap or pot for lobsters. Blackfish, porgies, mackerel and cod are still caught in such a helpful order of rotation that no one ever needs to complain of a day in the year when he cannot fish. Blue crabs, round clams, eels and other seafood are plentiful, and may be readily sold in the local market. Lobsters bring ten cents a pound, and codfish four. Blue crabs sell for two cents apiece, and clams at twenty cents a mess, or pailful. Lobster pots can be bought, ready to set, for a dollar each. A boat could be rented for as little as one dollar and twenty-five cents a week.

"Why don't you try fishing?" I asked. "There ought to be a little money in trapping for lobsters, I should think."

[234]

"There is, if you have a big yacht," he said. "There ain't any money in trying for them right around here."

"How about clam-digging?" I inquired.

"There's a bay up there where there's a lot of them," he returned, quickly,—"round clams."

"Why don't you try for them?"

"Well, you could," he said, "but you couldn't get a steady market for them. They're only bought here once in a while."

"Did you ever try to get work on one of the fishing boats?"

"No, they don't pay nothing."

His obvious weariness with local conditions reminded me of the mail carrier, whom I mentioned.

"Yes," he said, "people give him things 'cause he's a cripple."

I received this explanation from several others who could see no opportunities in the prevailing conditions; and, finally, I decided to go to the cripple and ask him how he got his start, and what his intentions as to his future were. Coming out of the post office one day, I encountered him.

"They tell me," I said, "that you have picked up all you have to do in Noank from favoritism. Is that so?"

"I don't know what you mean," he replied. "Is it this work I'm doing? Is that what you mean?"

"Yes," I said, "somebody told me that it was given to you because people wanted to be kind to you."

"Maybe they did," he said, cheerfully; "I don't know. I know I have it to do all right."

"Who got you the job in the post office?" I inquired.

"I did."

"How did you get it?"

"I heard that the man who had it before me was going to resign, and I went and asked for it."

"Was it given to you just on your asking?"

"Well," he said, diffidently, "I offered to do it for a little less than I knew they had been paying the other man."

"How did you get the school janitorship?"

"I applied to the school board."

"Did you go, yourself?"

"Yes, sir."

"Did you get anyone to help you"

"Well, I went to men who knew me, and told them I'd like to have it."

"What about the fire-house work?"

"That was offered to me."

"After you had these other positions" "Yes, sir."

"How did you get the newspaper route?"

"Well, I built that up, myself. There wasn't anyone delivering newspapers here, and so I decided to try to get a few customers if I could."

"And how about the parcel-carrying you do?"

"I did that work just as a favor, in the beginning. I didn't expect anyone to pay me for that."

"Well," I said, "what are you going to do with your money, anyhow?"

"I don't have so very much, after I pay all my expenses. Living is expensive nowadays."

"Expenses?"

"Yes; I live with my family."

I learned, afterwards, that, with his father, who really earned less than the boy, he supported his mother, two sisters, and a younger brother, contributing freely to their maintenance.

"Do you expect to stay in Noank forever?"

"Only until I can get something to do."

"Have you fixed your mind on anything better you would like to do? What is your ambition?"

"Well, I've thought something of the news and book business."

"Where?—In Boston?"

"No, sir, you don't catch me going to Boston,"

"What's the matter with Boston?"

"It isn't business-like enough for me."

"You've been there, have you?"

"Yes, sir."

"How about New York?"

"Well, I wouldn't mind going there, if I could. A person might build up a good business there, if he had a chance."

"How about New London?"

"That's a good town," he said; and, with that keen appreciation of opportunities which makes a successful businessman, he began, in answer to my questions, to dilate in a particular way upon several of its advantages. He knew about all the great manufactories there. He knew its successful men, and of its industries that were likely to develop.

"How do you know all this" I asked.

"I've looked about, some, down there," he replied, sagely.

"What do you think of the opportunities of a boy anywhere?" I inquired.

"O, he can always pick up a little something," he replied. "It isn't always that you can get a start in a town, but you can pick up something."

"Have you any idea what you are going to drift into eventually?"

"I haven't," he said. "What I'm trying to do is to save a little money, just now. When I get that, I don't know what I'll do."

"You won't let it get away from you?"

"I don't know," he replied. "You never can tell,"—but he looked as if he knew better.

I left him, and he went busily about his affairs. During the remainder of my stay, it was always as it had been. Everybody seemed to like him. He was the typical village product of energy.

One day, I said to the leading grocer of the village, a man of considerable energy and commercial ability:—

"What do you suppose will ever become of that cripple that carries the mail? He seems to be a very bright young fellow."

"Oh, he'll get along," he replied. "He's the best boy in town. You can rely on him. He's perfectly honest."

"It's too bad he's so crippled."

"That won't make any difference with him. Everybody knows him. I hear that the general passenger agent of this division is going to make a place for him next year. He's seen him a good many times taking the mail on and off, and I guess he likes him. Other people have spoken to me about him. He'll get along."

"It pays to be energetic, doesn't it?"

"Indeed it does. If a lot more of the boys about here would hustle around a little more, they'd do better. As it is, we've got to put up signs to keep them off our doorsteps. Yes, Harry's a good boy," he concluded. "He's perfectly honest."

QUIRK REVISITED

By Stephen Jones

If you ease down the steep east side of Main Street to the Old Town Landing Place and find yourself a bench in the pocket park at the water's edge, you can look out across the harbor. There, a half-mile to the east, is the subject of this book. The Isle o' Quirk is the one in the middle of the three obvious islands that line up to form the shelter that protects the mooring field. At the moment there are three trees out there, but they remain hostages to weather and, like the cabin in the book, may not be present by the time you arrive.

The village of Noank is almost exactly halfway on the railroad line between New York and Boston at the very eastern end of Long Island Sound. The first recorded settlers were Pequots who used the shore as a fishing camp in the warmer months. Noank is but a shortened kind of white man's grunt left over from a much longer word in the Pequot dialect signifying *neck of land*. While technically a peninsula, Noank is itself, like Quirk and the other harbor islands, a random collection of glacial erratic islands glued together by the combined work of littoral and riverine currents. It is attached to the mainland by a pair of roads over former wetlands, but if the book's two principal characters were to arrive today they might be confused. Neither of the present roads existed in their day and the two that did are now fenced off grade crossings. It is no accident perhaps that the mentality of the locals has often seemed to outsiders somewhat insular.

By the mid 19th-Century the native fishing camp had been cleared out and a new wave of Yankees, followed by Nova Scotians had come to make a living by fishing. Later they built boats to fish further out as they consumed the local stock. In the last decade of the century a few people arrived to merely recreate themselves, ministers and office workers from inland. Such were the people who inhabited another one of the harbor rock piles to the west of Quirk across the anchorage a mile, Mouse Island.

When Dorothy Cramer, the daughter of a Rhode Island accountant, was a little girl at the beginning of the 20th century, the most exciting time of the year was when her family packed up their seaside clothes and moved out to Mouse Island. All winter the island upon which perched three little buildings and three trees, sat out there at the mercy of the storms. The worst weather, of course, was from the east, but Mouse Island was protected from the fetch of the Atlantic by those three companion islands across the harbor, one of which was Quirk.

The largest of the islands across the harbor was known to the locals as Mystic Island, but was and is called on the chart, Ram Island. Like the other land features in the harbor area, Ram Island was made up of a few scattered erratics held together by the sand transport of the littoral. Connected to the big island at extreme low tide were two little, fuzzy rock clumps to the north. These had until recently no names. Then along had come some "people from New York" who camped out on the little island nearest the big one. They would have you believe the name for that island was now "Quirk," and that the one just to the north should by the same whimsy be called "Ahoy." The man from New York had a cabin built on Quirk. He took along two grown women, neither of whom was married to him, but who evidently liked to swim, a pastime in those days not yet accepted as a legitimate activity, especially for those of the gentler gender. Furthermore, he had the audacity to write a book about all this co-cabinating and splashing about. Two decades after he had left, so great was the scandal that little Dorothy was not allowed to look east from Mouse Island.

"This, of course, made me very, very curious," she told me one afternoon some sixty years later. We were standing inside the former Grace Episcopalian Church on Sylvan Street, the new site of the fledgling Noank Historical Society. The fieldstone and timber building was in the first year of its deconsecration and there was still very much the feeling of piety lurking up there in the open rafters. Dorothy was the first official historian of the society and in that capacity she handed me a copy of the scandalous book, called innocently enough *An Island Cabin*. It was by a man with a bland enough name, Arthur Henry. "Of course," she said, "we were all pretty damn curious."

There are two editions of this account of life on Quirk Island. The one Dorothy had put in my hand was her very own, the blue one with the tiny watercolor on the cover reminiscent of the popular Childe Hassam paintings of Maine's Celia Thaxter's 1894 *An Island Garden*. "This is the first edition," she chuckled, "and it came out in 1902, the very same year this church we're in was built."

A former math teacher in a private school, Dorothy herself was central casting's idea of a historical society maven, but her twinkling eye and smoke-weathered alto signaled that in the years since her own island childhood, she'd managed to satisfy at least some of that curiosity. "It's not to everyone's taste," she said, tapping the book.

"Oh?" I flipped it over. The back was blank.

"Some people find it too idyllic."

"Idyllic?"

"Too flowery. Some find it too... well, what we used to call *risqué*."

"Sounds perfect," I said.

"Well, you can give it a try. Dreiser's in it."

"Theodore Drieser? The great American oaf?"

"*American Tragedy*," she said. "*Sister Carrie.*"

"Sure, that guy, the American Dostoyevsky or something... as a novelist up there with Henry James, Fitzgerald, Hemingway. What's he doing in here?" I poked into the book.

"He's called 'Tom,'" she explained. "He and Arthur Henry had been buddies. They weren't really from New York, only recently. Making their move on the big time. They were really Midwesterners on the *Toledo Blade* out in Ohio. As a matter of fact, at the time, Arthur Henry was the more well-known."

"And the women, the two woman who so conspicuously... *bathed*?"

"Actually there were three. Drieser brought his own. And later added a maid, so that all told there were two men and four women."

"And Arthur Henry had *two*?"

"That's what seemed to shock everyone on the mainland."

I held the book a little further away. I could feel the not entirely deconsecrated Episcopal pulses. "Idyllic, eh?"

"Hell," she said, "it's really not that much *hot stuff*. It's just damn interesting about the place in the old days."

And damned interesting it turned out to be and not all that flowery, unless you include poison ivy. As for too idyllic, there's plenty of petty squabbling and in addition to the poison ivy, rats. Far from my glib dismissal of Dreiser, his enormous reputation can perhaps be best summed up by 1995 Merriam-Webster *Encyclopedia of Literature* as a "Novelist who was the outstanding American practitioner of naturalism, [who] led a national literary movement that replaced Victorian propriety with the unflinching presentation of real-life subject matter." Richard Lehan, editor of the Dreiser volume in the canonic The Library of America, says, "Theodore Dreiser is arguably the most important figure in the development of American fiction in [the 20th century]. Lehan quotes H.L. Mencken, America's foremost literary critic of the era, as saying, "American writing before and after [Dreiser's] time, differed almost as much as biology before and after Darwin." As for all those *relationships*, as we'd call them these days... well that's taken some poking into.

PRELIMINARY INVESTIGATIONS

I began this inquiry by obtaining my own copy of *An Island Cabin*. Returning the book to the Noank Historical Society, I was able to find a copy in 1968 up at Charlie Vincent's ramshackle excursion into serendipity, The Old Mystic Bookstore. Since Charlie has died, his shop has been converted into a bed and breakfast, but you can still see the old gentleman, or at least a

Dickensian likeness, swinging from the inn sign opposite the general store at the headwaters of the Mystic River.

"This is the one that caused all that stir down the river," Charlie warned me.

"I'll be careful," I promised.

Charlie's copy was also the March 1902 edition with the painting on the cover. (For years I knew no other. The first seemed miracle enough.) In the back were ads which revealed the literary milieu into which *An Island Cabin* was born: Anthony Hope's sequel to his successful *Prisoner of Zenda*, *Tristam of Blent*; a Booth Tarkington novel, and an exposé on Wall Street featuring "vivid pictures of the cutthroat campaign carried on under the standard of the dollar," a performance which the editors of what we now call the "old (pre-Luce)" *Life* found to be "rattling good tales." Also advertised was the best war around, the struggle in South Africa, the contours of which were limed by none other than Dr. A. Conan Doyle: *The War in South Africa: Its Causes and Conduct* and *The Great Boer War*. Charlie quietly pointed out that it was for Conan Doyle's work in a South African hospital and not the Sherlock Holmes yarns that he had been knighted.

As for the mysteries of the Isle o' Quirk, there were, of course, all sorts of mainland theories down through the years. Robert Palmer "Chip" Anderson told me that some of his relations in previous generations had performed scholarship of the inadvertent genre by means of errant telescope work. "Apparently one couldn't help but pick up some data while scanning the horizon with the family optics."

Even now, I suppose, one of the drills in reading *An Island Cabin* is trying to track just who is swimming on which side of the island wearing what. (Masons Island on the back side of Quirk seems to have no tradition of Quirk ogling, the big island being then largely farmland.) The ocularly ambitious of Noank must have been constantly in a dither.

Arthur Henry's *An Island Cabin*, however, was only half of the literary product of that summer at Quirk. Dreiser himself had published non-fiction on Noank. The editors of *Noank: Celebrating a Maritime Heritage* have salvaged a news item from January 17, 1920. The bland "social notes" tone belies what a half century later seems to be the community's unhappy memory of the Dreiser's literary reception:

LOCAL MEN FIGURE IN BOOK

A book entitled *Twelve Men* by Theodore Dreiser contains much of interest to the villagers, two of the twelve American characters being Noank men. One chapter, "A Doer of the Word" is about Captain Charles T. Potter and the opinion of all who have read it is the story is [a true picture] of a remarkable character. "A Doer of the Word" was first published as a short story. The other chapter of interest to Noank is called "The Village Feudists" and, although the name of the principal character is omitted, he is easily identified by anyone familiar with him in life. Besides these two principals, many other villagers, the most of them dead now, are mentioned. Among them Aaron Main, Robert Palmer Sr. and William Johnson. It will be remembered that Mr. Dreiser spent considerable time in the village some years ago, while the guest of Arthur Henry, the author of *An Island Cabin*, at his home on the Isle of Quirk.

The first serious Isle o' Quirk scholar I ran across was Professor Robert "Bob" Coltrane of Lock Haven University of Pennsylvania. He came into Noank one day seeking information about Dreiser's stay. Coltrane was working for his Ph.D. at Penn State where he had been studying under Professor James L.W. West. As part of a Dreiser revival, West was heading up a virtual Dreiser industry with University of Connecticut Professor Thomas P. Riggio and others to produce a new uniform edition of Dreiser's works. Bob was focused on editing Dreiser's collection of short, non-fiction pieces, *Twelve Men*, which he put into context for me.

Although his focus was on Dreiser, the Professor, I was to pleased to see, had equipped himself with a copy of the second edition of *An Island Cabin*.

It had a grass-cloth cover, and while it lacked the painting of the island, the second edition made up by containing a number of black and white photographs. Professor Coltrane was soft spoken, but his black beard bristled with questions he'd come up with from a fresh scouring of the texts. He was eager to set forth into the no-man's land between literature and life. Most of my own recent time had been spent hanging out with the marine scientists whose laboratory was directly across from Quirk so I had grown into the odd habit of taking field notes when accompanying academics out in the harbor. The account that I sketched out that week of our foray to the island went something like the following—

AN EXCURSION TO THE SITE

We rowed out to the island in a ten foot dinghy before a soft sou'west wind. Judging from the photo in the second edition, our vessel was about the size of Henry's boat. I had not gone clear over there under oars since rowing my kids out ten years before, and even running before the wind the Professor and I quickly came to appreciate the distance. It was not anything you'd brag about, but it was far enough that even in good weather you'd think twice. "It's a respectable distance," said the Professor, "This goes to the book's credibility against those who say it's all exaggerated."

Out on the eel grass flats we moved through the moored fleet of fiberglass. No longer the "picket line" Henry describes, the entire mooring field was saturated with boats. On the far side we were out in the channel again and a twin screw, fly bridge sport fisherman screamed past. We wallowed in its triumph for a moment or two, the Professor clasping a gunnel in each hand as if he might by sheer willpower, still the boat. I rested on the oars until it made sense again to try to put the blades back in the water. We congratulated ourselves on only having shipped a few drops of the harbor.

"That's something Henry and Dreiser never had to contend with," I said.

"No, but they could see it coming." As so did the Professor who refused to unclench his grip and was duly rewarded when another sport churned past us.

"Where is the *brush buoy*?" said the Professor, perhaps hoping that a navigation fix might aid our stability. "He keeps talking about a 'brush buoy.'"

I poked an oar past where we had just been. "I've always suspected it was the oyster ground marker," I said. "There's still a granted ground over there and it goes back to Henry's day. The Malloy family's had it now over fifty years, but small boat sailors are afraid they'll run into the brush marker in the night and rip it up."

The can turning in the tide at the north end of the islands was marked #7. In Henry's day it was #3. "It would seem that the bifurcated channel leading into Noank has been reversed. In Henry's day, the government thought it was wisest to come in this way from the east. Now the numbering begins out in the west branch. I don't know when the thinking changed."

"Is this an important fact in the life of Dreiser?" said the Professor.

"I suppose not," I said. "It wouldn't be anything he or Henry'd notice. In fact Henry never mentions any buoyage except the oyster marker which he doesn't seem to recognize for what it was. To me the reversal of the preferred channel buoyage would indicate which way Noank was thinking of itself: New York and the markets or Boston and the fishing banks."

"I think you're right," said the Professor. "There's clearly a level of detail about maritime Noank which was beyond our two men."

As we approached the northernmost island of the three the Professor let go of the gunnels and gestured. "Now, this must be the one he calls 'Ahoy.'"

"That didn't take," I said. "*Quirk* was ok, at the very edge of tolerance, but *Ahoy*... The best you can salvage is that some people like Dorothy Cramer called it Quick, just as a cutesie paring, sort of a homage to Henry, but even she was somewhat embarrassed by doing that."

I raised the oar blades out of the water and let us glide past. Through the thinning water we could see the yellow-green ribs of an old hull. "Locals say this was the *Ram Island Lightship.* "I paused and the oar blades dripped across the surface. "Captain Ben Rathbun was born right across the harbor here in 1928, and he says she was from down the Sound toward New York. In any case, she had been retired to the breaker's yard back over there in Noank. About all that was left of the old Palmer Yard in the book. One of the hurricanes shifted her over here."

The Professor peered down at the ship's bones and adjusted his spectacles. "There's less of her every time I come out here," I admitted.

He reached over the side and touched the water, but the ribs remained below. "Cold," he said.

The birds were in a fury by now, wheeling and screaming uncomfortably close to our heads. "Herring gulls," I shouted and the Professor nodded.

We landed as gently as we could on the pebbly beach of the middle island and I lifted the bow further up.

"This is not a sanctuary, is it?"

"No, but be careful where you step."

I tossed the anchor just shy of the historic poison ivy. From previous landings I knew that there would be no archeological scraps or shards at the old cabin site as there were on Gates, a comparable islet a half mile to the east where the chimney of a cabin had remained for years. Quirk was chiefly rock and had been washed clean by too many storms even in my time, to say nothing of picnickers beachcombing every little tweak of a potential artifact.

The Professor first wanted to confirm that we had landed on the correct island. I admitted he had a point as even locally there had been much arm waiving about which of the two islands north of Ram had been the site of the infamous cabin. Back in Lock Haven he had familiarized himself with the point in the text where Arthur Henry and his pals are standing on Quirk and talking to the caretaker on Ram Island. (The caretaker had been identified to me by Captain Adrian Lane as a relative of his, one Gilbert "Gibby" Wilcox who, with his wife Nora, wintered at the corner of Main and Riverview. This was the very house I was living in at the time of my talk with Captain Lane. Captain Rathbun remembers Wilcox "as a well known character around the Noank waterfront [in the 1930s]... renowned for his ability to write different words simultaneously with each hand."

Ram was the island most familiar to locals and while mentioned in the book, I agreed that when you met it in person it did seem out of proportion and uncomfortably close if one were trying to make the case for Quirk's isolation. The Professor was clearly disappointed in its proximity. As I tried to explain, the problem is that "Quick" or "Ahoy" do not really exist outside of Henry's book or references to it. Furthermore the two actual hunks of earth are inextricably bound with Ram, not only geographically, but historically. Aside from Henry's book, there is no separate history of the satellite islands, and while the Professor made an effort to assimilate Ram's undeniability, I apologized for its presence by filling him in on its recorded past.

Through the years I'd picked up various bits of information including a wonderful lecture that E.B. Read of Masons Island had delivered to the Noank Historical Society. Louis Allyn of the Mystic River Historical Society later provided me with a transcript of that lecture and another paper Ms. Read had done on the Ram Island light vessels. There was also, of course, Carol Kimball's work originally published as a column in the *New London Day* and later reprinted by Flat Hammock Press. There was Captain Rathbun's diggings in his lighthouse book and interviews at his house on Riverview Avenue which faces the islands across the harbor. These accounts do not always quite match as to specific dates and academic historians of the Noank Harbor islands best go back to the primary sources in *The Stonington Mirror* and the National Archives. Ms. Read has an excellent bibliography at the end of her Ram Island paper. What the Professor and I were interested in was the flavor of the islands and what Henry had put in and left out in his book.

Pequot Indians used the islands as fishing stations in summer until the horrendous atrocity a couple of miles upriver at Mystic in 1637. Near the site of the present Mystic-Noank Library, Englishmen under the command of John Mason, in cahoots with a party of Narragansett Indians, slaughtered some seven hundred Pequots, mostly women and children. With the area now "safe for civilization" as the Daughter of the American Revolution plaque on the old Mason statue once trumpeted, the river mouth islands were ripe for Puritan John Winthrop, Jr. who was awarded the thirty-acre "Ram-Goat Island" upon which the New

London County record says, "he puts his ram goates." In 1769, the African slave later called "Venture Smith" went to Ram Island where he cut enough wood to buy his own two sons out of slavery. (Venture is now an icon of the African American history and the subject of much academic interest by Professor Nancy Steenburg and others). About a decade later a small pox hospital was opened on the island to administer the new inoculations. The doctor in charge was arrested and sent to prison and it wasn't until three years later that small pox inoculation were declared legal. A year after the new law, a different doctor reopened the hospital to give inoculations. The isolated site presumably allowed the mainlanders to relax while they waited to see how the cases worked out while the patients bided their quarantine by fishing.

According to E.B. Read it wasn't until 1881 that the "disposition of the islands in the Sound" was clarified as to the New York-Connecticut border. (Rhode Island is in sight two miles to the east and the border of all three states comes together at what was once was a small island as late as Prohibition. (The 1938 Hurricane put the intersection under water.) By the middle of the 19th-Century Ram Island's Puritan function had been radically altered and even the Temperance picnics seemed gala. The island became the site of a big hotel with a cultivated garden, known as Nawyaug House, later the Mystic Island Hotel.

This was a huge place after the manner of the great 19th-Century "watering holes." Read tells us that there were rooms for 150 guests. The hotel provided lavish "shore suppers," breezy rooms, even a scattering of bathrooms down the hall, and lots of veranda space for rocking chairs. The more ambitious danced in a special pavilion where "they navigated the waltz, two-step and polka." The tipple was Moxie and Phosa, and visitors "nibbled pink candy bananas and large round peppermints." All the hotel's vegetables were grown on the island which also had its own dairy. This was in the era of Charles H. Osgood from Norwich, the heir to a patent medicine fortune based on a cure for "fever and ague... Osgood's Indian Cholagogue." Osgood even went so far as to float in complete bowling alleys on barges from New London. It was Osgood who planted the European silver poplars that yet twinkle across the harbor in summer breezes and give some of the old Schofield tintypes a kind of George Seurat *Sunday Afternoon of La Grande Jatte* ambiance. The brochures and travelogues all praise the island's freedom from mosquitos and flies.

Not all was so pleasant on the island. For years locals told me there had been an illegal, marathon bare-knuckled prize fight that went 150 rounds involving John L. Sullivan. E.B. Read found the lengthy account in the *Stonington Mirror,* checked that out and discovered that the 1870s fisticuffs merely staggered through some 40 bloody rounds. The pugilists involved were mere mortals Billy Edwards and Sam Collier. To exacerbate the horror of the fight itself, apparently a number of New York's most notorious "roughs" attended, men who kept "dog pits" in Gotham. The *Mirror* editorialized that there should be a law against such "brutal and disgusting exhibitions." As late as the 1960s there were rumors that cock fights were held at some indeterminate time past on the island, perhaps vestiges of the New York "roughs" with their dog fights. On a more elegant level, there were also huge regattas, church picnics, Civil War reunions. These events in some cases brought thousands of people to the island without "rowdyism."

"None of this backstory of the place gets into Henry," said the Professor.

"The amazing thing is that it was Charles Osgood Jr. himself who was the key connection through the mother of Arthur Henry's girlfriend. Without Osgood's generosity, there's no *An Island Cabin.*"

"Not the kind of thing you'd want to own up to as a rugged Robinson Crusoe."

"Well, in fairness to Arthur Henry, he seems to have been here during that little null point in history when the nymphs have departed but the poets have not yet arrived."

"Maybe," said the Professor, "That's why he brought along his own nymphs."

"Exactly."

"Well, the Wilcoxes must have been taking care of something besides ghosts."

"You know Henry's very cagey about that, isn't he. I know that as late as

1893 the *Atlantic Coast Pilot* recommended the "large hotel" on the southern end of the island as a reliable sea mark. Historian Carol Kimball has a piece about a couple of fellows camping out on the island in 1919 and the hotel was still up, though the windows were out and the stairs perilous. The two campers saw the guest register and one of them even played the piano."

"Good Lord," said the Professor. "That's virtually twenty years *after* Henry was here. And the piano was still playable! You'd think that Henry with his love for music would have had a whack at the old keyboard and Dreiser—his older brother Paul wrote 'My Gal Sal.'"

"I suspect the reason the Wilcox couple was standing there talking to Arthur Henry was that the owner paid them to keep an eye on the place. Maybe he didn't want some folks from New York wailing on the old ivories."

"That would be a bitter pill for Henry to swallow, I imagine. Leave *that* the hell out of the book."

"In a dilapidated seaside hotel—to be denied the plangent cry of an out-of-tune piano..."

"Yes, right—the book does say they shouted back and forth across some water. I believe he called it 'a narrow run.'"

"*That* water," I said and pointed to the few dozen yards of liquid moving between us and Ram. "'The narrow run.' Hell, you can walk it at dead low, certainly moon low, but that may be recent." I passed on something of what my scientist friends across the harbor had explained about the local dynamic sand transport. Most of the hydraulic action was out to the east where Fishers Island Sound opened past the reefs into the open sea. I pointed far down the Sound toward Sandy Point, Rhode Island, which sometimes almost seemed underway. "They have to discipline it with dredging."

"Henry doesn't give any sense of this drama."

"Well, he was only out here for the summer and he probably had enough problem with what he saw as the unstable women."

"Yes, for an attempt at finding serenity, a very turbulent environment."

Before things got too shifty I quoted the Noank Postmaster Bill Banks who'd said that as a boy he'd played in the ruins of the cabin on the middle island and that the 1938 Hurricane had finished it off. "This was a similar storm which had dragged our friend Noank lightship, over here."

"Is this Bill Banks still around?"

I had to admit that our source had passed away.

We did have an obvious indicator in the huge, almost squared off glacial erratic balanced on the north end of the middle island. It was prominent in the photos looming behind the cabin. In the text, the big rock, whose flat top was the "size of a living room," was the scene of the after dinner perch to which Dreiser was want to retire with Henry.

"Ah, the Observation Rock," said the Professor tapping the book.

The rock's top flared out toward the south, just enough to be alarming if you were thinking about standing on that lip.

Sea birds and poison ivy make small New England islands, when actually landed upon, disappointing, and one's first impulse is to get off as soon as possible. It was, of course, too soon to leave, so we attempted to deal with the unpleasantness, by escaping upward.

By scrambling aloft on the side away from Noank we reached the top of the observation boulder, a prospect from which we could re-orient ourselves to the physical world of the book. Up there, the air was yet acrid from sea birds and our eyes burned. The wind was just strong enough to make us reach out for invisible walls. Our stomachs were uneasy and we were glad that in our excitement to get out to the island we had left our sandwiches on the kitchen table. Could the ammonia, iodine and rotting crab and clam bits have likewise so spanked the nostrils of our literary subjects? I recalled that Captain Rathbun often reminded the nostalgic that the whole village of Noank reeked of lobster bait, tar and questionably maintained outhouses, and that this condition had permeated the air well past World War II. Also teeming New York City from which Henry and Dreiser had fled could have been at least as pungent.

"Of course," said the Professor, "if Henry and Dreiser were living out here on a daily basis, the birds might not have been so bad."

"I don't know, didn't he call this place 'An Island Eyrie'?"

"That was in a photo caption, and I think he was being metaphorical. You know, a writer thing. Usually he called it simply: 'The Observatory Rock.'"

We looked around on the top of the rock to observe *writer things*. There were bird feathers rippling in thin, rancid pools of bile-green water, "I wonder if this is ocean spray up here or rain water," said the Professor. "I mean we're up here above where the roof of the cabin was and the salinity of the water in these pools would give us some sense of the power of the sea literally to reach Arthur Henry and Dreiser."

"There's one way to find out."

He stooped a bit toward a puddle and wrinkled his nose. "Think I'll pass."

"One wonders how they handled their own sewage," I said. "On the Town Shellfish Commission we had to get after Mouse Island."

"I believe," said the Professor drawing himself up to his full dignity, "They 'cast their refuse into the crucible of life.'"

"Ah, yes, and that included, if I recall, the economical baiting of crabs with the 'remains of supper.'"

"Well, what do you think the standards were on land at that time?"

"There's a deed restriction on the house I live in. It was put on a few years after Arthur Henry and says, 'There shall not be any obnoxious buildings on the described lands.' From what I can figure out *obnoxious building* was a term of art for outhouse."

"So you mean the villagers just straight-piped into the harbor?"

I admitted that my fellow Coast Guard mates had done no differently on the Harbor of Refuge Light Station off Delaware in the 1960s, and the village of Noank into the 1960s had also availed itself of the simple straight pipe. Captain Rathbun often recalled the need for learning the breast stroke if one was to sport aquatically.

We found ourselves turning away to the open sea toward which we had been so eagerly rowing earlier and facing the village from which we'd been at such pains to put our backs.

"Another ugly item Henry leaves out," I said, "is what must have been the excruciating noise of the caulking hammers at the Palmer Yard over there."

The professor peered to the west, but saw nothing but the gleam of fiberglass and glitter of chrome and windshield glass, a kind of visual shrieking muffled by his dark glasses.

"Howard Davis's father and grandfather worked over there," I said, "his grandfather as a caulker, and he himself was a caulker up at the Mystic Seaport. People asked if he learned the trade from his grandfather. 'Not a bit.' Howard told me, 'he'd never talk about it. Didn't want me to be a caulker.' Howard pronounced it *corker*. Said that the *pinging* of those mallets—the big ones were the size of croquet mallets—sixteen inch handle by sixteen inch head—*lignum vitae* or live oak. The live oak, Howard said, was a little lighter. You never had any carpal tunnel problem because to ease the shock on the forearms the heads were split—held together by metal bands, but this is what made the blows resound. The acoustics were sacrificed to the ergonomics."

"How about their ears? The poor 'corkers'—their ears?"

"Howard said most of the corkers went a bit deaf, especially in the right ear if they were right handed. He put in ear plugs after a while. Most didn't. Never thought of such a thing in those days. Same thing with safety goggles and all that."

"After a while, I don't imagine they heard much of *any*thing."

"Howard said it was 'a highly penetrating pinging'—a dozen of them going at once—'could be heard echoing over a great distance.' Since the yard is directly upwind in the summer sou-westerlies it must have been painful even over here. I know what it was like recently when they were knocking in pilings at the Yard. My father's description for a hangover—'The little men with hammers inside your skull.'"

"And remember the eight-hour day didn't come in until Warren Harding's administration."

"Six days a week, too. Starting at least at 7:30."

We considered for a moment the working day of the old caulkers. What we had was the hum of muscle boats.

I explained that the Noank skyline was different then. There were three water towers, at least two visible from here. The village was just coming off wells and cisterns even when I bought my house in the early 1960s. One water tower was for the Palmer Yard, the other the new hotel built just as Henry came here called "The Palmer."

"Palmer is certainly the name to reckon with," said the Professor.

"And that tall Baptist tower over there, really more of a Congregational model, that was not there in *An Island Cabin* days. There were two shorter towers, more typically Baptist style. That was called 'Deacon's Palmer's church'—but a fire in the late 1950s gave them—Deacon Palmer's descendants—the chance to alter the design. The new spire makes a good beacon coming in from sea and the church takes up a special collection to keep it lit. Of course, in Henry's day it was just kerosene lamps over there."

The Professor stared at the distant shore. Was he lost in a thought of the might of the Palmers or a reverie of what it must have been out here at night with merely the fuzz of kerosene lamps ashore?

"I think," said the Professor, "Henry fades out the caulking mallets into pleasant salty activity in the distance. All those men with hammers."

"And he doesn't seem to have been a drinker."

The Professor offered further scholarship: Henry was satisfied to pad Observation Rock with a blanket. Dreiser, however, insisted on lugging up a rocking chair from which he expounded upon the Universe—while below at the water's edge, the women did the dishes. We tried to estimate from the top just where the rock's flare began, the overhang that might find us... well, hanging over. We both laughed a little nervously, as much at our failure to transcend the tyranny of the moment and come up with grand Dreiserian theories of the universe. We had to be satisfied by noting that Dreiser's labored affair with the furniture struck an odd life-imitating-literature note. Were not the last lines of *Sister Carrie*, the book Dreiser's had just published, the heroine's meditation upon her fate as conducted in a rocking chair?

Oh, Carrie, Carrie!... In your rocking-chair, by your window dreaming, shall you long, alone; In your rocking-chair, by your window, shall you dream such happiness as you may never feel.

"Well, as he had just published it, yes," said the Professor, "but in our restored edition that is the penultimate chapter. As for rocking chairs, the biographies are full of Dreiser sitting in rocking chairs all over the place—all through his life," said the Professor. "Usually he'd be knotting and unknotting his handkerchief. Drove Mencken and others nuts."

"Henry left that part out, didn't he? I don't remember any knotting and unknotting the handkerchief business."

"He might have thought that would make 'Ted' too identifiable—or maybe just too ridiculously compulsive."

"Maybe Dreiser had not started that habit by then."

"You could be right. He seemed to get nuttier after he left here, I'll have to check that: *Dreiser, handkerchief compulsion, commencement of.*" He made a mock knot in the air.

We did feel it necessary, however, since we'd bothered to come all the way out to the scene, to follow our own compulsion to complete a scholarly survey of the actual world of *An Island Cabin*. There to the southwest on its drumlin island was the mansard roofed South Dumpling Light. Both Richard Lingeman and W.A. Swanberg in their biographies of Theodore Dreiser have their subject living on "Dumpling." No doubt they mistake the generic term *dumpling*, a word that Henry does use to describe the geological formation of his island.

"Ah," said the Professor, "now this goes to the credibility of the biographers."

True, the *dumpling* mix-up was a small error from the perspective of a Manhattan publishing house, but two and three-quarters miles makes a long row if you're the one who has to do it. We continued to pan about the horizon, taking attendance of the sea marks in the book. Behind us, to the east, was the odd hummock out.

"That's Gates," I said. "And that would have been a better island to make Henry's point about isolation."

"But, that would be pretty spooky out there," said the Professor. "Maybe asking a little too much."

"Well, it was indeed the site of a cabin comparable to Henry's. A little after Henry was here, perhaps even inspired by him. The story in the village is that the family who lived there were quarantined by the 1918 flu epidemic and had to remain longer than they intended. I've seen photos of the place and visited the site when its fireplace was still recognizable. There had even been a 'For Sale' sign on it with a legitimate broker."

"Still, asking quite a bit," said the Professor and gave a shudder at all that open water beyond.

"It seems to get smaller ever year," I said. "Whereas Quirk here seems to get bigger, at least the sandy base of it. Old charts in Henry's time show a foot at mean low water between it and the island on either side. Now you can pass from one to the other without getting your feet wet at low water."

"And over there," said the Professor "I take it is Latimers Reef Light—the end of the known universe."

"There are days when it seems from Noank that if it weren't for the spike of that tower the whole Sound would slip right out the Watch Hill Passage into the open ocean."

"You have to wonder how they managed before the lighthouse was built."

"You do," I said, "Captain Rathbun says Latimers Light was only out there a few years before Henry came to town."

Around to the northeast, up against the Connecticut mainland was Dodge Island, where Henry and Dreiser rowed at times for their fresh water. At hand, but a half mile to the north was Masons Island, which figured in a comic circumnavigation by the two worthies in search of water. And having clocked around full circle we were looking at Noank.

As in Henry's day there was what seemed "almost a parade of sail bearing up and down the Sound... with all kinds of smaller craft crisscrossing..." Unlike those times, however, there were very few gaff-rigged vessels. Almost all of the sails nowadays are Marconi rigged, the high aspect ratio of the triangular sails reaching up to catch the light summer breeze to windward or going the other way, there were pastel spinnakers in bloom. It was a soft southwest breeze, but the wakes of motorboats roughed the water and kept the sails in constant agitation, the spinnakers wrinkling and collapsing like a withered garden as the din of muscle boats echoed off the islands.

"In Henry's era most of this traffic had been commercial," I said, "This is all in the name of recreation."

"Yes," said the Professor "we learn in one of the Dreiser pieces that the locals are 'against yachts and Sunday pleasures.'"

"True, but there is that wonderful description in 'Cabin where the old guy with the long beard is sailing his little sloop through the 'narrow run' here between Ram. You remember how Arthur Henry tries to imitate the old guy's cavalier manner of salutation, but can't quite pull it off?"

"Yes, but definitely the exception—that old fellow. A village eccentric."

"To me, the most delicious passage in the book. But, you do have to worry about the old guy's chances of getting back against the current that time of day with the wind due to peter out."

"Yes, and not much of a boat, either."

We stood there a moment mentally smacking our lips, looking at the narrow run between the islands, a bit concerned for the return against the tide of the old sailor who had so captured Arthur Henry's fancy and become a kind of icon for the local life.

"Jesus," said the Professor waking up, "It's like I-95 out here."

I can hear these muscle boats in the bathtub," I said, "or rather feel their throb resonating off the enamel."

Mixed in with the angry cry of the herring gulls and throb of engines we occasionally could hear a bell off to the south, coming from the far end of Ram Island.

"That would be where our friend the lightship was stationed?"

I agreed it would, that is if that were the same lightship over which we'd just glided.

"You say there's less of her every year."

"I know a duck hunter sets up out here on Quirk in the fall. He's got a handful of bronze drift pins from her under the seat of his pick-up."

"Isn't there a law about that?"

"This is all open through here in season."

"I meant scavenging from historic wrecks."

"Nobody's designated her a historic wreck yet."

The Professor wrote something in his notebook. "This lightship then, it would have been, in addition to the Wilcoxes, Arthur Henry's nearest neighbor." The Professor stared off in the direction of what would have been his subject's nearest neighbor. "The bell buoy there—"

We could just see it in the sun dazzle to the west of the southeast horn of Ram Island. "I only know that's it," I said "because I've seen it up closer. It's a common racing mark, but the reef beneath it was once was the menace for the deeper Sound steamers that plied this east-west channel between Stonington and New London."

"You sure that was her station?"

"It's in the 1893 *U.S. Coast Pilot,* same spot as the present bell. Also on the Eldridge Chart, same year."

We discussed what I knew from the local historians. The Ram Island station had been created in 1855 to mark the route of the "palatial" Stonington-New London steamers. Financed by the steamship company, the first vessel was a mere 47-foot smack and was sunk in the February gale of 1885. Captain James Sisson was aboard alone, as usual, and endured two days and a night bailing and chopping ice off the rigging. On the morning of the second day, having seen her through the night watch, he noticed with bleary eyes that his gunnel was now almost even with the water. He hacked the gaskets holding down his dory and stepped aboard. The wind was 75 miles per hour of close-packed winter molecules and out of the northwest. He was lucky to catch the rocky easternmost tip of Fishers Island just before being blown out into the open ocean.

The government didn't get around to replacing the sunken light vessel until the next December when *LV 19*, a government vessel nearly twice the size but already 42 years old, was put on station. Whacked by ice in winter storms she wore out and was replaced six years before Henry arrived by *LV 23,* a 94-foot converted Civil War brig. In addition to her war duty, *LV 23* had already served for a decade at Cornfield Reef to the west of the Connecticut River off Saybrook.

"You see what they were doing here," I said. "The government. They were still trying to invent a way to handle Fishers Island Sound, to make it habitable, or at least traversable."

"And there would have been human activity aboard this vessel?"

"Yes, certainly," I said. "Carol Kimball tells us she was crewed by a master, a mate, four seamen and a cook."

"A *cook*!"

"Sure."

"Thats a far cry from poor old Captain Sisson on his lonely vigil."

We shared a shudder at Captain Sisson's icy vigil.

"Of course, that was winter," I said.

"Of course—winter."

We looked around to check the season. An island, especially a small one, is apt to have its own climate.

"Henry never did winter here," said the Professor. "Hell, he ran out in mid-autumn."

"Yes he did. Put his cats up at the Ashbey House. Said he'd be back."

"You know," said the Professor, "I find it odd that Arthur Henry doesn't say that—that he—that he took comfort in their presence. The light vessel men. I mean with their cook and all, the smell of dinner on a—."

"Southeasterly."

"A southeasterly wafting of supper aboard could not have spoiled his book contract."

"It could only enhance it, I think," I said, "and the light vessel crew came ashore at Ram Island for water. Why leave out that community of off-shore brothers moment?"

"But, you know what he does do? What he does is write this crazy lyrical paean to the lightship's bell."

"You're right, he does that doesn't he! Maybe he's making up for not getting to play the hotel piano."

"Here it is." The Professor grew excited and flipped the pages. "Ah, yes, here it is: *the constant ringing of the bell... of them all*—he means the sounds of the sea—*the most important to me has been the lightship's bell, for it has given me a sound to the quality of mercy; it has made my ear familiar with the spirit of tender, watchful benevolence?*"

"It's funny he never mentions the *crew*. I mean they must have been visible on deck, doing their work."

"He talks up the guy who made the bell. Says that 'by chance or design,' he 'fashioned a masterpiece.'" TheProfessor lowered the book and peered over the page, looking above the top of his glasses. "It is—" he coughed—"the true voice of Providence." The Professor coughed again, "I postulate that's the kind of stuff got him in trouble with the flowery police."

"Absolutely. I only wished he'd rendered the crew at their actual work. I mean a half hour before sunset they'd be out there on deck, lighting the lanterns, hoisting one up in each of the two masts. Each lantern made of a ring of eight oil lamps."

"A ring of eight oil lamps." the professor murmured. "And fog? Fog out here would really make you feel isolated, but Henry seems to have reveled in it."

"In fog, the crew took turns cranking the fog horn."

"So he'd have that. The thought of those guys cranking away just on the other side of the fog."

"Well, *inside* the same fog."

"Sharing the shroud of the sea." Infected now a little more by the late 19th-Century, the Professor had Poe'd himself into another little shudder.

I felt it was time a cold dose of logistics brought us back. "To get their supplies the crew had to make the same row across the harbor to the village we just made—plus an extra half mile in more open water out to the reef. She maintained station until the mid 1920s when the Ram Island Bell Buoy replaced her."

"And..."

"And she ended up, I suppose, something like what we saw out here a few minutes ago."

"The closest neighbor."

"Yes, and Carol Kimball tells us there was a rescue made out there the very year Henry was over here. Something about a stranded sloop."

"Now you would think Arthur Henry would have said something about that. That would be a big topic in Noank. The 'Voice of Providence' in practice. Can't see the pious locals missing a chance to be all over that one."

"Might have happened after he left," I said, "or hey, maybe nobody bothered to tell him."

"There certainly seem to be such moments in history," said the Professor, "moments when nobody tells you." He gave Ram Island another grudging look. "Much as I hate to admit it."

Ashore that night we ate supper with my companion Sina Wright. Her house overlooks the harbor one way and the old shipyard site the other. Like our neighbors we had twenty years before turned the *obnoxious building* in the backyard into a tool shed. We sat in rockers on the porch. The islands had all gone back to the way I'd been seeing them for years. They were just lumps at the far side of the view. I remarked that the row to Quirk had turned out that afternoon to have been longer than I'd remembered it from years past.

"Yes," said the Professor. "We certainly authenticated the fact that Arthur Henry had not exaggerated the distance off shore."

"Well," said Sina, "I don't think I could swim it anymore."

The Professor and I looked at each other.

"It was not more than a couple of times," said Sina. "Maybe three. I was younger."

"Well, you'd be run down by boats," said the polite Professor.

As dusk eased in and the noises of the modern village subsided, the din of the waterway slacked off. Under the sound of our rocking chairs we could hear the bell from the reef where once floated the old lightship and the cries of the seabirds, rinsed by distance, as they settled into the night.

[262]

"Flashing red, every four seconds," said the Professor, "that's her."

"The lightship was a fixed white," came a truculent sea voice from some-where.

DREISER COVERS THE NOANK WATERFRONT

Ashore, Professor Coltrane explained the back-story of Dreiser's interest in Quirk. One of the reasons the thirty-year-old Dreiser sought refuge in Noank was to lick his wounds over the poor reception of *Sister Carrie*, his first novel. The year before, his own publisher Frank Doubleday had tried to duck publishing the book at all. When Dreiser was able to force him to issue the book, Doubleday got back at him by not promoting it or even distributing it in any meaningful way. When Dreiser stepped off the train in Noank he had made $68.40 out of the 450 copies sold. To add to his woes, that Christmas Day his father had died.

Dreiser thought he could justify his summer retreat by knocking out some more magazine articles in his usual uplift vein. For a number of years, it was by such magazine pieces that he kept the pot boiling. Eventually he pulled to-gether a dozen such sketches into the book *Twelve Men* which he did not get published until 1919 when it was well received by the critics but not the pub-lic. He had also planned to start a novel while on Quirk but for reasons that become obvious in *An Island Cabin* could not get underway. A decade later the book emerged to H.L. Mencken's dilection as *Jennie Gerhard*. Before Dreiser died after the Second World War, he had published a shelf-load of books. It is interesting to note that the only ones that have been canonized in the Library of America's two volumes were either spawned or completed at the time of the Noank experience: *Sister Carrie*, *Jennie Gerhardt* and *Twelve Men*. As for *An American Tragedy*, as we shall see one could make the case that the central murder derived its texture from the bizarre circumnavigation of Masons Island by Dreiser and Henry in search for an improved fresh water supply for the cabin on Quirk.

The overarching concept of *Twelve Men*'s collection of non-fiction was that these dozen individuals were somehow representative of the new, go-get-'em America at the turn of the century—an optimism that the Dreiser of the realistic novelist so often mocked. His best example was P.T. Barnum whose model city in late 19th-Century, Bridgeport, Connecticut, was a paragon of what we'd now call urban planning. Dreiser balanced this optimism in *Twelve Men* by including a portrait of his song-writing brother Paul who, after a glorious career in New York music publishing, had fallen on days of pathos.

The two Noank pieces in *Twelve Men* edged toward a more complex awareness. In contrast to Barnum's progressive vision, the Noank works were almost parodies of flashy success. Dreiser began one of them by describing Noank as "a little played-out fishing town," a phrase taken as an insult by the locals to this very moment, a hundred years later. Mention Dreiser outside Carson's (Est. 1907) coffee shop on Main Street and you'll get, "Oh, yeah, the guy who made that crack about Noank."

Just how "played-out" Noank actually was in 1900 has been the subject of considerable debate. Dreiser seems to set 1875 as the height of the village's prosperity, a full quarter century before his arrival. To a person who'd come from Chicago and New York, Noank might well seem pokey and the big city rhythms no doubt gave him a poor metric to judge the village activity. Yet only six years before he arrived, a Noank harpoon crew landed sixty-six swordfish averaging 300 pounds in a trip of just seven days. Two years after Dreiser left, a Noank boat off-loaded nine thousand pounds of blackfish from one trip, (*Noank: Celebrating a Maritime Heritage*)

Russell Bourne a *Smithsonian* contributor, in the chapter on Noank in his 1989 *The View from Front Street* writes of "the heyday that Noank enjoyed in the mid-1800s." He also notes that the locals are still unpleased with Dreiser's "played-out" crack. Following Captain Adrian Lane's lead, Bourne traces the evolution of the Noank fishing industry from the latter part of the 19th-Century into the early 20th. After the Civil War, Noank rose to prominence through its live-well smacks. These were gaff-rigged engineless sail boats that kept their fragile mackerel loads alive in bulkheaded compartments where sea water circulated through holes drilled in the vessels' bottoms. With the advent of better ice production, the live-well boats were replaced by "market fishermen" who took their catch directly to Boston and New York by icing the cargo. Bourne, however, sees the main change into the 20th-Century not so much on the issue of Noank's prosperity. For him it is the shift from the independence of "each (fisher) man on his own hook" to the paternalistic corporate structure of working ashore for the Palmer Shipyard.

In many cases, by 1900 it was not so much the fishing that Noank was known for. Dreiser might have better emphasized the booming shipbuilding. The whole time he was in residence on the island, right across the harbor the Palmer Shipyard was pounding and sawing away, establishing its reputation as being the largest wooden shipyard on the Atlantic Coast. Mystic Seaport Curator William N. Peterson found that between 1827 and 1914 when Robert Palmer Jr. died, the Palmers "had launched no fewer than 699 vessels. This is more than the combined total of all of Mystic's shipbuilding during that period." The Palmer Yards—at one time there were three separate ones in Noank—had "been active since the Civil War building barges, scows and car floats." Referring to the year before Dreiser deigned to drop in, Peterson uses words such as "frenzy" and "feverish activity" to describe the atmosphere. "In 1899 there were 500 men on the Palmer payroll which came to a monthly total of $23,000." In the very year Dreiser was in Noank listening to the caulker's racket, according to the *New London Day* the yard was working on 13 vessels under construction: which consisted of seven railroad car floats, one tug, one yacht and one lighter." Five years later the three Noank Palmer yards launched four schooner barges, thirteen car floats, three steam towboats, one side-wheel steamer, one screw steamer and a steam ferry boat." (Peterson in *Mystic Built: Ships and Shipyards of the Mystic River 1784-1919*).

When John A. MacDonald, the Palmer Yard supervisor featured in *An Island Cabin*, bragged that he'd "tumbled over more ships than any man in the country," we know that to help him accomplish this Bunyonesque task he employed at least five big dray horses. They were stabled in back of the Palmer General Store on top of the hill where five of their names yet hang over the stalls: Charlie, Henry, Harry, Beth and Doll. You can see horses hauling stuff around the Yard in the old Addison Scholfield glass negatives. There are no less than five pairs in one panoramic photo in the Noank Historical Society. Frederick Detwiller works them into his wonderfully strong drawings of the yard where a dray driver has a brace hitched up to what almost looks like a chariot and is whipping them Ben-Hur style into dragging a great balk of wood. The yard produced so many hulls that the mere chips and shavings built up a deep substrate under foot which came into play during the great fire of May 1924, when the buried wood acted like a slow fuse that kept the Yard smoldering for days. During that time an underground river of flame traveled in the residue and from moment to moment erupted behind the line of firemen with near fatal results. A good share of this punk had been laid down by the noisy activity in the year Dreiser was in town.

Noank certainly seemed promising enough to business interests in those years. The J.H. Paine & Sons Engine Company soon set up by the Town Landing in a building still there (The Shellfish Hatchery) and built the steam engine for the steamboat *Sabino* (a.k.a. *Tourist*), a vessel that yet operates on the Mystic River with that very engine.

The issue of Dreiser's impatience surfaces time and again in Henry's book and combines with the sour taste his name leaves to this day for many Noankers. Interestingly enough, there is an old edition of Dreiser's Noank pieces in the Noank Historical Society donated by High Street artist Harve Stein, who himself came from New York and Paris between the world wars to render some of the village's most enduring images. The introduction is by none other than Robert O. Ballou, who was John Steinbeck's early editor, and in the 1930s worked with William Faulkner on *The Sound and Fury, As I Lay Dying* and *Sanctuary*. After the war, Ballou was to be editor at the Viking Press for Mystic's Ellery Thompson on *Draggerman's Haul*. In 1928 it fell to him to write the introduction to the Modern Library edition of *Twelve Men*: "...the man who wrote *Twelve Men* is incapable of unkindness—but persons and the things they do amuse him in a friendly way." Ballou does seem to have anticipated an objection to some of Dreiser's portraiture, but displaces the harshness by shifting it slightly off-center. "Not one of the twelve biographical sketches here could have been written by anyone save an almost savagely curious person." Of course, "savage curiosity" is not exactly a virtue the citizen of a small town welcomes in a stranger. Ballou goes on to say that Dreiser's so-called realism is not the flat two dimensional realism of photography, but in "three or four dimensions," an anticipation perhaps of Hemingway's famous brag about his own multi-dimensional prose.

Metaphysics aside, sailor-painter Rockwell Kent said of Winslow Homer that realism was Homer's "*job* in youth!" Like Homer who began as an illustrator for magazines, Dreiser was a journalist, providing the text as Homer had knocked out the cuts. For all the professorial talk about Dreiser's "realism," it strikes me more and more that he is poet's soul trapped in this journalist's career. When in the poetic mode, he often runs behind the skirts of his female characters, most notably Carrie (who is apparently based on his sister.) These women seem to live in a blur between the American Dream seen in material terms and a longing for something ineffable out there beyond the buck. It seems that in his life Dreiser used the fey dreamer Arthur Henry as his stalking horse for beauty. In Henry's battle plans, the Isle o' Quirk was to be the field of action, or at least a staging area from which to launch an attack on the vast continent with its grim, unfeeling, out of scale metropolises.

One of the most interesting places to watch Dreiser's struggle with beauty and money is in his sketch of his once famous, songwriter brother Paul in *Twelve Men* ("My Brother Paul"). Paul's enduring song celebrates the paradoxical nature of his gal Sal who is both "frivolous" yet somehow "dead on the level," and so, "a real pal." (And, as with Carrie, "Sal" is to the biographers, Dreiser's real life sister.) "My Brother Paul," was later the basis for the 1942 20th Century Fox musical "My Gal Sal," starring Rita Hayworth and Victor Mature as Paul.

Of course, if you read the Dreiser's Noank pieces you'll find that he is actually quite enchanted with the place in 1900, finding its undeniable funkiness the chief charm. In "A Doer of the World" he introduces the Noank of *An Island Cabin:*

Noank is a little, played-out fishing town on the south-eastern coast of Connecticut, lying half-way between New London and Stonington. [Which is to say half-way between New York and Boston]. Once it was a profitable port for mackerel and cod fishing. Today [1900] its wharves are deserted of all save a few lobster smacks. There is a shipyard, employing three hundred men, a yacht-building establishment, with two or three hired hands; a sail-loft, and some dozen or so shops or sheds, where the odds and ends of fishing life are made and sold. Everything is peaceful. The sound of the shipyard axes and hammers can be heard for miles over the quiet waters of the bay. In the sunny lane which follows the line of the shore [Riverview Avenue which now connects up Snake Hill to Palmer Court], and along which a few shops struggle in happy-go-lucky disorder [but were swept away in the 1938 Hurricane] may be heard the voices and noises of the workers at their work. Water gurgling about the stanchions [pilings] of the docks, the whistle of some fishermen as he dawdles over his nets, or puts his fish ashore, the whirr of the single high-power sewing machine in the sail-loft, often mingle in a pleasant harmony, and invite the mind to repose and speculation.

If there is anything to take offense at in Dreiser's sketch of turn-of-the-century Noank it is a remark he makes a page later when he marvels at the "uniformity of opinion" about the protagonist, which comes to Dreiser as a surprise in "this restless, religious, quibbling community."

In "The Village Feudists," however, Dreiser initially plays it a little cozy for some reason, setting his scene "In a certain Connecticut fishing-town sometime since, where, besides lobstering, a shipyard and some sailboat building there existed several shops and stores which catered to the wants of those who labored in these lines..." It is quite clear, however, that this is the same village as previously identified in "A Doer of the Word," and eventually Dreiser does get around to naming it Noank. "Old Mr. Main" is certainly one of the numerous Noank citizens by that name, one of whom, George S.

Main, married *An Island Cabin*'s "Elizabeth" ("Beezie" Seery Main).

Under the excuse of buying the obligatory rocking chair, Dreiser enters a store at the Town Landing Place (what seems to be what is now the Chester-Latham Store) and after taking an inventory of the store's diverse wares, comments: "I have never seen [a store] so remarkable for its disorder." [A contemporary ad now in the Noank Historical Society touts Elihu H. Potter's establishment as featuring "The Conqueror—Every Wringer Warranted" and "Provisions, Ship Chandlery, Hardware, Crockery."] Dreiser's "Burridge" tells the visitor he has no rocking chairs in stock, yet when Dreiser returns on another day an assistant reveals a back room in which "here are rocking-chairs, lots of them... just the kind I want."

More to the prowling writer's larger purpose, Dreiser has stumbled across a little drama in progress between two men, a scenario that seems ripe for the making into as symbolic, long-time tussle for the village's soul: Elihu Burridge (Elihu H. Potter?) versus Deacon Palmer. Dreiser says that "Elihu" interests him as an example of "the rural man." "Example" seems an odd word as all the data the reporter has collected would seem to point to his subject's willful uniqueness. Dreiser's thesis perhaps is that it is the "rural" nature of Noank, that "restless, religious, quibbling community" of "truculent sea voices" that inevitably squeezes such an eccentric to the periphery. In a similar move, Dostoyevsky has a footnote in "Notes from Underground" that would have us believe that his narrator protagonist is the inevitable product of modern St. Petersburg.

On a quick reading, Dreiser's Deacon Palmer, apparently based on Robert Palmer Sr. (1825-1913), (Robert Anderson's great grandfather) may come off as the heavy. The validity of such a characterization is vehemently taken exception to by his descendant, by marriage, Noank historian, Mrs. Robert Palmer Anderson: "I would say that Dreiser's picture of Deacon Palmer merely confirms the official library designation that decrees *Twelve Men* is fiction." The *Record of the New London County of Connecticut* in 1902 certainly bears out this view of the Deacon whom it finds:

...a man of industry perseverance and activity in every direction...

outspoken... stern and unyielding in principle... [whose] whole life is an example of Christian charity. His liberality might almost have been called a fault, for no cause of distress brought to his notice, was ever forgotten or disregarded, worthy or unworthy.

The change in Noank during the Deacon's lifetime, largely attributable to the growth of the shipyard was dramatic, as he reported to the *Record of The New London County* that he "distinctly remembers that time when [Noank] consisted of but thirteen houses." (The 1904 map indicates three times this many houses just from the Deacon's home to the Lighthouse.)

A reading of "The Village Feudists" itself shows that Robert Palmer makes only a cameo appearance, in which Dreiser spots him "most considerately helping a cripple up the lane to the local Baptist Church." To Dreiser the Deacon is "a keen, fine-featured, energetic individual, with excellent commercial and strong religious instincts [who] by dint of hard labor and a saving disposition [had] obtained, soon after the Civil War, a powerful foothold." Dreiser saw Palmer as "reticent, unobtrusive" and felt that he was no more "narrow and religionistic as the region in which it [his shipyard] had its rise." In the story, Dreiser otherwise renders Palmer through the perspective of the bitter "Elihu." It is a vision Dreiser consistently wrings out through extensive interviews with village characters who reveal "Elihu's" distortion. Indisputable, however, is the fact that Deacon Palmer does have what Dreiser calls "the color of power." He practices "quondam leadership." He owns not only most of the town's chief industry, the Palmer Shipyards, the company store, the coal yard, sail-loft and the new hotel but, after the church and business model of the day, he plays the role of head deacon of the dominating ecclesiastical unit in the village, The Noank Baptist Church. The Noank Historical Society note on its Palmer Shipyard exhibit states: "When Deacon Robert Palmer died at age 87 in 1913, the *Herald Tribune* said: 'During his life Mr. Palmer built 674 vessels. At times he employed between 500 and 600 men.'" Clearly poor "Elihu" never had a chance in the contest, if there ever were one.

Dreiser's second Noank story, "A Doer of the Word," demonstrates a more barefoot, Sea of Galilee slant on religion by featuring a loquacious Noank waterfront character Charlie Potter. Charlie takes in orphans on a houseboat at what seems to be the foot of Potter Court which faces across the harbor to Quirk. Nowadays we'd probably call him a hippie guru, or maybe a freelance social worker, but to Dreiser he was a true "doer of the word [of God]".

Dreiser's magazine journalism had thus far covered a wide field, anticipating the *New Yorker*'s John McPhee in specializing in the examination of the growing technology and the people who were involved. An examination of Professor Yoshinobu Hakutani's brave dredging of the files of 1890s magazines reveals that Dreiser ranged from the apple business to carrier pigeons, the manufacture of guns and cartridges, the making of stained glass windows, metal working, photography, American women who play the harp and the ongoing epic of the Chicago sewage system.

With this interest in technology, Dreiser combined the travails of those striving to achieve their place through the manipulation of these arts and trades. Each piece turned on the struggle with the society whose ladder these innovators sought to climb. The perfect market for this niche was the magazine blatantly named *Success*, for which Dreiser knocked out a whole string of what the *New Yorker*'s founding editor Harold Ross would later call "fact pieces," but which in Dreiser's day were heavily besprent with the aspirations of the eager practitioners of technology.

Certainly a test for anyone's ambition is a physical deformity. The tolerance of any community is challenged by a disabled person living among the citizens. This was especially so in the days before political correctness when deformities were often welcome objects of sport for "played-out... grass-grown"... village which is "seemingly so unpromising as Noank." Dreiser wrote about such a person in a sketch dug up by Professor Coltrane. In his personal papers Dreiser called the piece "The Noank Boy" but the magazine *Success* in February 1902 titled it: "A Cripple Whose Energy Gives Inspiration." Other pieces he wrote in this series included interviews with Chicago meat packing mogul Philip Armour, and department store king Marshall Field and as he moved the quest east, Thomas Edison and the nature writer and friend of

Teddy Roosevelt and Henry Ford, John Burroughs. There was even an anticipation of the small-town take in "A Village Boy's Gift of Oratory Earns His Wealth and Fame-Chauncey M. Depew."

While the Noank piece ostensibly is an upbeat performance championing the virtues of hard work in the face of handicaps, it is, when considered with all of Dreiser's Noank journalism, the most stunning indictment of the place. Here the village is not merely a quaint backwater, but a repository of hopelessly unemployed young men who blame their lack of good fortune on the recent influx of "Canucks" who have driven down wages. While the usual feeling in Noank now is that the Canadian immigrants were worthy citizens who contributed to the quality of life in the village, as certainly their progeny have in our time, in Dreiser's day there was evidently a strong xenophobic feeling among the resident Yankees. In "The Noank Boy" one of the swarming indigenous loafers (none of whom are spotted by Arthur Henry) sourly complains to Dreiser of the shipyard:

"They don't hire anything but Canucks from up in Canada, who, when they get a dollar and quarter a day, imagine they're in heaven... They ought'n't to get anything,—them fellows. If they didn't come down here, wages would be a lot higher than they are. It's them that's keeping the people around here, that would work, out of jobs."

So pervasive is the depressing presence of these lay-abouts that all the local merchants have had to post signs at their establishments warning off "loafing." (A bit of local color passed up by Arthur Henry.) What jobs exist outside the shipyard are either not worth the wage or have been scoffed up by the "cripple" who is pampered by the older populace who exploit him to run errands.

Say what you will about the content of the comments in "The Noank Boy," Dreiser, who had honed his ear on the utterances of the *vox populi* in Chicago and New York, certainly captures the acrid tone of the down side of small town America in a way that no other documents of the time, including *An Island Cabin*, are equipped to handle.

The "boy" himself—Dreiser calls him Harry and puts him in his late teens—was a young man who had grown old in his tasks, a *boy* only in the sense of his duties as errand *boy* or paper *boy*. Unlike the Horatio Alger model of the times who starts humble as a gofer to rise to the top by dint of hard work and marginally ethical ploys, the Noank exemplum is not promoted beyond his original position. Fame or as the magazine sees it, "success" comes entirely in the perfection to which he hones his responses to his given mission, and the transfiguring élan of his performances.

Withheld by the author from republishing in *Twelve Men*, the *Success* piece lay little known during the 20th-Century, though Dorothy Cramer seemed to carry an almost racial memory of it its dark picture of Noank's youth. She did recall, however, the "boy," who had a leg defect since birth and stuttered. Years after Dreiser had written him up, when Dorothy was a little girl living on Mouse Island, the "boy'" loved to give her rides in his express cart. The vehicle was more than a mere logistical trick, but an extension of his personality: an improvised contraption, "part soap box derby racer, part double-ripper." To Dorothy it was both intriguing and terrifying.

"I'd sit in the front of the damn thing. We'd start at the top of the little slope that crests at the corner of Pearl Street and Palmer Court where Deacon Palmer's big old gingerbread looms [Now Dr. & Mrs. Ferguson's]. I'd feel a shove and he'd jump on the back like an Eskimo and down we'd rush—around the corner at the Ashbey House—*boom* past the great rock that overlooks the shipyard—then zip right through the yard that usually seemed to go on forever when you were on foot—on all the way out the other end to Morgan Point where the lighthouse is.

"Usually he was quiet, stuttering when he spoke at all, but on these excursions he'd become another person—*ki-ying* all the way to the end of the line when he'd come to a quiet stop at the water's edge. I'd adjust myself, thank him and stagger to my skiff. As I rowed out to Mouse Island I could see him dragging his rig back up the long hill, but I never felt sorry for him. It always seemed he'd have it no other way. I just always supposed I was his excuse for raising hell."

"I can see him now," Charlie Abate told me, "that funny cart. Name was Ashbey—lived across the street from the railroad station and he had a job to meet each train at the station and wrangle the mail sack to someplace where the postmaster could get to work at it."

Nor was this a sleepy, once-a-day job. According to the brochure for The Ashbey House, "There (were) five incoming mails daily, and four going out." When time came for the Boston-New York express Ashbey had to hang the outbound sack from a yardarm next to the track.

"It was a long sack," Abate said. "To reach the yardarm, he had to climb up a step ladder. The clerk in the mail car would pluck the sack as the train whizzed past, reaching out with a hook. You had to time it just right. One day, he's hobbling about on his bum leg, and was just a tad late in removing himself from the sack. The train spun him like a top. Poor fellow hollering away. But he hung on. The train just kept going without the sack."

In his *Memories of a Noank Boy* (Groton Public Library, 1991), George Wilcox Hewitt had similar recollections:

> When the mail came in by train to Noank, a little crippled man wheeled the mail from the depot to the post office on Pearl Street. We called him "Hic" Ashbey. He got the nickname because he had the hiccups quite regularly. That cart he pulled always had two or three bags of mail. He would come rain or shine. In snowstorms, he would use a sled. When a big package came, someone would give him a lift in their car.

Somehow, he who was blasted at birth was now sheltered by providence and was not harmed by the train's passing. The incident, however, went on as part of his legend. People, otherwise lacking entertainment at the moment of the express, came to the station just to witness this schtick. How often the near disastrous performance was repeated is unrecorded, perhaps never, but so interesting had been the premier that the show attracted audiences for years. The same could be said for the frequency of Dorothy Cramer's descents on the express cart down the spine of Noank. Perhaps tales of the Noank Boy's transcendent mobility were a comfort to the villagers whose daily routine was merely to witness his labored locomotion.

IN THE FOOTSTEPS

Going in the footsteps of the *An Island Cabin* crew is a game of quasi scholarship. It's open to all readers of Henry's book and the three Dreiser stories. Professor Coltrane and I tromped about the village on just such a quest. We found various *An Island Cabin* characters in the Noank Valley Cemetery which lies just across the railroad tracks at the foot of Prospect Hill. Inside the village, right back of the firehouse, (now converted to a residence) was a good candidate for the barn where Henry bought hay for the "tick" which served as the mattresses when he first got off the train.

Thanks to *The Claude Chester Papers*, the first book published by the Noank Historical Society, we found the house of John A. MacDonald. He was the busy superintendent of the Palmer Yard who urged Henry to "get the sentiment in" to his book so that "I can have it when things don't go right." MacDonald (whom Henry spells as Irish) seems to have been a Scot born in Prince Edward Island, Nova Scotia around 1844. Pre-eminent among the Nova Scotia shipbuilders who made their way down to Noank in the 19th-Century, MacDonald began as a foreman in the yard and was later promoted to superintendent. Chester characterized him as "popular and congenial." Noank historian and boatbuilder Arnold Crossman told me that there had been some eight MacDonalds working at the Palmer Yard, "all in a row." Arnold wasn't sure if they were all related to each other, "but *MacDonald* is a strong name at the yard." It would seem John A. MacDonald was accurate when he claimed to have "tumbled over more vessels than any man in the country." With wife Sarah, MacDonald also launched two children, Anna C. and John F. who in turn extended the family through children of their own. His great granddaughter Barbara Servidio, long-time clerk of the Noank Fire District, informed me one evening at Carson's Store that MacDonald had been asked to run for the state legislature, but turned it down. "As there was then no Catholic church in the village, he bought a lot at the edge of the Palmer House property on Front Street and sold it in turn to the Catholic Diocese for a dollar to build what became St. Joseph's Church in 1908. One day in 1911 he came home for lunch from the Shipyard and died. He is buried in New London." (Deceased Catholics then unwelcome in the Mystic Valley.)

The MacDonald house has had a succession of colorful people within its walls. It was there in 1931 that aviatrix Amelia Earhart was married to her publisher, George Palmer Putnam, by Judge Arthur Anderson (the Deacon's grandson). Later the house was lived in by the artist Katherine "Speedy" Forrest, who was succeeded by the eccentric independent scholar and collector David Fentriss. This house is now owned by Noank Fire District Executive Committeeman, boat restorer and sailor Paul Bates. The Professor and I found the MacDonald house half-way down Church Street on the west side, a two story, yellowish clapboard affair with a roof so flat as to be out of sight.

"My God," said the Professor, "it has no roof. What do they do when it rains?"

I assured him that while I myself had never seen the roof, either, I had been inside on the second story and had found no evidence of water damage. There had been another floor above, but Paul Bates tells me that the 1938 Hurricane had done its editing. In the backyard we came upon a ramshackle boat shed surrounded by a number of interesting old wooden hulls nuzzling the walls as if vying for admittance.

Years later when preparing for this edition, I learned from Arnold Crossman that John A. MacDonald had also built the big white house on the north side of Spring Street and moved his family in there. As with MacDonald's house on Church Street, some maritime continuity remains. Arnold reminded me that Maynard Bray, the technical editor of *WoodenBoat* magazine, and author of a number of wonderful books on wooden boat culture, had lived there when he was in Noank working for the Mystic Seaport.

In a mood for poking about more backyards which might contain old boats, or at least adumbrations of them, we next searched for Captain Green who'd built Arthur Henry's sharpie. By making various inquiries and deductions, we found ourselves down at Lighthouse (Morgan) Point looking at Captain Green's house, its fancy bit of carpenter gothic ropework in the soffit a testimony to the Captain's impish skill. On the east side of the street was (and is) a modern house, but we had a photo from the Historical Society of a long building that stuck out over the water. The picture seemed to fit Henry's description from Quirk of watching Captain Green vanishing from sea right into such a structure. We concluded this was the location of the shop where Captain Green built Henry's sharpie. In *Noank: Celebrating a Maritime Heritage* you may find your man (with an added *e* on his name) by a somewhat circuitous route:

> September 5, 1915: Work has been commenced on the boat shop which is being built for Frank S. Brace & Co. on the property of Walter E. Coe at Morgan Point. The building is an extension of the boat rigging lot formerly owned and operated by the late Captain A. Greene.

Captain Green's old house is presently owned by Mr. & Mrs. John Butler, an old Noank family.

The house with the well under the cherry tree occupied by the man Arthur Henry calls "Captain Louis" is by local tradition on Potter Court. The story goes that he was born in France in 1817 and as a more or less homeless wharf urchin in Marseilles was taken aboard a Noank vessel and given the name which was the only thing remotely English he could then utter, "Louie." In the Noank Historical Society there is a marvelous oil painting by a Danish artist of his "jackass brig" *Frances Lewey*, named for his wife. His son Ellison was in command when *Frances Lewey* was run down and sunk in four minutes by a steamboat off the China coast. Six of his thirteen crew were drowned instantly. After a miraculous head-bashing eruption through the skylight of the sinking vessel, Captain Lewey himself managed to survive and write a brief memoir later re-published in *Noank: Celebrating a Maritime Heritage*.

There was a more recent Lewey presence. A census search seems to indicate the daughter of Captain Ellison Lewey (b. 1843) who was the son of Captain John Lewey, he of the trifecta maritime disasters and the irascible parrot in *An Island Cabin*. In the early 1960s I knew here a Mrs. Annie Lewey who lived in an unpainted house with a rusty tin roof at 62 Main Street. It was, despite its cosmetic difficulties, a house of beautiful proportions, often "discovered" by people breezing into town looking for the essential quaint Noank house for the proverbial song. Mrs. Lewey herself, then in her nineties, was a kind of geriatric Scheherazade holding court by spinning yarns of the old island cabin days to two elderly gentlemen, each vying to out-wait the other before going home to sleep. (One of these suitors was David Fentriss, who would eventually tiptoe back down the hedge-tight lane in his carpet slippers to sleep in the MacDonald Church Street house, a structure whose job, it seemed to be, to keep weaving the old *An Island Cabin* associations together).

Of interest to anyone reading *An Island Cabin* in concert with the three Dreiser pieces is their antiphonal relationship—or what in "The Village Feudists," Dreiser calls in a Whitmanesque phrase: "side elucidations." (At other times, he reveals a more desperate aspect admitting, "I had so little to do at the time, the very idlest of summers"—an interesting statement when cross-referenced with Henry's complaints about "Ted's "laziness in helping about the cabin.") When "Ted" goes off on a petulant foray ashore, Henry tells us he is painting and sketching locals and it all seems a bit pretentious if not buffoonish. In the three pieces, however, Dreiser shows us the sort of reportage he's actually working on. (In "The Village Feudists" he justifies his journalistic excursions by saying cryptically in what sounds like a line from Wallace Stevens: "The summer wanted evidence of a particular life accumulated.")

"Ted" loses an oarlock in *An Island Cabin* and we never hear from Henry what was done to replace it. In "The Village Feudists" Dreiser as reporter tells us he goes into Elihu Burridge's store one day for "row-locks." Henry tells us "Ted" sits up on the "Eryie" in a rocking chair which in "The Village Feudists" Dreiser tells us he goes in search of in the same store.

Dreiser finds the village barber "a lean, inquisitive individual with a shock of sandy hair and a conspicuous desire to appear a well-rounded social factor." This is the man *An Island Cabin*'s "Elizabeth" later marries. One of "Ted's" absences in *An Island Cabin* can be accounted for in Dreiser's "A Doer of the Word" as a steamboat excursion all the way to Norwich and back on "the afternoon boat." (A good candidate for the boat Dreiser took was *The Summer Girl* which ran between Mystic and Norwich and was built in the Palmer Yard four years earlier.) Once in Norwich Dreiser identifies himself as one who "lives in a little hummock at the east of Mystic Island off Noank." This is the same fellow who as "Ted" seems hardly to be "living" on Quirk in any but in the most tenuous of visitor status. (Also the "little hummock" is more significantly north than east of Mystic Island.)

Our graveyard search turned up the time-eaten headstone of Elihu Potter.

"My gosh," said the Professor. "It says he was a corporal in the Civil War. In fact that's all it says about him."

"Nothing about the rocking chairs he hoarded. Nothing about the Conquerer Wringer he advertised with the voluptuous woman supine. Nothing about the feud with the great deacon."

"Well, it's a small stone."

A further scouring of all four texts would yield more "side elucidation," adding up to evidence of a summer in which "a practical life accumulated."

A PARALLEL LIFE IN THE HARBOR

We can take a parallel account of life on Noank Harbor from May to October 1900 as lived by Captain Charles Ira Chester, a lobsterman who kept a journal now in the Noank Historical Society. Some readers of the journal are disappointed because "all he talks about is the weather and going to church." It is perhaps no accident that Wallace Stevens, the insuranceman-poet who wrote "the gods come out of the weather," lived sixty miles from Captain Chester.

The weather that Captain Chester is chiefly concerned with is the easterly wind in off the open end of Fishers Island Sound, or the back side of Quirk that is away from the village. The easterly is not only the vehicle for the great storms, but the much more common overcast damp day saturated with rain or fog or both. This is the wind that can really get, almost literally, under your skin. I recall the first morning I woke in my quarters under the hill in lower Noank and saw the ancient, arthritis-racked lobsterman who lived behind and above me peering off at the harbor from his back porch. "Goddamn *east-wind*," he sniffed, "all the time damp."

On Saturday June 4, 1900 with Arthur Henry already installed on the harbor island, Captain Chester decides to "get some of [his] lobster pots down to the shore" from where he presumably has been storing them by his little free-standing shop in the back yard up the hill. From this moment on he is pretty much exclusively concerned with keeping account of when he works on the gear and when he washes. The need to track the lobster pots is obvious, but the compulsion to note each time he "washes"—two or three times a week, strikes the modern, appliance-happy reader, as bizarre. Yet I recall the diary of a next door neighbor in Iowa City in 1961 as made up of some thirty years of solely two entries: a weekly sojourn to Waterloo on Tuesdays and a "wash" on Thursday.

What lends drama to Captain Chester's ablutions is his nemesis, the east wind which not only makes going to sea difficult, but prevents drying. It is not mere mercantile frivolity that the featured item in "Burridge's" store at the bottom of the hill is "The Conqueror," a hand cranked mangle that promises to vanquish the saturation, if not all the damp from your life. As one pages through Captain Chester's spring, summer and fall of 1900 the word "easterly," needing no modifier or further comment, seems to leap from the page. It is enough merely for him to set down the seven letters to account for all that occurred and was prevented from occurring. In fact I find only two other entries recording any other kind of wind by name and these are two notations of southeasterlies which I suspect then, as now, will prove unstable and rot before afternoon into all-out easterlies.

The easterly is one of those issues that Arthur Henry leaves out of his book. That Henry did not make more of the east wind is consistent with his "philosophy of happiness," and as Alfred Kazin points out, Dreiser found to be a weakness in philosophers in general who "do not make sufficient allowances for the natural elements in our philosophy." We hear of dishwashing and bathing. When it comes to laundry, the "trying to get clothes to dry" as Captain Chester puts it, Henry makes one great orgy of it. Bedding flies from the attic windows; "Then came great bundles tied in bath robes." The washtub is courtesy of the flotsam gods and, of course, there is an epic which compels them to "set sail for our distant laundry" on Dodge's Island, a voyage that arouses in the girls a sense of "danger." The thrust of the scenario has thus shifted from the wearisome contingencies of domestic life to the epic maritime challenge of Arthur Henry Versus the Sea. Once on Dodge's Island the handmaidens of ammonia and soap are rewarded by another one of Henry's by now famous sailing lessons. In later days Henry refers to damp only as the putative issue between him and "Ted" over ventilation. "Damp and foggy," the *leitmotif* of Captain Chester's version of Noank Harbor that summer, becomes merely a counter in the domestic politics for Henry. This, I suppose, is part of Henry's Doctrine of Happiness: to turn the drudgery of what literary histories writing of the era liked to call "poor real life" into some sort of sudsy dithyramb. I suppose it does beat: "Thursday. Wash."

When not struggling with damp clothing, Captain Chester is dinking about with his gasoline engine, a novelty at the turn-of-the-century, that permits him to range out to The Race, Gull Island and Bartlett's Reef. These are places some dozen miles to the west or the better part of two hours chugging each way. Without that engine, it is a voyage that could even now pass for a bit of epic splendor. I'm guessing his vessel must have have been some variation on the vernacular Noank sloop—perhaps with her gaff rig cut down a bit in deference to the new engine. This would be the kind of craft in the mid-twenty foot range that formed what Henry called "the picket line" on the eel grass flats that constituted Noank Harbor inside Ram and Quirk. Beset by "strong tides and poor slacks from [the] solstice," Captain Chester would need an engine to haul his eleven trawls of probably three pots each in the Race. Even in normal tides he is frequently at the mercy of "eddies," currents swirling counter to the main direction of the ebb or flow and which wander from place to place on each hour of the tide, and which became more predictable only with this century's advance in hydrodynamics.

On Friday August 12 the currents have created "a snarl this morning" which Captain Chester can only free "by cutting" the warp or pot line, an evolution he must soon in any case abandon when "chased by easterly." The following day he finds some of the lost gear, but has to take the next day off for church. On Monday he has a bit more success in recovering lost gear until "eddies" and "easterlies" again send him home. Ashore he tries to capitalize his time by making more buoys. It's a six day work week with Sunday off for Deacon Palmer's church which he attends with his wife, except when one week her absence is noted, but not explained. During the time Henry is in Noank, Captain Chester praises two of the sermons, one of which was delivered by "a missionary." (I'm not sure whether Noank was considered to be a place *for* missionary work. Absurd as it sounds, I recall attending the Noank Catholic church with my grandfather in the 1940s and hearing a clergyman address the summer people in behalf of the poor folk of what he called *"Non-a-nank,"* blighted souls who must get through the watery winters on the momentum of their seasonal guests. Nowadays, the Noank Baptist Church is known for sending money and blunt-ended scissors to African missions.)

Captain Chester's chief expense is gasoline which he buys by the jug and "rigging" ($15.30) which he presumably pays to Captain Green, the man at Morgan Point who built Henry's sharpie, but seems to have been more known as a rigger of small craft. The presence of strangers from New York on the middle harbor island who were also putting out lobster pots, however, does not make it onto the page of Captain Chester.

Henry himself does not mention venturing from Noank during his May-October tenure, nor does he let on about Dreiser's Norwich steamboat excursion. As a benchmark for travel from the village, Captain Chester in the same period makes it up river to Mystic no less than three times. Mystic abuts Noank and the centers are noted on the appropriate signs as being two miles apart.

Even the most loyal of Noankers now feel compelled to touch base with downtown Mystic at least once a day and I have been frequently called out for not having managed to have "gotten out" of the village during the day, as if I'd spent the daylight hours crouched beneath the bed midst lint and cat fur. On the other hand, having made it to Mystic and back now seems to be considered prima facie evidence of having accomplished something. Whether Henry stays put out of a commitment to the premise of his book contract or out of fealty to the Aristotelian unities, it is curious he never mentions Mystic except as the inland boundary of Noank. In discussing the chimney on Quirk, Captain Ashbey mentions that a mason lives in Mystic, but indicates this geographical fact alone puts the craftsman so far beyond the pale that Ashbey himself is forced to do the job. Perhaps the reticence on Henry's part to admit to the relevance of Mystic is less a comment on the sketchiness of the pre-trolley River Road as it is an endorsement of the self-sufficiency of insular 1900 Noank.

HENRY'S BIOGRAPHERS COME TO NOANK

It wasn't until some years after Professor Coltrane, I met Arthur Henry's granddaughter Maggie Walker, and began to probe the strange tensions that for some spoils the "idyle" of *An Island Cabin*. It was a journey I wasn't always sure I wanted to continue as I had already formed my own opinion about the two writers and their female companions out on that island in the good old days. Like Arthur Henry, I wanted Quirk to work out. Who needed Tahiti when you had it right there, shimmering eternally on the far side of the harbor?

Maggie Walker, however, was a force to deal with. She was in company with her union organizer/writer husband Mark Walker. They were working on a biography of her grandfather and had come to the Noank phase. A lean, handsome woman with a Midwestern twang, Maggie had spent a lifetime working on newspapers as a writer and city editor and she quickly demonstrated to me that she was well-trained to follow a story where it led, regardless of family connections. In her husband she had the perfect collaborator. Breaking the stereotype of a union organizer for the maritime trade, Mark was a mild-mannered man of decorous vocabulary from rural Maine. Among his works was a fine book about his childhood Down East and another about his days as a stokehold organizer, *Working For Utopia*.

To Maggie Walker the problem between Dreiser and Henry was more in the literary business between the two men than in the sexual rivalry for those extra women that apparently had so titillated the locals. As for Henry's legendary sexual appetites, the biography that Maggie and her husband Mark wrote later would suggest that if Arthur Henry had any erotic abnormalities it was more on the side of under performance than satyriasis. The Walkers point out Dreiser's take on the relationship between Henry and Anna as thinly fictionalized in Dreiser's "Rona Murtha," in which "Winnie and Rona" stand for Arthur and Anna:

Perhaps a superficial flaw was a somewhat dubious, albeit pretentious, plantonism between Winnie and Rona... I also noted, with a marked absence of that salt of desire... He did not enough wish to be alone with her.

For corroboration of this "dubious... platonism," the Walker's point to the text of *An Island Cabin* itself, where Henry sums up his idea of Anna ("Nancy") in the two paragraphs beginning with "Wisdom is all." And ending with "You are doing this most of all because you see truly what is lovely in character and because you love these qualities, and because you posses a sunny, warm and generous nature." To the Walkers, "underlying these uplifting words is the dismissal of desire as inimical to happiness."

Some of Henry's attitude, Maggie reasoned, toward sex seemed to lurk in her grandfather's upbringing.

Arthur Henry was born in the aftermath of the Civil War, November 26 1867, the year of Matthew Arnold's popular "Dover Beach," a seaside celebration of true love against the confusion of armies fighting by night. His father James Henry was a Quaker who opted for one of those fights via the 185th

Regiment of the New York Infantry Volunteers, an enthusiasm whose consequences he somehow survived. It was Henry's mother, however, who was the
true battler. Sarepta Henry was a fighting comrade of Frances Willard, forty
year head of the Women's Christian Temperance Union. When she penned
The Pledge and the Cross, a tome cum tract, Sarepta demonstrated to her son,
if nothing else, at least what power a writer could have. She augmented the
might of her pen by dragging little Arthur and his brother to the famous Rock-
ford (Illinois) Woman's Temperance Union's "Swearing in the Troops." This
was her own Utopia, not an island but a paramilitary force—the 500-strong
"Cold Water Army." *Forward march!* and there they all were afoot off on a
torch-lit march about the village green singing away like some anti-Woodstock
Woodstock. Little Arthur and his brother, swept up in the communal orgy of
austerity, shouted out the "Triple Pledge." Henceforth they would eschew al-
cohol, tobacco and language profane and impure. All this a generation before
Carry Nation hit the headlines.

In addition to taking on demon rum, tobacco and semantic defilement,
Sarepta progressed in later years by going after "hygiene" itself—especially
what she saw as the great menace to health of her time, "secret sin." Toward this
end she wrote *Studies in Home & Child Life* a book which emerged in 1897.
By now her son was thirty. He had passed through an apprenticeship in
Chicago's daily newspapers. He had met the womanizing newspaper reporter
Theodore Dreiser and become his coconspirator in modern literature. They
were, in fact, about to make their move on Quirk Island with all those women
in tow. Of especial interest was Sarepta's chapter "The Little Body" in which
she takes on, in chaffing detail, the clandestine menace of tight undergarments.

It is pleasant to think of the turn into the 20th-Century as a benign pasture
between the Civil War and the first of the great world wars, broken only by
two comic opera "splendid little wars" in exotic locales. To newsmen such as
Henry and Dreiser whose profession had educated them to see the world as
their beat, living at this time was to be on the edge of turmoil. The idyllic aura
that seems to hover over The Isle o' Quirk is actually a willful construct by

Arthur Henry in which he tries to find validation in Dreiser, the future icon of American realism. Henry had already worked on this utopian idea on a summer vacation with Mr. and Mrs. Dreiser in Ohio. It was then he had come up with what he called "the doctrine of happiness," a kind of tongue-in-cheek take on all the other dismal doctrines then hovering about. Like Thoreau's pond a couple hundred miles to the north, Noank Harbor was to be for Henry's little crew the moat surrounding the bolt hole out of which might emerge a kind of desperate rear guard action. The enemy, for one required to build any utopia, an enemy,—well, that was something like, shall we say, the unintended consequences of industrial progress of the late 19th-Century, or as Henry puts it more universally, "the world of men groping, greedily reaching, toiling and contending." (Ergo, let's pretend that instead of having the constant cacophony of a huge shipyard to windward, we have "a played out fishing village," ho-humming and aye-yuping through "the happy-go-lucky disorder" of sunny waterside shacks.)

A biopsy of nineteen hundred alone reveals the mix of progress and disaster that was to haunt the coming era. The zeppelin made its first flight. The New York subway was begun. The Paris metro actually opened. Chicago seemed to have cured both its sewage and logistic difficulties by opening its great canal linking the Mississippi system with the Great Lakes, (Look out below!) an event about which Dreiser wrote a long non-fiction pageant. The first great modern corporations made their move as Andrew Carnegie formed his steel company and the Vanderbilts merged three large Pennsylvania railroads: the Reading, Lehigh and the Erie. (Dreiser wrote about Carnegie and other business dynamos).

The push back came from Labor with coal strikes in Pennsylvania and in Europe strikes for the eight-hour day. Labor Day, now the bookend with Memorial Day for the summer season, was then not an excuse for picnics and back-to-school sales, but a six-year-old, rear guard action by the government in an attempt to hold off growing labor unrest. On a less positive note there were outright riots in New Orleans during which large numbers of blacks were beaten, riots in North Carolina between the "Red Shirts" and populists. A black accused of murder was burnt at the stake in Colorado. In Europe the seeds of World War One were already sprouting with unrest in the Austria-Hungarian Empire and at the eastern edge the revolt of the "Young Turks" sprung up against the Ottoman Empire. Most vivid perhaps in the new age of sensationalist journalism was the Boxer Rebellion in which American newspaper readers were treated to breakfast photos of Chinese brandishing the severed heads of missionaries on uplifted pikes outside Peking.

The uprisings had consequences beyond their immediate locale. The Russians, for instance, took advantage of the instability of China to invade Manchuria. In what we would now see *a la* Jared Diamond's analysis of global geographical influence, millions died of starvation in India. There was an epidemic among Eskimos in Alaska that killed half the population in some villages. Furthermore, the perceived threat to the Atlantic coast by the Spanish battleships in 1898 had inspired a string of forts, one of them visible from the top of the "eyrie" rock on Quirk hardly a half dozen miles to the east at Watch Hill (but curiously not noted by Henry who on easterlies of Captain Chester that summer might well have heard some of the construction sounds). Even the "splendid little war" in Cuba turned ugly after its ostensible conclusion as hundreds of returning vets died of yellow fever and malaria. As Charles Thompson Post put it, "Each morning we would hear bugles blowing taps." During demobilization at Camp Hero on the eastern end of Long Island, there were a far greater number fever casualties than had been at the hands of Spanish Mausers in Cuba. These same mosquitoes that had bitten soldiers on Long Island eventually made their way to Noank. The malaria ridden coves and backwaters surrounding Noank became a problem that was not significantly alleviated until Civilian Conservation Corps workers in the alleged boondoggle during the Great Depression opened up coastal wetlands by ditching. The romantic Boer War of South Africa where Winston S. Churchill made his reputation as an embedded war correspondent, and Conan Doyle received his knighthood, was now seen to be "dragging on." It is significant that when Boston, Detroit, Milwaukee, Baltimore, Chicago and St. Louis got together to form a second major league in baseball, journalists characterized the move in this context of unrest as the "upstart American League." It is a perhaps the most telling sign of the times, however, that William McKinley and Theodore Roosevelt could win the White House on so meager a slogan as "four more years of the full dinner pail."

The man whose writings might have made the most sense of all this died largely misused. John Ruskin was inventor of what we would now call urban planning and organic analysis of the relationship between the working day, craftsmanship and community, but was largely seen as a mere aesthete. Comforting to some were the deaths of three trouble makers: the satirical enemy of the complacent bourgeoisie, Oscar Wilde; the scourge of the smuggly religious, Frederic Nietzsche; and the brilliant documenter of slum life and the evils of war, Stephan Crane. The three most enduring books of the year were Polish exile Joseph Conrad's *Lord Jim*, the study of the ultimate futility of setting up an alternative society on an island; Sigmund Freud's study of the subconscious's alternative world *Interpretation of Dreams* and Beatrix Potter's tale of the consequences of imperialism, *Peter Rabbit*. Perhaps the most innocent seeming was the revolutionary text of Max Planck's vision of change cloaked safely in his theory of quantum mechanics.

Then, of course, there was in 1900 the publication of what was later seen to be the beginning of the anti-romantic novel in America, *Sister Carrie*.

There was that other Carry. On June 6th of the year of the island cabin a large woman dressed all in layers of black from bonnet to shoes approached a small Kansas town in her worn buggy. It was hauled by a gelding she called Old Prince. In a burlap sack on the seat next to her jostled bricks from her outhouse, a structure that had been but recently demolished by her unsympathetic neighbors. She was about to hurl them into the glassware of no less than three separate liquor establishments and thus begin her country-wide fame which she hoped would echo her name: Carry A. Nation. After years of local forays, 1900 was the summer that Carrie Nation took her act on the road and became a force no longer possible to ignore. One wonders what Henry, the newsman, thought of her. It must have been on some level of his awareness as if his mother Sarepta had gone irrevocably amok. (Maggie Walker says that a generation later his favorite topic was not islands but Prohibition and when Repeal came in, he seemed poignantly stripped of his major material.)

Not to worry, however, Queen Victoria was yet on the throne.

FURTHER FOOTSTEPS

My job with the Walkers was once again to lead the in-the-footsteps forays which culminated in the voyage to Quirk in my old Noank lobsterboat, a trip to which Maggie Walker refers in her introduction to this volume. In the evening listening to the Walkers around my friend Sina's dinner table, I began to appreciate how Arthur Henry was a much more complex man than I had thought from my reading of *An Island Cabin* and the passing references to him in Dreiser biographies. As for the relationship between the two men, the Walkers pointed out how extensive it was. It had gone back not only to newspaper days in Ohio, but other summer vacations where the two men had holed up in waterfront houses owned by women in order to become writers with a capitol W. And after all, didn't they actually pull it off? *The American Tragedy*, if not *Sister Carrie* was the Great American Novel in the desk drawer of every frustrated newspaper man; Quirk was the escape island, not in the Caribbean or South Sea but in New England. If these were cliches, Henry & Dreiser were very near the minting of that particular stereotype in America.

There is another great American myth about how memorable composition gets done. These yarns are best applied to tune and lyric collaborators, but there are plenty of literary ones. One thinks of Mark Twain and Charles Dudley Warner working on *The Gilded Age* (or Twain and Ulysses Grant on the General's memoirs); Stephen Crane and Joseph Conrad working at opposite ends of a long table; Ezra Pound and T.S. Eliot on *The Wasteland*; Fitzgerald and Hemingway on the end of *A Farewell to Arms*.)

As we have seen when Dreiser came to Noank, he was brooding over the failure of what eventually was to become the groundbreaking piece of realism that is *Sister Carrie*. What I had not realized was the extent to which Henry had been involved in the inspiration, composition and editing of that book.

(It might have helped if I had read the dedication.) It had been Arthur Henry, the man who had hired Dreiser on the newspaper and who himself was, as Maggie Walker puts it, "the successful author of pot-boilers and hack work," and who had first inspired Dreiser to write a novel.

While Captain Ashbey built the cabin on the island in the winter of 1899-1900, Henry was lodging in Manhattan with Dreiser and his wife Ruth. Meanwhile, in England, British publisher William Heinmann sought to bring out *Sister Carrie* in a cheap edition if he could reduce its bulk by 40,000 words, (the length of the entire *The Great Gatsby*.) Dreiser threw up his hands at the task. Seeing a second chance for the book and the friend he believed in, Henry set aside his non-fiction book *A Lodging in Town*, which was to be the first of a kind of back-to-the basics, do-it-yourself trilogy of which *An Island Cabin* was planned to be the second. He instead went to work on *Sister Carrie*.

Alfred Kazan argues in his introduction to the Penguin paperback of the University of Pennsylvania edition that some of Henry's cuts were perhaps hasty and harmful to Dreiser's intent. James L. West III, the textual editor says:

> The original typescript was corrupted by Dreiser's typist [in Anna Mallon's pool] and was revised and cut by his wife, [in *An Island Cabin*, "Ruth"] and his friend, Arthur Henry. The first edition was further flawed by the interference and censoring of Doubleday, Page & Co., Dreiser's publisher. Only the manuscript (before Sara and Henry revised it) preserves the original text of *Sister Carrie*.

While great sport can be had in debating such aesthetic matters as parallels with Ezra Pound's cleaver upon T.S. Eliot's "The Waste Land," there can be little argument that without Henry's work we would probably not be talking about *Sister Carrie* today, or even Dreiser as a novelist. His original manuscript was just not going to get published. As Kazin himself puts it:

> [Dreiser] had never thought of writing fiction until pressed to do so by Arthur Henry, his sometime employer on the *Toledo Blade* and

then his most intimate friend. Henry was himself a fluent, although not particularly interesting writer of fiction, but he had great sophistication and was an "emancipated" husband and assertive thinker in the rebellious style favored by end-of-the-century newspapermen. Like Dreiser's future friend and supporter, H.L. Mencken, Henry provided a figure of authority to Dreiser, who was to show awesome force as a social novelist but little personal self-confidence.

The nuances of the editing issue are best run down in Professor West's commentary and notes in the Pennsylvania edition. For the purpose of fully appreciating *An Island Cabin* it is merely necessary to recognize that all this high literary activity was going on during the period leading directly up to, including and easing away from the Noank project. It would seem that *Sister Carrie*, rocking chair and all, was the 800-pound gorilla in the corner of Quirk's rough hewn cabin. It was as important for Henry's own literacy project to keep Dreiser's book off the island as it was to fend off the arrival of his own wife. Indeed, *An Island Cabin* is as interesting for what is not aboard as for what is.

In any case, by 1900 the chemistry of their collaboration had reached the point where Henry could write: "We lived and worked together—often finishing each other's articles. If I read them today I could not tell what was his or mine." With the longer fiction, however, "Our stories were our own. We talked them over together but wrote them with less collaboration." Henry sliced and spliced the unwieldy *Sister Carrie* manuscript into shape so that it was publishable in the cheap English edition. With the positive reception to the new, trimmed book in England, *Sister Carrie* rebounded to its native shores and finally became a success, but only after *An Island Cabin* was out.

Before he cut *Sister Carrie*, however, Henry had had to push his hack journalist friend into writing a novel at all. Burton Roscoe sets the stage:

One evening in October 1899 a diffident and discouraged reporter, working on a newspaper in Cleveland Ohio, sat for some time, after his day's work was finished, peering at the clumsy keys of an

Oliver typewriter on which, by ambitious practice, he had learned to play the usual tunes of news reporting in a fairly competent one-finger technique.

.... he had made a compact with Arthur Henry, his side-kick, buddy, room-mate, partner in adversity and in literary production. Arthur Henry, when he took Dreiser under his wing, was already a successful writer of pulp yarns and run-of-the- mill commercial fiction. He knew the formulas, the tricks of the hack-writing trade. But Henry sensed in Dreiser a genius far transcending his own boy-meets-girl fiction-writing facility. Like a doting mother Henry tried to bring that genius which he suspected Dreiser had, into some fruition.

Here is how Roscoe says Henry accomplished this:
One night he pulled an umbrageous scowl over his otherwise amiable and easy-going continence, picked a quarrel with Dreiser, told him he was a bum, had no talent, and that he had better learn how to run a trolley car or something, for he would never be worth a tinker's dam as a writer.

Henry then flung a challenge at his friend. They would both write their first novel, prize to the first one to finish, and get it published.
The football coach ploy worked and Dreiser was eventually off on *Sister Carrie* although Henry actually got there first with what Roscoe calls a typical "bon-bon" of the times, *A Princess of Arcady*. While you can read all about this in the Heritage Press limited edition of *Sister Carrie*, you will be hard put to find *any* surviving edition of *A Princess of Arcady*.

"MURDER IN A SMALL BOAT"

When they arrived back home the Walkers went at the Arthur Henry biography. Just how they divided up the writing eludes me. I do know that Mark and I spent some telephone and letter writing time trying to thrash out "The Great Circumnavigation of Masons Island" in *An Island Cabin*. The fruits of this cooperative labor are available in the Walkers' *Dreiser's Other Self: The Life of Arthur Henry*, published in 2005. It is a fascinating look into a place, a time and a level of the culture which while quintessentially "American," is often neglected for the periods before and after.

In the case of the circumnavigation of Masons Island is the wonder of how Dreiser and Henry actually managed their boat. A causeway which, according to the 1893 and the 1990 Eldridge charts, was already in place. The little excursion is hardly a major moment in American sea voyaging, but the problem at the bridge is one I've personally faced a number of times with pretty much the same equipment as Dreiser and Henry. The scent of that brine-saturated, iodine weed as the current quickens through the sudden darkness is in my nostrils.

The cross-plank sharpie Captain Green had built for them was not much more than a glorified rowing skiff with a short, un-stayed mast stuck through the bow thwart. Rigged thus, the spar could be easily lifted out by competent sailors, laid along the gunnels as the occupants manhandled or paddled the boat under the bridge. Once out from under the span they could and quickly re-step the mast. One can even grant them the luck of a fair tide. Given Dreiser's general inflexibility of body and spirit, however, it is hard to picture him comprehending, much less mastering this un-stepping and stepping procedure and the need to grab at the concrete and fend off. Henry necessarily remained aft at the helm which by then had degenerated through a gudgeon-pinion failure into an oar in Henry's clasp. Nor was it likely for the author to pass up this farcically rich opportunity to expose their bogus seamanship. Yet, he does not mention their approaching the low bridge down wind before a building sou'wester towing a water cask—a circumstance that given the talent aboard, could have only produced, at the least, a flying fiasco.

My partner at Flat Hammock Press, ex-Coast Guardsmen Robert McKenna, speculates that any attempt to render some sort of literary version of Dreiser and Henry at the Bridge would have involved such a massive job of technical editing as to be uneconomical to the narrative flow. Still, I would have given anything to be standing on that span when the "Outstanding Practitioner of American Naturalism" advanced unflinchingly in a real-life situation under sail upon the rude bridge.

Perhaps Henry was saving the climax of the foray for the subsequent thrash back to windward up the west side of Masons Island. Now, presumably against the current, the skipper becomes so frustrated with the ineptness and arrogance of his crew that he yells at him until "Tom" petulantly lets go of the sail entirely:

> There was a moment's ominous silence after this, in which we glared at each other, while the boat went its own way swiftly, blown sideways toward the land.

The sharpie shoots up into the wind in a comic kerfluffle of luffing which snaps the tension. Both men agree that their friendship should not break up over such a matter. Once they gain control of the boat again and seem well under way, however, the future author of *An American Tragedy* makes a prophetic comment: "Well," said Tom, "you can easily see how just such a thing a miserable little mess like that might end in murder."

Once again we see the bizarre way life and literature interact with Dreiser. By 1925, "murder in a small boat," of course, is the key to the plot of his greatest work, *An American Tragedy*. While Dreiser grabbed the yarn from newspaper accounts (and thus created the first American non-fiction novel decades before Truman Capote), where else but the voyage with Arthur Henry did he get the texture of the climactic murder scene in the rowboat? Mencken had come to know Dreiser and his literary methods as well as had Arthur Henry, and wrote in his introduction to the Modern Library edition of *An American Tragedy*:

> ...all those novels are based upon things actually seen, heard or heard of... It was seldom that he departed from what he understood to be the record, and he never did so willingly... When he described a

street in Chicago and New York it was always a street that he knew as intimately as the policeman on the beat... When he sent some character into an eating-house for a meal it was always some eating-house that he had been to himself, and the meal he described in such relentless detail was one he had eaten, digested and remembered.

Here is the maritime heart of the murder scene in the novel, chiefly stripped of the three pages of verbiage particular to the hero's psychology and amorous dilemma:

> He paused in the rowing and put out his hand, then resumed. He would not row directly to that island in the south. It was too far— She was looking at the very same point of land that he was–a curved horn of land that bent to the south and yet reached quite far out into the water... The little inn and the boathouse to the north were growing monumentally smaller... At the point of land favored by Roberta, into a minute protected bay with a small, curved, honey-colored beach... And after that, further on down the west shore... in this little boat, to that island... And then at last, after fully an hour of rowing, brooding, singing, stopping to look at some charming point of land, reconnoitering some receding inlet... connected by an inlet or passage to the larger one, and yet itself a respectable body of water. The manner in which to the east, the north, the south, the west, even, except for the passage by which the island to the north was separated from the mainland... And as they glided into this, this still dark water seemed to grip Clyde as nothing here or anywhere before this ever had—to change his mood... And yet, what did it all suggest so strongly? Death! Death! More definitely than anything he had ever seen before. Death!... They would not come on shore again together. Never! Never!... that island and this dark water around and beneath her... His wet, damp, nervous hands!... All that he needed to do now was to turn swiftly and savagely to one side or the other—leap up—

upon the left wale or right and upset the boat; or failing that, rock it swiftly, and if Roberta protested too much, strike her... And apart from that, nothing—a few ripples—the peace and solemnity of this wondrous scene...

Arthur Henry may have had a closer call than he knew!

THE OTHER WOMEN

One of the curious things about the whole Quirk episode is that the scandal seems to have grown considerably *after* Henry and his entourage left Noank. As long as the "Quirk Islanders" were in sight they seem to have been treated with a courteous curiosity and much helpful sympathy. The locals apparently bought Henry's explanation that the second woman was a maid of the first and a chaperone to the couple. (This was a distinction no doubt facilitated in person by the difference in the strength of the Irish accent between Anna Mallon and Bridgett Seery, a point made by Maggie and Mark Walker.) It was only after the book came out two years later with Henry's vague assignment of roles to the two main women that the notion arose that little ol' Isle o' Quirk had been harboring *a ménage a trois.* Further evidence of the ostensible blandness of Henry's arrangement is his actual wife Maud's remark years later that she had "hadn't been suspicious about this affair while I was there [on the island]." Time passed and Henry's Noank friends, most of whom were elderly when he met them, passed on. There were fewer and fewer people who had actually met the Quirk Islanders, and Bridgett, who stayed on, had quickly married into one of the old families.

Dorothy Cramer put me onto the closest person to *An Island Cabin,* yet living, Mrs. Walter Lowe, nee Alice Seery Main, the daughter of Bridget Seery, nicknamed "Beezie," whom Henry calls "Elizabeth" in *An Island Cabin.* Born in Ireland in 1878, "Beezie" emigrated to America in 1884. Of the four island women of the book, "Elizabeth" early almost steals the show. It is her swimming lesson that takes precedence over Nancy's sailing instruction. You would never know in the early part of the book which girl Henry was romantically involved with. There is nothing to indicate that she is actually Nancy's maid, as there is the case with Ruth Dreiser and her maid Susan. Maggie Walker says, "A year earlier, while on the island, she [Beezie/ Elizabeth] met and married George Main, Noank's barber." What would it do to poor Arthur Henry to think the whole time he was merrily enjoying the spirited company of "Elizabeth" that her real-life prototype was actually being courted by a barber from the mainland a quarter century older than she? (Perhaps this smolders in Dreiser's remark in his journalism that he finds the Noank barber "almost offensively social.") And furthermore, to know this man had courted so successfully *"while on the island"*!

Fortunately for Henry, a look at the census records reveals that the Seery-Main nuptials did not occur until 1903, two years *after* Henry left Noank's shores. Alice, their daughter, was born the next year. (In Dreiser's shore-side sketches "A Doer of the Word" in addition to the social barber Main, the Mains make an appearance through "old Mr. Main" whose first name is Henry and who serves as the interlocutor in a gam in a fisherman's workshop.)

While it is not inaccurate to do as Maggie Walker does, and characterize Beezie as Anna's "best friend," the relationship actually began in as much more formal and commercial way. In the fuller account in Maggie Walker's biography of her grandfather, she explains:

> [Beezie] had originally entered the Mallon household as a maid but was now considered one of the family. Anna's was a substantial middle-class Irish-Catholic family, a home of refinement, means and good taste... Beezie was to become Arthur and Anna's chaperone and confidante for the next several years.

Beezie's daughter Alice lived on Pearl Street in Noank across from her late grandfather-in-law, the catboat fisherman Aaron Main. When I knew Alice in the 1980s she was a handsome, white-haired woman, the widow of a non-maritime man named Walter Lowe "from away." Her husband's job had taken them far inland to Tennessee for years, but she'd persuaded him to return to Noank in their retirement. After her husband's passing, she was watched over by her nephew, the iconic Noank lobsterman, Captain George Main, scion of a long line of lobstermen. Captain George and his father before him have always named at least one of their lobster boats after her. (One of the little side streets running west of High Street is called "Main Place.")

Alice told me how her mother had first met Anna Mallon in Grand Central Station armed with a letter of recommendation for employment as a maid. Alice even produced this handwritten paper from before the turn of the century, a document so crucial to the assimilation of Brigitte Seery into the old Yankee family. I got the distinct impression that her mother and Anna Mallon had not met face-to-face before the Isle o' Quirk interlude. There had been the letter and then the actual encounter in Grand Central as Anna was boarding the train to come to Noank. That they became more than employer and employee, does seem to be true, however. In the hallway leading to Alice's neat parlor was an example of Anna Mallon's "refinement and good taste" a relic of Isle o' Quirk days, a now electrified brass kerosene lamp with the green glass shade which Anna had given her mother as a token of her affection. While there is no evidence that Arthur Henry ever returned to Noank after departing the island in the fall of 1900, Alice Lowe indicated that Anna Mallon had come back at least once and that the lamp in the front hall had been the product of one of those visits. Alice told me this was the very lamp that the Quirk islanders had set in the cabin window to guide them across the harbor when they returned from Noank at night. With the passing of Alice Lowe I suspect it now has to be in the attic of her old house.

A less pleasant recollection of Alice's was how summer boarders down Pearl Street at the Ashbey House would read *An Island Cabin* then amble up, parasol in hand, and poke at Alice's house. "When I'd walk by the piazza down there at the Ashbey House, I'd see them with nothing better to do than sit in those rockers, reading away, stoking up. I think they were always disappointed my mother didn't emerge from our house in some sort of outlandish rig." It was, of course, the Ashbey House that furnished "harborage for the winter" to

Quirk's cats—and since Henry never returned, presumably became home for the rest of their lives. Since Henry makes no mention of altering his pets, can one assume that there are to this day leaping in and out of the village hedges at dusk, or underfoot in parlors, off-spring of Quirk's cats? In any case, there are relics of the Ashbey House in the Noank Historical Society. A brochure reads:

> The Ashbey House is ten minute's walk from the railroad station; six minutes from the trolley [not quite yet in service when Henry was in Noank] and four minutes from the post office. There are five incoming mails daily, and four going out.
>
> The Ashbey House gives special attention to the service in the dining room. The table is provided with homelike, New England cooking, fresh vegetables and the added advantage of abundance of fresh fruit and vegetables.

Poking around some more in the Historical Society, one eventually turns up the fact that The Ashbey House was built by Captain L.D. Ashbey and realizes that this was the same fellow who built Henry's island cabin.

An Island Cabin does not level either as to just who Anna Mallon "(Nancy)" really is. The Walkers have traced down her background. Like Arthur Henry, her father had been in combat in the Civil War, but had not been as lucky:

> Her father, James Mallon, who had been a colonel in command of the 42nd New York Infantry regiment, was killed in action at the battle of Briscoe Station, Virginia, in October 1863. Her grandfather had been an officer in the Revolutionary War.

Like Arthur Henry's mother, Anna's mother was a woman of command, "a woman of some means, owner of several properties of which Anna appears to have been to some extent the overseer."

At the time Henry lived with her on Quirk, Anna was not yet married to him, a solemnization of the relationship that did not take place until a year after the book came out when he was 35 and she six years older. When Henry was on Quirk, not only was he not married to Anna, but he was still betrothed to Maude. His wife was a fellow *Toledo Blade* reporter by which he'd fathered a daughter before heading east to find his fame and fortune in the Big City (and meet Anna in the steno company to which he'd taken his literary typing.) Chaperoned by the maid or not, "Platonic" or laced "with the salt of desire," for Arthur Henry and Anna Mallon the Isle o' Quirk interlude was the sort of honeymoon in reverse, a sequencing which in those days, of course, was less popularly recommended.

In what may seem as the most perverse of Henry's actions regarding the relationships between his wives and his books, he dedicated *A Princess of Arcady*, a book he began while still living with Maude, the *Toledo Blade* reporter, the mother of his daughter, to Anna but dedicated *An Island Cabin* to Maude! Just how the first wife got onto the dedication page of what should have been the second wife's book is something that cannot be inferred from reading *An Island Cabin*.

What with all of the wives and the maid, each with a nickname in real life and a pseudonym in the book, the simple fact of the dedication reversal had eluded me until I read the Walker's book for the second time. The dedication unlocks the secret to the most bizarre of all the omissions from *An Island Cabin*.

Forty-four years after the business on The Isle o' Quirk, Maude Henry wrote to Robert Elias on March 14, 1946, a piece of correspondence unearthed by the Walkers. It needs to be noted that in spite of one's memories of *An Island Cabin*, Henry spent at least half the time alone on the island. First he went out there to prepare for the women and the Dreisers. Later he was left alone when the Dreisers bolted prematurely and Anna and "Beezie" went back to Manhattan during the week to work. In spite of the businesslike schedule, it was not during one of these opportunities that Maude, languishing long in Ohio with the daughter, (by luck or design?) somehow arrives on Quirk. The motive for Maude's visit seems to have been the unfinished business of their divorce. Her four epistolary paragraphs deserve to be folded into the account of that summer on the idyllic isle, not only for the information, but for the voice which reminds us what people actually spoke like when not consciously literary:

I gave Arthur a divorce after that summer at the cabin—1901—because "he thought he ought to marry Anna." Naturally I was surprised, but replied that I did not know that I had any objections, except there was [daughter] Dorothy. He said, "Lord, I'll take her or you can." And I said, "No, Arthur, you will not take her," adding, "but you told me last year in New York that you were not in love with Anna anymore than you were with your grandmother."

"Well, I'm not in love with Anna, but her mother is sitting over there in Noank trying to watch this island with a telescope (or field glass or some such thing) and I felt I ought to marry her." (That mile-off mother always struck my funny bone.)

Arthur said Dreiser told him he thought I wanted to be released from our marriage in order to marry a certain Toledo physician... Then Arthur reminded me that I had told him I wasn't sure what he meant by love one night in a Maumee [Ohio] garden... (that) "I was an interesting woman but an impossible wife." "Ahem—maybe so," I replied, Not any more impossible than you are, Artie."

Well, to cut this—off-the-record stuff short—Arthur rushed over and offered himself back to me, but I shook my head—no. Anna had run from the cabin and I got up and followed her as she was climbing into the sharpie. "I wouldn't have Arthur Henry for a million dollars if you want him," she said pretty wildly. Of course she did want him—although I hadn't been suspicious about this affair while I was there. My reply was that she could have him—but I warned her that there would be trouble. Women and finances... I told them they would have to wait a year before I could take time off to give him a divorce. He got his friend Brand Whitlock to represent us in a three-minute trial with two or three questions asked almost in a whisper—and Arthur met me in the old Boody House here immediately afterward with a resounding smack and the remark that I would never know how much he cared for me. As Dreiser would say, "so much for romance."

Never mind Dreiser's take. One can only wonder what Captains Green and Ashbey made of all this ferrying back and forth out there.

The Walkers have discovered no evidence that Anna's mother was one of those on the shore with the telescope or other ocular device, but it is clear Arthur believed she was. (Could he have, at that distance, mistaken one of Deacon Palmer's relatives?) More to the point, it was after all, Mallon's mother who seems to have arranged with her friend, Norwich patent medicine king Charles Osgood, a kind of lease on the unnamed island north of Ram. Captain Rathbun in his meticulously researched *Capsule Histories of Some Local Islands and Lighthouse in The Eastern Part of L.I. Sound* writes:

> I have found no way to verify the statements in Arthur Henry's book that no deed to the island had ever been filed until he fill[ed] out the papers establishing his claim; neither is there any record of an official name for it prior to Henry dubbing it "The Isle of Quirk" so perhaps he was not stretching the truth when he wrote it.

(Today as all three islands are connected to each other at dead low tide, property taxes from the Town of Stonington treat Quirk, Ahoy, and Ram as one island owned by Ann and John Ragsdale.) As Maggie Walker tells us, Mrs. Mallon also provided some of the ready by which expenses were met such as the building of the boat to get there by the seventy-year old Captain Greene. Mrs. Mallon also seems to have underwritten Captain Ashbey to build the house at $275. (An Anthony Ashbe was John Winthrop Jr.'s overseer in the district in 1645 and built a house where Eccleston Brook debouches into Palmer Cove and so became the first "settler" in Noank. Part of his house remains. What is now West Cove was called "Ashbey's Cove" in Henry's time and the point at Blue Meadows was "Ashbey's Bend." Ashbey (with the *e* and *y*) is yet a common Noank moniker used for first names, last names, restaurants and streets. There are also plenty in the cemetery.)

Oddly enough it wasn't until Anna Mallon's mother noticed that her daughter actually was marrying the bohemian writer Henry well after they left Quirk that she disowned her daughter. Anna, however, was not rendered insolvent, adrift in the feckless hands of Henry. She had long been running her own office worker pool business in Manhattan and was one of those "New Women" go-getters that the magazines Henry and Dreiser wrote for feasted upon.

In *An Island Cabin* Henry would have you believe these uninhabited islands are lying about within a rowboat's pull of the Connecticut shore just for the picking up. This was a necessary bit of dissembling in order to get the book published. *An Island Cabin* was part of a trilogy of back-to-the land, self-help narratives Henry knocked out within a few years: *An Island Cabin*, 1902; *The House in the Woods*, (Catskills) 1904. *Lodgings in Town*, (Manhattan) 1905. It was an editor friend John Phillips of McClure, Phillips & Co. who suggested Henry capitalize on the back-to-the-land fad by exploiting his experience on the little New England island. Henry had actually begun working on the last book first as that was his experience of the moment.

The island part was key to the literary project for if it were just a matter of hanging out in quaint Noank, in addition to the Ashbey House on Pearl Street, there was a brand new hotel built the same winter Captain Ashbey was working on Henry's cabin. The Palmer, named after Deacon Palmer who provided the inspiration (and Mary Anderson says not a little of the finances) was a big ark of a place overlooking the harbor in the Block Island and Watch Hill tradition and was run by a genuine salt, the high-wasted, rotund Captain James H. "Jimmie" Sistare (Now the site of the Village Boatyard). The contemporary write-up that historian Carol W. Kimball has salvaged shows the contrast with Henry's island structure:

The spacious building was to be up-to-date in every respect with all the modern conveniences, including electric lights and steam heat, second to none along the coast. By Jan 11 the rooms were lathed, awaiting masons who would come as soon as the furnace was in service.

Captain Jimmy's brochure touts "The Summer hotel that is different" has easy access by train from New York, New Haven and Hartford and "by the New London boat from New York, sailing from Pier 40, North River." (Oddly enough the Captain makes no attempt to solicit guest from the east, perhaps realizing that the resorts from Watch Hill to Cape Cod may have that trade sewed up. There are accommodations for up to sixty guests with "rates on application. Special rates for June and September, and for families for the Season." Potential guests are advised to "write at once" to the Captain who assures them they can "find rest and plenty of broiled live lobsters awaiting them at The Palmer." The proffered blandishments of The Palmer provide a contrast to the stark life style Henry eked out on Quirk and serve even more than the Ashbey House brochure, as a kind of alternative text to *An Island Cabin*:

> The house is hospitably and comfortably furnished and is lighted by electricity. All sleeping rooms are large, light and airy and special attention is given to the beds, woven wire springs and first-class mattresses being used exclusively. There are bathrooms on each sleeping floor, containing hot and cold, fresh and salt water baths.
>
> The dining room is large and commodious, extending entirely across the house and contains many large windows, facing both East [where Quirk would be in the "view"] and West, from which an abundance of light is obtained.
>
> A special feature of The Palmer is its cuisine. A well supplied table is considered by the management one of the essential requirements to meet the ever increasing appetite, stimulated by the invigorating sea air. Fresh vegetables from nearby farms are picked and delivered daily, and choice sea foods taken daily from the water are

served in abundance. A specialty is made of broiled live lobsters.

One of the chief attractions is the "Aunt Edie," a very staunch able fifty-foot schooner with a fifty horse-power auxiliary engine. Almost daily invitations are extended to all guests for sailing and fishing trips. Some of the places visited on these trips include, Block Island, Gardiners Bay, Bartlett Reef.

Veranda sitters are invited to partake of the magnificent view of "Fishers Island, Race Rock [not actually visible from the hotel], Mystic [Ram] Island, Cabin Island [Quirk?!] the Ram Island Light Ship [available only from the cupola], Latimer Light and beautiful Long island Sound [only by courtesy of calling Fishers Island Sound part of L.I.S.]."

For more active sports:

The fishing trips to Montauk [some 20 miles straight out to sea] are most enjoyable, a large catch being the result of each trip. Through June and July, many sword fishing trips are taken, and fine sport is had in taking these gamey fish, weighing over one hundred pounds, from the water.

To those who enjoy sailing and sea fishing, this opportunity is found in no other hotel on the coast.

The rocking chair fleet is invited to consider that "Noank has long been and favorably known [as] "surrounded by many places of great historic interest, and some of the most pleasing romances of literature [which] have received inspiration from the character of its early settlers, chief among them being the hero so beautifully portrayed in the story of Caleb West."

Caleb West, of course, was hardly "an early settler," having been the protagonist in F. Hopkinson Smith's (1838-1915) novel *Caleb West, Master Diver,* a fictionalized version of Smith's experience as architect and engineer in the challenging construction of Race Rock Light, first lit in 1879. Smith, also architect of the base of the Statue of Liberty and of the Mosquito Inlet

Light in Florida mentioned in Crane's "The Open Boat" was a popular writer in his day, writing a shelfload of fiction and non-fiction with outdoor themes. *Caleb* went through a least two editions. At the end of his life Smith re-packaged the lot in a uniform edition, collected works *a la* Conrad and Henry James. His character Caleb West seems loosely based on Smith's close associate, the Race Rock construction foreman, New London's Captain Thomas A. Scott (1839-1907). Dorothy Cramer, who introduced me to Smith's work, always told me Caleb "was" a Noank man whose last name was Shirley and who is buried in a pinkish, beach pebble monument in the Noank cemetery. Where she got this information beside a hand-me down from her Mouse Island crowd, I could never ascertain, but a memorial artifact answering to her description does indeed exist in the Noank Valley Cemetery. Smith's composite novelized descriptions of the shore sites in *Caleb* have always struck me as more New London than Noank and even the small fishing village of which he speaks seems too generic to evoke the actual village in the way that Henry and Dreiser's accounts do.

As for another "pleasing romance of literature," two editions of *An Island Cabin* must had been available by the time Captain Jimmy's brochure writer wrote as evidenced by the fact that the publication mentions the trolleys. The brochure's reference to "Cabin Island" in a sequence of Masons Island, Mystic Island and the Ram Island Light Ship would also seem to at least speak to an interest in the architectural remains of that "romance."

Captain Rathbun says the great Palmer Hotel structure lasted until the 1938 Hurricane gave its leisurely dilapidation the *coups de grace*, "as that storm did for so many other artifacts that were just barely hanging on out of Noank's past." Abbott's Lobster Co. had its cannery there in my youth. The spiffy Noank Village Boatyard presently occupies the site.

Of course for Henry, the publishing hook was not to be high-end, seaside living in a quaint fishing village already in place. The whole idea was that the land came as a kind of homesteading, a notion that Henry smuggles dramatically into the mouth of old Captain Green: "...You can rig her up and claim her and she's yours," the captain replied. In terms of grand literary parallels, the fib seems no more reprehensible than Thoreau's not telling us that Emerson let him stay rent free at Walden. Or, take a story out in the same year Henry arrives on Quirk in which "Joseph Conrad" evades admitting to us that Conrad Korzeniowski's aunt got him the job on the *Roi des Belges* that led to "Heart of Darkness."

FALL OUT

The Noank summer idyle reached the public first in the dead of winter of 1902 as a Saturday night serial in the *New York Post*. When the book came out, the reviews were positive. The Walkers have collected a few. The *Bookman* praised *An Island Cabin* for "The fresh ideals and hopes... The strong, salt breath of ocean air that blows through its pages... a book which awakes a nostalgia for the broad reaches of sea and sky, and dim-veiled glimpse of distant coasts." There were the inevitable evocations of the bachelor poet of Walden Pond as *The World's Work* which called Arthur Henry "A homespun Thoreau because he writes without literary pose." The *New York Sun* drew other literary parallels stating that the book combined "The delightment of Sancho Panza with the adventures of Swiss Family Robinson." (Perhaps seeing Henry as playing the realistic squire to Dreiser's windmill tilting Don, or would it be the other way around?)

And what was the personal fall out of *An Island Cabin*? We have mentioned some of the local reaction, but this seems the usual sort of small town *tsk-tsk*, nothing compared to *Look Homeward Angel* or to pick a modern New England example, *Peyton Place*. The deep cut was between Dreiser and Henry not Henry and the community. Although they did make up years later, the two writers quite simply were never the same toward each other. How much of this was truly the treatment of "Ted" in the book, how much the actual behavior of Dreiser which led to this rendering is unclear. While it was ostensibly to cull local color for the series of uplifting magazine pieces that Dreiser was visiting his old editor friend, the fact was that Dreiser seems to have been on

the verge of a nervous breakdown. As much as to seek material, he had come
to Noank for a rest cure

The strain of writing and publishing *Sister Carrie* had somewhat un-
hinged his already fragile psyche and he was looking to his old savior Henry.
When Henry said he had an island, the situation seemed perfect. As *An Island
Cabin* shows, the results were anything but therapeutic for him. Whether
Dreiser's stay in Noank delayed his eventual breakdown or accelerated it is the
stuff of his biographies, but readers of *An Island Cabin* can certainly wonder if
beneath the comic camping out stuff there isn't some real neurosis a-smoldering.

Long before *An Island Cabin* came out Dreiser had left his wife Sara
Osborne "Jug" White, (called in the book "Ruth") and launched on what
was to become one of his manic waking tours, striding off down to the
South, and was unheard from for weeks at a time. Australian natives call
these excursions "walkabouts" and I suppose we could credit Dreiser with a
kind of American version of this sort of homeopathic foot marathon if it
weren't so, well, Dreiserian.

In what purports to be an eulogistic essay on his brother Paul, Theodore
gives a glimpse into his own post Isle o' Quirk depression:

> ...I had become so disappointed in connection with my work and
> the unfriendly pressure of life that I suffered what subsequently ap-
> peared to have been a purely psychic breakdown or relapse, not phys-
> ical, but one which left me in no mood or condition to go on with
> my work, or any work indeed in any form. Hope had disappeared in
> a sad haze... Apparently there was but one door, and I was very close
> to it...

It is this low moment in Dresier's life that provides the key for E.L. Doctorow's own method in *Ragtime*, that marvelous late 20th-Century recreation
of America's swing into modernity in the *An Island Cabin* era. Doctorow even
gets in Dreiser's rocking chair fetish as paradigm for his own point of narration.

Coincidentally this was the time in our history when the morose novelist Theodore Dreiser was suffering terribly from the bad reviews and negligible sales of his first book, *Sister Carrie*. Dreiser was out of work, broke and too ashamed to see anyone. He rented a furnished room in Brooklyn and went to live there. He took to sitting on a wooden chair in the middle of the room. One day he decided his chair was facing in the wrong direction. Raising his weight from the chair, he lifted it with his two hands and turned it to the right, to align it properly. For a moment he thought the chair was aligned, but then he decided it was not. He moved it another turn to the right. He tried sitting in the chair now but it still felt peculiar. He turned it again. Eventually he made a complete circle and still he could not find the proper alignment for the chair. The light faded on the dirty window of the furnished room. Through the night Dreiser turned his chair in circles seeking the proper alignment.

What pulled Dreiser out of his suicidal despair was what we would now call an intervention by his buoyant older brother Paul, then at the crest of his career as one of the top songwriters in what was to become the burgeoning Tin Pan Alley trade. Paul all but kidnapped his brother into his own world, paid his flop house bill, set him up with food, money and most important, restored by the "unlimited generosity of his mood and deed."

By the time Dreiser was done with his breakdown he was pretty much through with the sort of literary partnership relationship he'd had with Arthur Henry anyway. Some of this shift may be merely what happens as people grow out of a strong, mutual dependency. When Dreiser got around to reading *An Island Cabin* in its second, 1904 edition, the break was, for a time, complete. At his old Midwestern friend's hands, he had by now undergone what literary critic Alfred Kazin has characterized as his "painful preparation for literature."

Dreiser's debt to his former mentor was, for so fragile an ego, no doubt a burden and one that became greater the more his own fame and "success" bloomed. He soon had the foremost literary critic of his time, H.L. Mencken, in his corner. In any case, the Walkers figure Dreiser "more than evened the score" for *An Island Cabin* 27 years later when he took a shot at Henry and Anna Mallon in "Rona Murtha," one of the thinly fictionalized pieces in *A Gallery of Women*.

Having cycled through a number of women, Dreiser eventually had effectively rinsed out the effects of *An Island Cabin*. Dreiser charges up his complaints about the housekeeping on the Isle O' Quirk to the offstage demands of what to others had seemed to have been his ostensibly cheerful wife. The Walkers, however, see Dreiser as running behind an invented shield to cover his moroseness over the failure of *Sister Carrie*. The fate of Dreiser's novel was especially troubling in his present company when contrasted with his host's modest triumph with the fluffy *A Princess of Arcady*. Henry's novel had at least made no one angry and had in fact brought in a small royalty which even kicked in a little income toward the household expenses on Quirk. Furthermore, Dreiser had made no progress on the work he'd intended to get well under way on the island, his next big literary project, the novel that was to become *Jennie Gerhardt*, a book Mencken called "...the best American novel I have ever read, with the lonesome but Himalayan exception of *Huckleberry Finn*." Instead of accomplishing major work, Dreiser said to Henry and maybe a little bit to himself, that he had escaped the irksome domestic tension on Quirk merely to futz around ashore, chatting up the locals. To him time wasted away from the big book could hardly hope to be recouped through magazine pieces.

Dreiser was able to at least keep the pot boiling through magazine work, even becoming in 1907 editor of *The Delineator*. This was a magazine published by the Butterick Pattern Company that catered to the growing market for females who stayed at home and knitted or sewed and maintained their psyches in the evening on a diet of practical instruction spiced with buoyant fiction. By now republished with Henry's editing, *Sister Carrie* had begun to establish its reputation. Promoted to run Butterick's three magazines, however, Dreiser ironically could not find time to write further realistic novels. His fortunate fall back into serious literature came when the woman's pattern company fired him for becoming "infatuated" with the eighteen-year-old daughter of one of his secretaries, the irresistibly monikered Thelma Cudlipp.

Slowly there was a kind of reconciliation between Dreiser and the author of *An Island Cabin*. At work on major literature once again, Dreiser dined at Henry's New York apartment with theater friends, and in a reversal of their former literary fortunes he tried unsuccessfully to peddle some of Henry's stories to his own publisher, Horace Liveright. Dreiser could now afford to accept both Henry and *An Island Cabin*, eventually even to the point of writing Henry's daughter upon her father's death: "I still see Arthur as the author of *A Princess of Arcady, An Island Cabin, The House in the Woods*, and *Lodgings in Town*. In them lies the Henry that I best knew."

Of the five principals on the Isle o' Quirk, the first person to die was "Elizabeth," the ebullient Irish immigrant *Bridgett "Beezie" Seery Main who passed in 1921, on the fifth day of the eleventh month of her 42nd year,* as is recorded in pen and ink in a gloomy tome in the Noank Historical Society. She is interred in the Noank Valley Cemetery, lot #374. The relationship between where most people are buried these days and their lives lacks much sense of continuity. Transitory lives follow their shifting careers; the very neighborhoods morph out of all recognition. The paths from the cradle to the grave celebrated by the classic poets seems but a fusty piece of literary bric-a-brac. To walk in the Noank Valley Cemetery, however, is to be transported back to the days of front parlor poetry. Standing at Beezie Main's all but lichen-smothered headstone, you find your eye is guided south by a tunnel in the foliage. There at the end of this natural telescope you have, picked out in the last rays of an August day, that other harbor island from which it was in Dorothy Cramer's time, forbidden to look upon the spot where once Beezie Seery swam. The large stone which commands the family plot announces:

MAIN

1876 GEORGE S. MAIN 1957

HIS WIFE

1878 BEEZIE S. SEERY 1921

THEIR DAUGHTER

1907 MARGUERITE S. MAIN 1908

1913 CAPT. WM MAIN 1974

1915 BERTHA M. MAIN 1999

Alice Main Lowe is evidently elsewhere, perhaps with her husband Walter. A few strides to the north is Captain Ashbey who built the cabin on the island and took in Henry's cats. The rest of the cast of *An Island Cabin*, like characters in Thomas Grey or Edgar Lee Masters, Thornton Wilder or Dylan Thomas, are not far.

As for Henry himself, he published the next two books in his light-hearted life-style mode as Dreiser went on to his heavyweight novels. Henry obtained a divorce from his first wife Maude, she of the daughter and the *Toledo Blade*, and married Anna Mallon in Manhattan. The marriage was not as successful as the premature honeymoon on Quirk. Henry found himself swept up in the New York theater world writing plays, the most successful of which was called *Time* and debuted in New York November 24, 1923, the same day that the Coast Guard towed into harbor the queen of the rum runner fleet, William McCoy's *Arethusa*. (One recalls that Henry's favorite topic was Prohibition.) After a number of years of Henry's indifference to Anna, they divorced. Anna came to a sad end, seemingly the victim of depression which had been developing in her *A House in The Woods* days when the "doctrine of happiness" no longer seemed to be kicking in. She was by now physically as well as emotionally far away from Henry who was aflutter in New York show biz. On a day in May of 1921, she was moodily walking along the banks of a river in Washington state—when she who had survived the salt water challenges of Noank Harbor—somehow ended up overboard. Her coroner suffered the Ophilian conundrum: did the waters come to her or had she come to the waters? The Walkers print a letter written by Arthur Henry's brother that eventually found its way to Arthur:

We do not know any details of poor Anna's death. She loved to walk by the swiftly flowing river bank and sit there and dream.

In either case, Henry immediately married someone he'd met in his show business life, Clare Kummer, a popular songwriter who later with Henry's help, became one of the more successful playwrights of the era. Clare was a divorcee six years younger with one child and after spending time in the theater world of Manhattan, the family moved to Narragansett, a modest rival to Newport across the bay in southern Rhode Island. Maggie Walker recalls playing with her grandfather when he was in his 60s:

I remember him [in 1927] as a man of immense presence and warmth, spreading about hugs, kisses, and endearments to all—even the family dog and cat. Our home was somehow enlarged in all its dimensions when he came periodically to spend time with us... he was a handsome man, with rosy cheeks, smooth skin, clear gray eyes and an infectious laugh. Even in old age he retained much of his youthful appearance.

Though he continued to knock out commercial prose, and frothy plays, Arthur Henry never got anything down on paper half so charming as his little comic idyll about a few months in a cabin on an island at the far side of the harbor of a "played out" New England fishing village. For him it was, with the two other little memoirs, the isolated literary product of a few years in the first half of his life in what does seem in retrospect to have been a halcyon time between the Civil War and the great wars of the 20th-Century. Reading Maggie Walker's biography of her grandfather, one feels there to have been a darker side to him. That he chose not to connect with this sort of profundity, as did his old pal Dreiser, may have cost him a larger reputation, but it is hard to see how such a note would have helped *An Island Cabin*. It is what it is, even though it seems to have taken us so long to see what that might be.

Although we tend to remember the various social interchanges in *An Island Cabin*, most of Arthur Henry's time on Quirk is in fact spent alone. He doesn't approach this in a self-conscious manner as his mission is more communal, but what we can sense of his use of solitude is a happy by-catch. Certainly the Dreisers withdrawal can be nothing less than a defeat for the project, especially when one considers the past success the two writers had with this sort of arrangement in Ohio, a part of their lives Henry in the required focus of his project, he ignores. The book deal, after all, was not to create a salt-water *Walden*, but was to be more in the homesteading spirit, a Brook Farm, if one needs the transcendental excuse. And yet one gets the sense that the author's finest moments were perhaps when he was alone with his cats and dog. (Minus the ghastly failure with "Dump.") Or at least it was so until the iron lid of the coming New England winter began to lower on his now "desolate hummock."

It is part of Henry's framing technique to keep world events off the pages of *An Island Cabin*. Nonetheless he must have heard in his forays to Noank what the New York papers had brought into the busy little train station from which so many barrels of lobsters were sent west to the metropolis. On September 8th and the following weeks reports circulated of the worst hurricane to hit the United States. Some seven thousand were swept off the narrow barrier beach at Galveston, Texas and while it was to be nearly forty years before anything remotely like it hit Noank, there was no guarantee of Quirk's immunity to wind and sea. It would seem that the "sunny little lanes" of Noank would have been abuzz with such an event, conversations featuring comparisons to the Gulf Coast city and its position versus the home town and the local vulnerabilities. As it is, the 1938 Hurricane did strip the island of the last remnants of Henry's scheme.

There is, of course, the question of why Henry never went back to Quirk. The whole last movement of the book is dedicated to the idea that he will be back. Captain Green may build them a new boat—Henry puts the limiting factor off onto the captain's age, not his own frivolity. The cats and dog are not given up, but merely put into an over-wintering regime at the Ashbey House. Henry would have everyone believe, perhaps including himself, that he is just like any other cottager counting on the locals to watch out for the place while he regretfully returns to the city grind. It is all autumnal wistfulness in minor, diminished chords. The Walker's biography, however, seems to indicate that he was taken up with the next part in his lifestyle literary project, *The House in the Woods*. He already has his mind on it when he's finishing up the season out at Quirk and thinks to himself "I would prefer a cave in the woods" to another week on the island and asks himself, "Shall I choose the inland fields, the mountain forest or the city?"

By the time he was done with both the house in the Catskills and its book for which he was running out of enthusiasm, his companion in the two projects, Anna Mallon, seems to have reciprocated. That he should just walk off from a summer house on an island is no more surprising than that he walked off from his daughter back in Toledo. None of his intimates seemed to have expected more from him—except perhaps his-long departed mother, Sarepta, she of the Cold Water Army. He died at 67 of heart disease on June 2, 1934, with his third wife Clare at his side which, according to his *New York Times* obituary "fulfilled an often-expressed wish—to die quietly before the age of 70." For those who wish to make the pilgrimage, the author is buried in Narragansett Pier, Rhode Island.

The gloomy Dreiser would get through the Great Depression and the Second World War, dying December 28, 1945.

QUIRK AFTER

The trio of islands on the east side of Noank Harbor have continued to exert their lure, though the human history of the little chain has been one of long decline. The great hotel on Ram became so dilapidated that even the Wilcoxes could not defend it. We are indebted to Masons Island's E.B. Read's account that one night a rag-tag fleet of Noankers rowed out in a kind of Dunkirk Armada and stripped the place. Somebody called up Anna Malon's friend Charles Osgood in Norwich and described the scene. The patent medicine king laughed and said, "Let them at it. Times are hard over there and I'm sure they can use the lumber." Indeed Osgood's passiveness was once again appreciated. The lobster shacks that so picturesquely lined Riverview Avenue before the '38 Hurricane were largely cobbled together from scraps of the old hotel as was the paneling in my studio.

In the 1920s African explorer Mary Jobe Ackeley bought Ram from Osgood. She and her husband Carl had set up the Primate Hall at the Museum of Natural History in New York and had summoned Teddy Roosevelt to Africa after his presidency. Roosevelt's resulting book *African Game Trails* inspired Ernest Hemingway whose subsequent books on Africa were instrumental in the safari stampede. While on safari, Carl Ackeley died of a fever on a rocky mountain and could not be buried. It was now entirely up to Mary Jobe to run the safari out of the jungle. In order to keep her husband from passing the troop in the jaws of a panther, she had to pile rocks on him. In her widowhood she turned the Noank islands into a summer camp for girls, and Mildred Phelps told me that Mary Jobe made her girls earn their passage by rowing out from her home some three miles up the Mystic River. Or, in less robust moments Mary Jobe skippered her charges down stream aboard her motor launch *Northern Lights*. She used the old hotel foundation as a venue for ghost stories around the camp fire for the girls. Quick and Ahoy were further islets of discovery. In the late 1920s Mary Jobe shut down her camp and the island became a huge vacant lot for those with a small boat to get there. E.B. Read has a memoir from one former camper who recalls chiefly the mosquitoes and rats that despite the old brochures, not only are on the island, but swarm. At night there are three sounds, the buzzing of the mosquitoes, the tintinnabulation of the rats knocking down the plaster as they are capering in the old ballroom and Mary Jobe in the next tent snoring.

During Prohibition some thirsty villagers stole a cask of wine that the village shoemaker had set aside for a christening and took lobsterman Tony Pezzolezzi's sharpie to ferry the goods and customers to the islands for a bacchanal. In the excitement they failed to bring a proper bung starter and improvised one with a screw driver and a caulking mallet. They succeeded in breaching the cask by also driving the volunteer sommelier's thumb through the oak head. When Tony told me this in the 1960s, he pointed out to the islands with his gnarled stick. "I wasn't worried where my sharpie went. You could hear them hollering from here."

In the 1930s Neil "Ma" Haring ran a rowboat livery at the bottom of Snake Hill with her husband Al, an out-of-work geologist for the state. She used to rent flat iron sharpies much like Arthur Henry's and Tony Pezzolezzi's, to her customers from what she called "the hinterlands."

"Because of the lubberly nature of the clientele," she told me, "we instructed the "captains" and their "mates" not to stray beyond the islands. Naturally all of them went right over there and got drunk and sunburnt and tested the poison ivy as a love patch and they were incapable of returning under their own power. Al had an old catboat with the rig cut down and one of those Lathrop Company, marinized cement mixer engines. At sundown he'd go over there and start collecting the customers off the islands. By the time he'd got them all strung out it made for a tow that reached about half-way across the damn harbor."

For years village kids played in the crumbling house that Arthur Henry had dreamed up and somewhere in all this, the shack lost its identity as a human structure. The 1938 Hurricane finished it off. The island, topped by its precarious great erratic, remains, its foliage waxing and waning with the great storms and the birds who reseed it.

In the 1960s, when the Akeley estate was being settled there was a moment when the three islands were offered up for public recreation. The price was $300,000 (now hardly half the cost of a single home on the banks of the estuary overlooking the island). The idea was that the towns of Stonington and Groton would split the costs. With matching federal grants, the price sank to something like $75,000 per town. Fearing liability issues, both towns turned the offer down.

From time to time sunburnt picnickers yet set up on the thin beach and the overly amorous tempt their partners with the seclusion of the poison ivy. In the 60s, before the present owners took charge, there was a man who attempted to run a campground on Ram Island. To get the site ready for the invasion, he somehow brought out a battered tow truck from Steve's Garage, Hackensack, New Jersey (complete with Steve's phone number on the door.) His customers—most of them day trippers—would employ the Town Landing Place for their staging area, loading enough personnel and material onto a rag-tag armada of dinghies to simulate a parody of Operation Overlord. Those seeking more privacy than Ram afforded would spill over to Quirk, thence schismatics set up on Ahoy until the entire archipelago was festooned with the half-naked worshippers of solitude.

Developers built a cheesy "boatel" on part of the abandoned Osgood foundation with the hope that mariners anchoring in the east-side harbor might enjoy a night off from wallowing about. That harbor, which is between the horns of the island, does offer a pleasant spot for a lunch hook as long as the daytime summer southwesterlies prevail; it is a fatal lie should one of old Captain Chester's nasty easterlies come creeping in from the open sea under cover of darkness. (The Osgood setup had had no less than three piers, each covering a different direction against such wind shifts.)

Presently John and Ann Ragsdale own the islands where they have raised a generation of children and in the spirit of John Winthrop's colonial tenants several generation of sheep. They demolished the flimsy "boatel" and built a well-designed house utilizing part of the hotel foundation. In winter from my bedroom I can see their lights out there as if the house were a long, low excursion steamer anchored just inside the bell.

Most mariners today certainly do not refer to the lump of granite and weed as "Quirk," a designation which strikes them—if they think about it at all—as a bit quaintsy. Many locals do know something once went on out there at the far side of the harbor and that it was of a rather infamous and vaguely literary nature. In his *Capsule History* Captain Rathbun gives a gloss:

> Quirk Island's claim to fame lies with it being the setting for a book called "My Island Cabin" by a relatively unknown early 20th

century author named Arthur Henry, who was a friend of the well-known writer Theodore Drieser [sic] [Henry] paid some Noanker to build a summer cottage there the following winter. Come spring, bachelor Henry, accompanied by two attractive bachelorettes named Elizabeth and Nancy took a train from New York to what was then the busy Noank Station and set up housekeeping on Quirk for the summer. The book, now long out of print, recounts the summer's events in what can only be described as an "Age of Innocence" style which gives no hint that there was anything unusual, or sexual, about their relationship: this at the turn of the century mind you. How many years this idyll continued, I do not know, but when growing up in the 1930s the cabin was long gone, leaving only the remains of the cistern to show where the cabin stood...

There is an account in the Noank Historical Society in which another memoirist says, "Dad often spoke of the 'shack' that O'Henry [sic] built on the Isle of Quirk to do his writing." Arthur Henry's actual name is pretty much forgotten except as a footnote to Dreiser whose own reputation rises and falls, but always manages to hang around somewhere in the major rank of the American literary canon.

I recall one evening in the 1980s being aboard the 1911 steamboat *Sabino* when, just as the vessel was turning at the extreme end of her run at Quirk Island, her resident Dixieland band broke into Paul's "My Gal Sal." I had been reading in a Dreiser biography which told how Theodore had adapted his late brother's box grand piano into a writing desk, the closest material tribute he evidently could come up with. And here was the brother's song reconstructed—its tear-jerking barbershop minors, kidded by the syncopation of the drum and the campy grace notes of trombone and cornet under a canopy of seabird and clarinet obbligato. Was there something truly magical about the pull of the good old Isle o' Quirk that even after all those years the emanations Ariel-like, were seeping forth to the old steamboat? (Wasn't it, after all, brother Paul, the songster, who *Twelve Men* tells us had bailed him out after

[319]

the almost fatal depression Theodore had suffered following his 'idyle' on the Isle o' Quirk!)

When the last note sounded I pointed to Quirk, then but a mere fifty yards off to the starboard, (and fortunately still down wind) and asked the bandleader if he realized the significance of his selection. He shook out the spit from the water key in his cornet, stared at the scrubby rock pile a moment and said, "It just seemed time to get back to something in B-flat."

Starting in the 1970s there was, however, a Quirk Island Boat Club complete with burgee, floating clubhouse, a complete set of flag officers, small boats, most of which seaworthy—and the good sense to keep the hell off the actual island.

Atmospheric conditions over water make for a great variety in perception and there are times when from my rocking chair, Quirk looks like one of those cartoon islands upon which it seems anything said by the inhabitants is inescapably ironic. I think of old Dreiser over there with Arthur Henry. Dreiser is in his rocker atop his precarious Observational erratic and I try matching him profundity for profundity, so in twilight we are like a pair of harbor mortars volleying splashy lobs.

EPILOGUE

BY STEPHEN JONES

As for my churlish initial assessment of Dreiser, I've come around more to Nobel Laureate Saul Bellow's point which he expressed in a 1966 *Paris Review* interview:

> The development of realism in the nineteenth century is still the major event of modern literature. Dreiser, a realist, of course, had elements of genius. He was clumsy, cumbersome, and in some respects a poor thinker. But he was rich in a kind of feeling that has been ruled off the grounds of many contemporary writers—the kind of feeling that every human being intuitively recognizes as primary... He somehow conveys... depths of feeling that we usually associate with Balzac or Shakespeare.

The task of running down the details of *An Island Cabin* goes on and seems infinite for anyone who seems to insist on hanging around the site. As recently as this Memorial Day (2010), some of us were at a picnic in a backyard that is now separated from the former property of Captain Louis (Lewey) by a tarred road called Potter Court. Potter Court has been in place long before the memory of anyone now alive in the village, but during the visit of Arthur Henry it was merely the yard between Captain Louis' and his next door neighbor. Somewhere near the middle of the present road was the spot Arthur Henry was wont to visit in times of stress:

> There is an old fashioned well under his [Captain Louis'] cherry tree, with a bucket and windlass. It is the best water in Noank, and we went

there for water frequently for a drink or a pail full. Close to the well was a porch where an ancient parrot stood with ruffled feathers, rolling a wicked eye at me, and muttering to himself.

Sitting around the watermelon and the wine, we fell into a discussion of the whereabouts and proper ownership of Captain Louie's "well stone." Since Potter Court had been knocked through right over the boundary it had become unclear on which side the now obliterated well had been. While one might assume the well would be on the side of Captain Louis' house, the only surviving element is a large granite cap stone. According to Sandy Smith who has lived in the old Captain Louis house since the 1970s, the well stone had been buried under the Potter Court tar until the sewer line was cut through and it wasn't until the construction that it saw the light of day again.

Whether its worth as an artifact was instantly recognized or the excavator merely wanted to save the expense of its disposal, the stone ended up dumped on the lawn of the house immediately to the south across the street from Captain Louis'. A heated argument then broke out between Florence Oliver, the founding president of the Noank Historical Society, a direct descendent of Captain Louis, and the owner of the house upon whose lawn the stone now resided, an old Noank family named Ellis. The battle between the two elderly women went on for some time until Mabel Ellis decided to give the well-stone to Sandy Smith as the present owner of the Louis property. Sandy took the position that she did not actually want to possess the stone as she did not have the space, that land now being part of Potter Court. But at the same time she did not want to see harm come to the artifact which she considered part of Noank history. After all, her husband Robert was the last full-time draggerman in the village.

The two elderly combatants passed on, and the stone remained safely on the Ellis property until such time as the new owner, Sharon Cohen, came across it one day. To her it was a rock pretty much without context. In need of material for a wall she thought it would be sufficient homage to whatever vague history the stone had if she were to break up the big square piece and incorporate it in the new wall. When Teddy Wydler, the mason, moved in to perform his task, Sandy Smith walked across Potter Court. "That's my well stone," she said.

For a moment it seemed as if there was going to be a reenactment of the old battle over the stone between Mrs. Oliver and Ms. Ellis.

Fortunately Paul Bates, a friend to both sides, offered to swap for the historic stone some granite he had collected. Captain Louis' well stone now reposes among the rabbits and the dozen or so wooden boats in his backyard, the former house of John Macdonald, the Palmer Shipyard supervisor who Henry quotes as wanting him "to get the sentiment in."

Much is made of this well in *An Island Cabin*. Its importance begins, as does that of all wells, with its utilitarian function. There is no well on Quirk and much of the book's adventure revolves around the forays to nearby islands for fresh water. It is the well in the middle of Noank, however, which begins to pick up the kind of sacred aura associated with classic watering holes.

On a particularly bad day out on Quirk, Henry comes ashore in Noank. The ever questing Henry takes advantage of a shopping moment by Nancy to slip away and stroll "around [the corner of the store] to Captain Louis." With characteristic dependence on serendipity, however, our hero claims to be only partially aware of anything so driven as an actual mission. "I wished to see him, to talk with him and yet I but half new why." It becomes clear that he is interested in the well's guardians as much as the water and these figures become for him something like a trio out of the mythology of ancient wells: the nurturing mother of fruit preserves, the blue-water guru and the erasable "malicious" parrot-troll. The ensuing interview with the old captain and his ironic parrot focuses on how the skipper handled his crew through all those long years in foreign waters, an urgent point with Henry who has come to feel his command at Quirk slipping away. The old captain passes on his management philosophy, which up until this point he'd "never thought much about." Henry bows out with the sense that he has just been in the presence of the "sublime." The parrot's mocking malice reminds us of the traditional role of the trollish well guardian as it raucously undercuts an otherwise sentimental genre painting.

Such a scene seems to anchor the coastwise village at the heart of a larger maritime enterprise. The home of Captain Louis with its well and ironic genie becomes the moral center of the book, and for Henry exudes a power greater than either the orthodoxy of the shipyard owner's church or the portentous secular flapping of Dreiser upon his island eyrie.

As for the parrot, Sandy Smith tells me it lived on into its fifties, primarily perched in the cherry tree over the well where it shared afternoon tea with the ladies by sipping from a proffered cup.

I thought it might be a good idea to see just when Potter Court got itself run through Captain Louis' well and was on my way to the street records in the Town Hall when I saw Captain John Wilbur standing in his front yard directly across from Potter Court. "I don't know when it was run through, but I do know what my great grandmother said about it. Her name was Davis and she was very much alive in the time of Arthur Henry and all that. Somebody stopped right here where we are and said to her, 'Well, I see they're about to run Potter Court right through to Water Street [now Riverview Avenue.]' She sez, 'Yes, and I hope the first vehicle through is a hearse and that you're in it.'"

The well stone, the literal artifact itself is, along with the converted kerosene lamp Anna Mallon gave Beezie Seely Lowe, the most significant of objects surviving from the days of *An Island Cabin*. It is classic New England glacial granite four feet by four feet square, neatly cut a piano octave deep. It is smoothed on one side, rough on the other. In the middle is a round aperture through which passed the Captain's bucket when he hauled it to the well's lip with his windlass. A two inch vein of faded pink igneous intrusion forms a kind of muted festive ribbon across the gray stone. When Ted Wydler's backhoe lowered the piece into Paul Bates' truck, Sandy Smith feared for the vehicle's springs. A cottontail seems to have replaced the parrot as guardian spirit.

This just in: The Macdonald house on Spring Street that Maynard Bray lived in was actually owned by John A. MacDonald's brother (Servideo).

For *An Island Cabin* updates please visit www.flathammockpress.com

ACKNOWLEDGEMENTS

In addition to those mentioned in the text of the introduction, I wish to give a special nod to the memory of Dorothy Cramer without whom I would never have known of *An Island Cabin*. Her own story about her life on a Noank island is an epic and certainly went on a great deal longer than that of Arthur Henry's lyric interlude.

Born in 1908, in Rhode Island to Earl and Luella Clark, Dorothy's mother's maiden name was Sevin and it was George V. Sevin who owned a third of Mouse Island going back to the time July 6, 1897, three years before Arthur Henry's invasion of Quirk across the harbor. Dorothy attended Wellsley and in the spring of 1929 received a fur coat and a trip to Europe as graduation presents. Her family, however, lost most of its money in the stock market crash of that fall and she sold her coat and her ticket to raise money to send her sister to college. With their last liquidity, the family took the train to Noank and got off in the same station that Arthur Henry and his entourage had used thirty years before. Their old neighbor, the retired Noank Lighthouse keeper Thaddeus Pecor had been at Morgan Point since thirty years before Arthur Henry's day. He took them by horse and cart down the spine of the Noank peninsula to sea-level where they boarded a skiff to Mouse Island. No longer were they the carefree summer residents from away. In many ways their ordeal was the true island cabin adventure.

The tiny house on the rocky islet was to be their sole domicile. Although it was but about a hundred yards off the southern tip of Noank, in winter storms that might as well have been ten miles. The highest point on the island was thirteen feet. There they spent the winter of 1929-30 subsisting on root vegetables and fish provided by the lighthouse keeper. In later years Dorothy became a math teacher in a progressive grammar school in Massachusetts taking on grades 1-9 and teaching each student to his or her own level, and the family was able to hang onto the island and later returned after World War II. They bought a house on Prospect Hill to which they retired in the more dangerous months. During the 1950s, however, her parents were living on the island when a hurricane struck. She told me that her son had to go out during the eye of the storm and persuade them to climb out of the second story window into his Boston Whaler, a maneuver that they were loath to do, having, as they explained with typical logic, survived the first half of the storm in the attic.

The information about Dorothy's experience in the Depression came to me from Lewanda Singer who credits Dorothy Cramer's tutoring skills with getting her children, now all recipients of graduate degrees, through their early years of school in Noank. The information about Dorothy's schooling and her teaching came from her daughter Stephanie. It is a credit to Dorothy's blend of high academic standards and good humor that the Noank Historical Society got off on the right foot as both a legitimate repository and interpreter of the village's history and a community organization that is the force that holds the present together.

I would also like to thank my partner at Flat Hammock Press, Robert McKenna, for finding early Dreiser material and illustrations, and our office manager Greta Jones for her assistance.

A GALLERY OF
PERIOD PHOTOGRAPHS

Arthur Henry, Circa. 1900.

Theodore Dreiser, Circa. 1900

The cabin from Ram Island at high tide showing the channel through which ran the exemplary old sailor in his sloop.
(Mystic Seaport Museum, Mystic, CT)

Captain Ashbey, builder of the cabin on Quirk.
(Mystic Seaport Museum, Mystic, CT)

The "picket line" that Henry describes as guarding the Noank shore.
(Noank Historical Society)

"The Deacon." Robert Palmer
(1825-1913)

So effective at lobstering and in-shore fin fishing were these gaff rig boats that they were known as "Noank Sloops" even if built elsewhere. In the mid-twenty foot range, they were beamy enough to provide good working platforms and were sometimes rigged as catboats. The hulls were constructed with a bulkheaded wet-well to keep the lobsters fresh on the way in from the grounds. This was likely the sort of vessel Captain Chester employed. In the first decade of the 20th century fishermen began to add small auxillary engines such as the six horsepower Lathrop built up the river in Mystic. Deacon Palmer's descendent, Robert Palmer Anderson, had *Winsome*, a replica of the earlier sailing model built in the 1960s and she is yet moored off the foot of Latham Lane. The floating boxes in the foreground are lobster "cars" built to hold the catch for the best market conditions and constitute the sort of impediment that Henry hit with his skiff the night he tumbled into the bilge. The sloops were not anchored but tethered to pilings set out on the eel grass flats. Noank Light is in the background along with a four-masted coasting schooner at the Palmer Yard. Fishers Island is some three miles away in the southern horizon. Quirk is across the harbor to the left (east).
(Mystic Seaport Museum, Mystic, CT)

Dorothy (Sevrin) Cramer on Mouse Island with her back to the channel and the Noank Lighthouse. If she looked just a tad more over her left shoulder she would see the "sinful" Quirk Island. *(Mystic Seaport Museum, Mystic, CT)*

Dorothy Cramer's Mouse Island at the mouth of Noank channel across from Quirk. As of summer 2009, both large houses still stand. *(Mystic Seaport Museum, Mystic, CT)*

[332]

Mouse Island from Fishers Island Sound. Noank's Morgan (Lighthouse) Point is across the channel to the right. It was from these porches that the young Dorothy Cramer was forbidden to gaze across the harbor to the east (right) because of the lingering aura of scandal on Quirk. Amazingly, these two houses and a third to the right have survived a century of great storms. In the 1950s Dorothy's mother and father were extracted, reluctantly, from the second story of the house on the right during the eye of the storm. *(Mystic Seaport Museum, Mystic, CT)*

Mystic (Ram) Island in its glory in the 1870s. This is the pier that jutted out due south toward Ram Island Reef, subsequent location of the light vessel. It was here that the Long Island Sound steamers stopped. Quirk is on the opposite side to the north. *(Mystic Seaport Museum, Mystic, CT)*

Ram Island Light Vessel about whose fog bell Arthur Henry waxed lyrically, but regarding the crew and their activities he was silent. Ram Island is to the right and Quirk a bit farther to the right (north). Noank is on the western horizon blending in with Groton Long Point. *(Mystic Seaport Museum, Mystic, CT)*

A converted sailing ship, the Quirk Islanders' neighbor, the Ram Island Light Vessel was a fascinating spectacle that Henry largely ignored in his book. Each evening the routine included the crew's hoisting the lenses up out of the protective shacks on the masts and each dawn featured the spectacle of the lamps being lowered. Ram Island is in the background. *(Mystic Seaport Museum, Mystic, CT)*

Servant's quarters and guest house on Ram Island before Arthur Henry's time. Some of these buildings remained to be watched by Mr. & Mrs. Gaby Wilcox. *(Mystic Seaport Museum, Mystic, CT)*

In "The Doer of the Word" Dreiser describes Riverview Avenue "along which a few shops struggle in happy-go-lucky disorder." The "shops" are fisherman's workshops, not stores. The 1938 Hurricane made the site into a parking lot. For most of the 20th century the Rathbun family ran their fishing business out of this corner of Noank. The present fuel dock is behind the trees to the left. The road is one foot narrower than the porch of the house which is out of frame to the right. Ram Island is across the harbor with Fishers Island on the southern horizon. *(Mystic Seaport Museum, Mystic, CT)*

The Ashbey House, which could accomodate 40 to 50 guests, was one of the most popular summer hotels in Noank. *(Mystic Seaport Museum, Mystic, CT)*

Captain and Mrs. Ashbey. It would have fallen to the lady, as hostess of The Ashbey House on Pearl Street, to have taken care of Arthur Henry's cats for the rest of their lives. It is interesting to speculate if some of the numerous felines which seem to explode out of Noank's hedges at twilight are the descendents of the Quirk Island creatures. *(Mystic Seaport Museum, Mystic, CT)*

Under the hill at Main Street at the time of Arthur Henry. The gambrel roof house to the left finally collapsed in the 1938 Hurricane. Front Street, formerly Bootjack, comes in at the left. The Town Landing sticks out into the Mystic River with Masons Island faintly on the eastern horizon. Burridge's store is in the center facing up hill looking almost as it does today as the meeting house for the Noank Historical Society which has called it the "Chester-Latham" store. The town (village) pump is in the road just outside the door. The four structures to the right were stores, two of which were later apartments for graduate students in the University of Connecticut Marine Laboratory, which is just out of frame to the right on the river. These two buildings were not torn down until the 1960s. Riverview Avenue, Dreiser's "sunny lane which follows the line from the shore," runs south to the right. The house on the corner of Main and Riverview with the porch beneath the tree was the off-season residence of Mr. & Mrs. Gaby Wilcox, the Ram Island caretakers often visited by Arthur Henry. The house was built in 1809 and looks very much the same today in its 200th year. The tree which presently stands was planted in 1963; the one in the picture having blown down in the 1938 Hurricane which sent the harbor lapping up the hill to about where the person is crossing Main Street heading north. *(Mystic Seaport Museum, Mystic, CT)*

A four-masted gaff coasting schooner, the trailer truck of its day, lays at the Palmer Shipyard directly across from Quirk. A Noank sloop heads upstream under auxiliary power. The flat iron skiff on the ramp is similar to Arthur Henry's. The shack on the edge of the water provided shelter for working on lobster gear during inclement weather. This waterfront was wiped out in the 1938 Hurricane, but there is faithful reconstruction of shack, ramp and skiff at Mystic Seaport.
(Mystic Seaport Museum, Mystic, CT)

Looking from the Palmer Yard back across the harbor to the hotel on Ram Island. Fishers Island is on the horizon. *(Mystic Seaport Museum, Mystic, CT)*

Grass literally grew in the streets of Noank as Dreiser was quick to point out. This would seem to be Main Street, no less, looking east to the crest of Store Hill. The Noank School, now Noank Park, is to the left in the foreground. The Mystic River Home for girls is across the street with what is now Oliver Porter's house next door to the east. Carson's Store, though a venerable institution, is not yet across from Porter's. The corner of Church and Main is visible to the left and Pearl Street is almost directly across to the right. Over the hill and down would be Burridge's store and the Town Landing facing out to Quirk. *(Mystic Seaport Museum, Mystic, CT)*

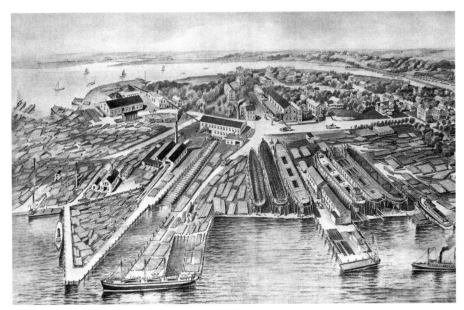

If Arthur Henry had been able to ascend in a balloon from Quirk this is the view he would have had of the great Palmer Yard. *(Mystic Seaport Museum, Mystic, CT)*

The photographer would seem to have been aloft on a large schooner at the Lower Palmer Shipyard. The yard is uncharacteristically devoid of vessels, but there are plenty of planks and men awaiting the first stages of construction. Captain Greene's work shed and house are between the shipyard and Noank Light. Mouse Island is offshore southwest to the right. Quirk is across the harbor to the left (east). *(Noank Historical Society)*

What the Palmer Yard was all about. A coasting schooner, "the trailer truck of its day," with her sails yet bent on alongside for repairs. The "donkey" engine whose stack and housing are to the right of the foremast, allowed for reduced manpower not only for hoisting sail and anchor, but cargo. Noank Light is dead ahead. In the distance, behind the starboard, aft ratlines is the long, low shed into which Henry, peering across the harbor from Quirk on the left, describes Captain Green's skiff vanishing.
(Mystic Seaport Museum, Mystic, CT)

Before the days of fork lifts, dray horses did the heavy hauling at the Palmer Shipyard, usually working in pairs. Here a pair wheel logs to the planing mill. Two framed-up schooners await planking. At night the horses slept up the hill in the stable in back of the Palmer Store, the present Universal Market. When the stable behind the store was under restoration in 2008 the names Doll, Harry, Bess, Dan and Charlie were still above the last five stalls on the southern end of the building. Della Pezzolezzi Kress recalled that as a little girl before the Second World War, she attempted to spend the night in the hay in Doll's stall. "I found out what all that nice hay was really for and when I came home my father found out exactly what I'd been up to."
(Noank Historical Society)

The end of each lane offered access to the harbor for typical Noank sloops, sheds and skiffs. Noank sloops were used for a variety of inshore fisheries, from lobstering to handlining mackerel flounder and small cod. Note the round cockpit combing on the boat at the left hand pier. Quirk is across the water.
(Mystic Seaport Museum, Mystic, CT)

One of the deep-water, offshore Noank fishing schooners that plied the George's Bank shares a berth with the inshore lobster fleet. As sails were canvas they had to be dried after rain at dockside. To air the material without allowing the wind to fill the driving pocket of the sail, the crew scandalized the peaks, that is left the sails half-way hoisted, the peaks of the gaffs parallel to the horizon. "Drying sail" was a favorite motif of waterfront artists all along the New England coast. Masons Island is in the background. Quirk is just out of frame to the right.
(Stephen Jones Collection)

Taken from Noank Light looking north up into the village of Noank. Captain Greene's house and the boat shed in which he built Henry's skiff, is in the foreground. The white picket fence that struggles up the great glacier erratic is still there. Deacon Palmer's spectacular home, built by his shipyard workers is in the center of the picture, his mansard style tower providing an ideal vantage from which to keep an eye on his shipyard. The house is still there, nicely restored by the last two owners having remained unpainted for generations through the Great Depression and the Second World War. The Ashbey House is across Pearl Street from Deacon Palmer on the west side. Quirk is across the harbor out of sight to the right. Note the relative lack of trees and also the scarcity of houses on the west side (the present High Street).
(Noank Historical Society)

The frequency of damp easterlies made drying a constant battle in Noank and certainly justified the hyperbolic military metaphor. It is difficult, however, to reconcile Dreiser's portrait of the dour Elihu "Burridge" whose prototype put out this ad featuring the voluptuous model who seems to have escaped from a harem. No doubt the Yankee storekeeper's association with the odalisque produced a few cackles around pot belly stoves and "Burridge" was challenged to justify the advertising image on purely mercantile grounds. (Noank Historical Society).

THE "CONQUEROR"

EXCELS ALL OTHER WRINGERS IN HAVING

1. A Forged STEEL SPRING, tapered and tempered, and the temper not "drawn" by galvanizing.
2. The EXTENSION CRANK, which gives double power, without loss of speed.
3. Composition METAL BEARINGS, which neither rot, rust or wear out.
4. Patent Solid WHITE RUBBER ROLLS, fastened immovably to the shaft.
5. Malleable Iron Swivel Clamps, which fit either round or Stationary Tubs.

ELIHU H. POTTER,

DEALER IN

GROCERIES,

Provisions, Ship Chandlery, Hardware, Crockery,

NOANK, CONN.

A less exotic version of Elihu "Burridge's" contribution to the ongoing war on easterlies in Noank. (Noank Historical Society)

Certainly one of the glories of the scene, stea
vessel *Summer Girl* heads down Mystic Ri
toward the railroad bridge. The swing highw
bridge is behind her as the present infamc
Bascule contraption was not built until 19:
Steamboat Wharf condos now occupy
point to the left on the west bank where
one-story shacks are. The Drawbridge
Cream building overhanging the edge of
west bank just above the bridge, has surviv
several fires. Cottrell Park at present behind
steamer, was in those days the Cottrell Lum
Company. *Summer Girl* is likely to have be
Dreiser's transportation across Fishers Isla
Sound and up the Thames to Norwich on
quest to interview Charlie Potter in "The Doe
the Word." That neither Dreiser nor Henry e
mentions the daily passage of *Summer Girl*
tween Quirk and Noank would seem to indic
how commonplace such an event struck the
Old-timers now, however, wax lyrically ab
Summer Girl and the Mystic Seaport's fif
seven foot, 1908, coal-fired steamer *Sabinc*
similar vessel, which confines itself to the M
tic River never fails to draw a smile. (Noank H
torical Society).

Looking up the Mystic River at the Palmer House Boat Landing on Noank's northeast end. This is pretty much the angle Arthur Henry would have had of The Palmer across the harbor at a half a mile. Built the year Arthur Henry came to Noank, The Palmer was the high end of the local seaside resorts. The white building beneath the water tower with the six doors seems to be lockers in an era when a complete change of clothes was required for every leisure "activity." The hills of West Mystic with Beebe Cove beneath them are on the horizon. The New York-Boston railroad line runs along the harbor in the upper right. Captain Jimmy Sistare's schooner took guests out to the deep water grounds off Montauk. Captain Sistaire's fleet is ready for guests even if the water tower is not quite. Note the swordfish pulpit on the schooner promising excursions to distant waters. Just to the left and back a block is the land that John A. Macdonald, supervisor of the lower Palmer Yard, donated for the building of the Catholic church. This is the present site of the Noank Village Boatyard. (Noank Historical Society)

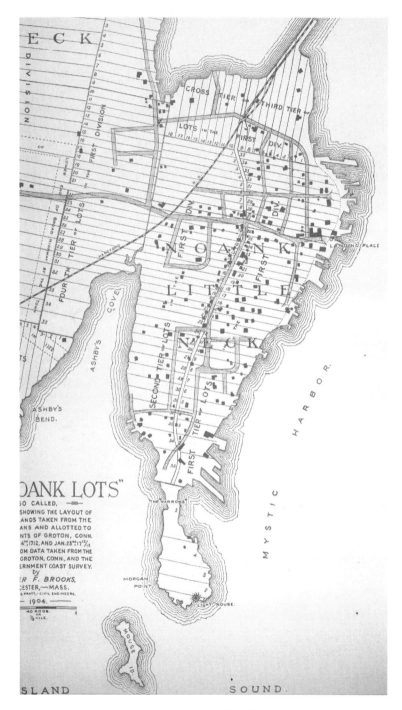

The head spins as the *An Island Cabin* reader tries to superimpose the present layout on Arthur Henry's Noank. There is just enough similarity to lead one on. The map is made from Noank lots as laid out in 1914 and updated with streets and structures as published in 1904.

The wide street that bisects the peninsula from the railroad tracks to the Landing is Main Street. The street that runs from north to south down the spine is Pearl Street but was originally Cliff Street. Captain Louis' house with the parrot and well is the fourth house down Main Street on the west side between the A and the N in Noank. The present Potter Court runs between Captain Louis' house and the one to its south and intersects with Riverview Avenue.

Ashbey's Ben is now called Blue Meadows; Ashby's Cove, little more than tidal flats, is now dredged and jammed with yachts known as West Cove. "Beezie" S. Main's descendant George Main's lobster business is at the end of the lane under the S in "Second Tier Lots." The two ways into the village from the Noank-Mystic Road were grade crossings at Main Street and to the north at what is now Spicer Avenue. Both are now closed by formal barriers and brambles. The two access roads are now Marsh Road, a loop around the head of West Cove, and Ward Avenue which passes over the railroad just above the V in "First Div." The Noank Valley Cemetery, final resting place of many people mentioned in *An Island Cabin* is within the rectangle of roads to the west just to the east of "First Division" in "Fourth Tier." The Ashbey House, spelled with the "e" was near the N in "Noank Little Neck." Deacon Palmer's house is across the street to the east. "Beezie" S. Main's house was just a few lots north of the Ashbey House on the same side of the street. What Dreiser refers to as the sunny lane that runs along the harbor is the present Riverview Avenue which in his day did not connect up Snake Hill to Palmer Court but ended just below the e in "Little" in "Noank Little Neck." Noank Baptist Church where Deacon Palmer held sway is on the north side of Main Street above the second n in Noank. The business district which included "Burridge's" store was concentrated about the Town Landing. Captain Greene built Henry's skiff in his shop close to the number 3 on Morgan Point just north of the Lighthouse. The Lower Palmer Shipyard occupied all the lots on both sides of the isthmus from the north to the beginning of "First Tier Lots" at the end of "The Narrows." Quirk is due east off "The Narrows." The elegant "Palmer" was located on the water on the north end of the peninsula marked "Third Tier." Mystic is two miles to the north and the map's designation of the water to the east of Noank as "Mystic Harbor" has had little actual use as the locals and even transients refer to it as "Noank Harbor." The railroad station at which the Quirk Islanders landed from New York and at which "The Noank Boy" met the mail is on the northeast corner where the "Hartford" (New York-Boston) railroad crosses what is now Front Street and is just above "First" in "Lots in the First Div." (Noank Historical Society)

Foot of "Snake Hill," now Riverview Avenue. Masons Island is on the horizon. The gambrel-roofed shingle building was the State Lobster Hatchery built just after Henry departed. The rest of the ramshackle waterfront would likely be as he'd experienced it. Note the curved-topped wooden lobsterpots and the size of the buoys in the foreground which would have been used in the deep, fast waters of the Race. This entire waterfront was swept away by the 1938 Hurricane except for what is now John Rathbun's house just across the lane from the hatchery. After the big hurricane the hatchery function was shifted upriver to the brick building at the foot of Store Hill which now houses the town Shellfish Cooperative. *(Mystic Seaport Museum, Mystic, CT)*

This would seem to be the cabin at some time after Henry's departure, although the neatness with which the windows have been removed suggests careful salvaging rather than mere vandalism. The villagers practiced great economy in reusing whole buildings and parts of buildings. The open porch faces Noank.
(Mystic Seaport Museum, Mystic, CT)

Quirk Island Boat Club, c. 1976. Ahoy to left, Ram to right. Fishers Island in background. *(Photo Geoffrey P. Jones)*

Quirk today at low tide. The trees have grown up since hurricane *Gloria* in the 1970s. The "Eyrie" is still much in prominence (minus Dreiser's rocking chair). The chain of rocks and sand to the left connect Ahoy. To the right is Ram (Mystic) Island. Fishers Island is on the horizon with Firestone's boathouse just to the left of Quirk. (Photo by *Furtive*)

(Continued from Back Cover)

The original text, published in 1902 as part of a lifestyle trilogy, is entertaining enough in its own right, but this Flat Hammock Press edition adds Stephen Jones' in-the-footsteps, back-story narrative of what happened before, after and even more surprisingly, during the summer of 1900. Arthur Henry's granddaughter and biographer, Maggie Walker provides an introduction. To flesh out the real story, this new volume also includes three short non-fiction pieces by Dreiser based on his awkward forays away from the island. A gallery of dozens of period photographs from 1900 Noank enhances a book which transcends local history to become a permanent part of Americana.

Arthur Henry (1867-1934), now a footnote to Dreiser studies, was at the time the better known of the two writers. He was not only Dreiser's frequent companion, but the man whose friendly wager challenged Dreiser to write his break-through novel *Sister Carrie*. Furthermore, Henry was the man who edited Dreiser's sprawling realism to make it publishable. A journalist, novelist, and playwright, Henry's varied career brought him together with many famous writers and social reformers.

Theodore Dreiser (1871-1945) is one of the giants of 20th Century American literature and in addition to the ground-breaking *Sister Carrie* is perhaps best known today as the author of *An American Tragedy* upon which director George Stevens based his Elizabeth Taylor-Montgomery Clift film *A Place in the Sun.*